A PHILOSOPHY OF EDUCATION

McGRAW-HILL CATHOLIC SERIES IN EDUCATION
Bernard J. Kohlbrenner, *Consulting Editor*

Johnston · *A Philosophy of Education*
Kolesnik · *Educational Psychology*
Lee · *Principles and Methods of Secondary Education*
McCoy · *American School Administration*
Power · *Education for American Democracy*
Power · *Main Currents in the History of Education*

A Philosophy of Education

Herbert Johnston

University of Notre Dame

McGRAW-HILL BOOK COMPANY, INC.

New York   *San Francisco*   *Toronto*   *London*

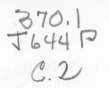
A PHILOSOPHY OF EDUCATION

For Nell, Fran, Tom, and Bill

Foreword

A good many years ago Mortimer J. Adler warned us that: [1]

> To know the truth in the philosophy of education . . . depends upon almost the whole of philosophy. There is no short-cut worth taking. If anyone has not the time, patience, or willingness, to study philosophy in its entirety, let him resign himself to being ignorant of philosophical truths about education. . . .

I do not think the situation is quite that extreme. Perhaps it would be more accurate to say that I consider it possible, as a prerequisite for reaching "philosophical truths about education," to telescope the preliminary considerations into an examination of the nature of man and of those powers that make him educable. This I regard as a barely sufficient minimum; but I think it is enough to do the job, and this book is an effort to do it.

A number of points should briefly be made here. One is that a philosophy of education is not an armchair version of any particular discipline, such as educational psychology in any of its forms. It aims at and sometimes achieves a different kind of knowledge.

[1] "In Defense of the Philosophy of Education," in Nelson B. Henry (ed.), *Philosophies of Education,* part I, The 41st Yearbook of the National Society for the Study of Education (Chicago: The University of Chicago Press, 1942), pp. 204–205. Copyright 1942 by the University of Chicago. Reprinted by permission.

A philosophical science, including a philosophy of education, does not ask or try to answer the same kind of question as a particular science, including the ones concerned with education. The first chapter will try to make somewhat more explicit the relations among these disciplines.

Another point is that this book is strictly doctrinal rather than historical in character. It is an exposition of a particular philosophy of education, with definite conclusions reached on the basis of what I hope is sufficient evidence. A history of philosophies of education would be an interesting and an important enterprise, but it is not the one attempted in this book. So, too, would an explanation of contemporary philosophies and their impact on educational theory and practice,[2] but neither is this enterprise the one attempted in this book. Any course in philosophy of education, especially at the graduate level, should include readings in both of these areas; yet the areas remain distinct from that of philosophy of education itself.[3]

[2] See, for example, the work referred to in note 1 above. See also Nelson B. Henry (ed.), *Modern Philosophies and Education,* part I, The 54th Yearbook of the N.S.S.E. (Chicago: The University of Chicago Press, 1955); John S. Brubacher, *Modern Philosophies of Education,* 3d ed. (New York: McGraw-Hill Book Company, Inc., 1962); George Z. F. Bereday and Joseph A. Lauwerys (eds.), *Education and Philosophy* (New York: Harcourt, Brace & World, Inc., 1957); John S. Brubacher (ed.), *Eclectic Philosophy of Education* (Englewood Cliffs, N.J.: Prentice-Hall, Inc., 1951); J. Donald Butler, *Four Philosophies and Their Practice in Education and Religion,* rev. ed. (New York: Harper & Row, Publishers, 1957); Joe Park (ed.), *Selected Readings in the Philosophy of Education* (New York: The Macmillan Company, 1958); Mortimer J. Adler and Milton Mayer, *The Revolution in Education* (Chicago: The University of Chicago Press, 1958).

[3] On the other hand, an anthology which fits directly the theme of this book and which would provide excellent sup-

This book is designed to serve as the basis for such a course at either the undergraduate or the graduate level. The approach envisioned is largely that of discussion arising from the inevitably controversial nature of the text itself and also from the questions and cases appended to the various chapters.[4] Many of the terms in these questions have deliberately been left vague in order to force those who deal with the questions to clarify the terms before they proceed. It will also be found that many questions are to some degree repetitious; yet even these provide the opportunity for a fresh attack on a problem from another angle. The great advantage of the case method is that, when carefully conducted, it involves the student personally in the work of the course to a greater degree than straight lecturing. This is not to say that lecturing is a bad method of teaching, or that the use of class discussion of particular questions is an end in itself. But for a course of this kind, the consideration of concrete problems seems to offer the ideal means of getting the student to see the practical nature of philosophy of education. He or she starts in the order of prudence with a particular problem, and finds that one must rise to the order of moral science for the knowledge in the light of which alone the problem will be susceptible of reasoned resolution. In this way a connection is made and retained, by constant reference to the terms in which the problem is posed, between the remotely practical order of moral science (of which, it will be argued in Chapter one, philosophy of

---

plementary reading is Malcolm Carron, S.J., and Alfred D. Cavanaugh (eds.), *Readings in the Philosophy of Education* (Detroit: University of Detroit Press, 1960).

[4] An effort has been made, though not on a philosophically profound level, to attack the study and the teaching of philosophy of education by means of a consideration of particular cases. See Robert L. Brackenbury, *Getting Down to Cases: A Problems Approach to Educational Philosophizing* (New York: G. P. Putnam's Sons, 1959).

education is a part) and the immediately practical order of prudence. This is not an effort to teach prudence, something which cannot be done directly; but it is an effort to keep the prudential and the scientific orders linked in the student's mind.

As all of us know who have tried it,[5] the initiation and control of class discussion is much more difficult than straight lecturing. Further, discussion classes have a tendency to degenerate into glorified bull sessions, involving little more than the heated exchange of opinion and prejudice and the painless passing of a fifty-minute period. But this is not teaching. Personally engaging the student in a problem is essential to teaching, for unless he sees the question, any answer is going to be meaningless. Yet personally engaging the student in a problem is the beginning of the teacher's job, not the end. For the only point of asking a question is to find an answer. The danger of the lecture method is that it risks giving the student all of the answers with none of the questions. The danger of the discussion method is that it risks giving him all of the questions with none of the answers. It is easy to go overboard in either direction; good teaching involves the avoidance of both extremes.

Each teacher will discover from experience which questions lend themselves best to lively and fruitful classroom discussion. He should be neither surprised nor disappointed if, at the end of such discussions, unanimity is as far away as ever. For even when demonstration can be reached within the order of philosophy of education, it is much more difficult to see than demonstration in the mathematical or even the natural sciences. And in the order of the particular problem, as will be explained below, scientific demonstration is impossible, though personal certainty is not. The

[5] This and the following paragraph are adapted from Herbert Johnston, *Business Ethics,* 2d ed. rev. (New York: Pitman Publishing Corporation, 1961), p. viii. Reprinted by permission.

text does not provide neatly packaged answers to the questions found at the end of any given chapter. It does, however, provide what I hope is a reasonable explanation of some of the things involved in the questions, an explanation on the basis of which alone a fruitful consideration of the problems can be made. This is not to suggest that such problems can be solved on philosophical bases alone; it is, though, to maintain that they will not be constructively solved without reference to such bases. The theory on which this book is constructed is that the student, through being constantly forced to refer particular educational problems to their philosophical dimensions, will develop the habit of doing so. This habit is precisely philosophy of education.

It is a pleasant duty to give thanks to my colleagues, Professors John A. Oesterle and Joseph Bobik in the Department of Philosophy, University of Notre Dame, for their patiently entering into lengthy and, for me, enlightening discussions, especially of the material in Chapters three and seven; to my other colleagues in the same department, Professors Kenneth M. Sayre and the Reverend Ernan McMullin, and to Professor Anthony C. Riccio of the Department of Education, The Ohio State University, for ready and helpful assistance with the material in Chapter ten; and to Professor Bernard J. Kohlbrenner of the Department of Education, University of Notre Dame, editor of this series, for his wise counsel concerning the work as a whole. A word of gratitude is also due my students, who supplied from their own experience many of the questions appended to various chapters, and who together formed the anvil on which the shape of this book was gradually hammered out. My hope is that it may be of some help to present and prospective teachers, on whose daily work the future of our society so largely rests.

Herbert Johnston

Contents

Contents

꒰꒰꒰꒰

chapter one

The Nature of Philosophy
of Education

It would be possible to get immediately into the subject of a philosophy of education without any lengthy introduction; the nature of the discipline [1] would then become gradually apparent as the various topics were discussed. Yet there may be some point in devoting an introductory chapter to an attempt to get at just what sort of knowledge is involved here. If the student can have a preliminary look at something like a map of the area, he is more likely to recognize, and to recognize in some sort of contextual

[1] Discipline is here being used according to what logicians call the first imposition of the term, that is, its original meaning; this is the first meaning given for the word in the College

whole, the various features of the intellectual countryside through which he is traveling. He may thus have a better chance of seeing the forest as well as the trees.

This preliminary excursion, then, into what the philosopher generally calls epistemology and the social scientist calls methodology is intended to provide the student with some notion of the nature of the discipline to which he is being introduced. It should also—and this is no less important—show him something of the relation of a philosophy of education to other areas of study and its place in the hierarchy of knowledges.

It is true that this investigation will require a certain degree of faith on the student's part, for it occurs before rather than after the study of philosophy of education itself. Faith, however, is of its very nature a temporary substitute, serving until the believer can come to see for himself. This fact holds true for the believer in divine revelation, whose faith will become unnecessary in the Beatific Vision, as it also does for the beginning student, who must trust his teacher until he can come to grasp with his own understanding the knowledge in question. Though the certainty involved in these examples is very different because of the difference between divine and merely human authority, yet in either instance the faith itself is quite reasonable.

The task of this chapter, then, will be to propose a theory of the nature of philosophy of education and of its relation to other

---

Edition of *Webster's New World Dictionary:* "a branch of knowledge or learning." It is in this way that the word will usually be used in this book. On occasions, however, and especially in Chapter ten in the section on Authority and Discipline, it will be used in the second meaning given in the same dictionary: "training that develops self-control, character, or orderliness and efficiency." The context should, in each instance, make clear which meaning is intended.

areas of knowledge, especially to the particular educational disciplines. The thesis that will be maintained is that philosophy of education is a branch of social ethics directed to the establishment, preservation, and direction of the educational society, whether at the level of the nation, the state, the system, the school, or the classroom. It will also be maintained that philosophy of education issues from and applies a combination of more general moral knowledge and such particular disciplines as educational psychology, and that it leads to conclusions which in turn serve as principles for the arts of teaching and administration in the sense that it sets up general directives at which the teacher and the administrator should aim.

THE DISTINCTION BETWEEN SPECULATIVE AND PRACTICAL KNOWLEDGE

In the investigation of the nature of any discipline and its relation to other fields, perhaps the basic question at issue is whether it falls within the order of speculative or of practical knowledge.[2] The following outline of what is meant by speculative and by practical knowledge is based largely on the teaching of St. Thomas and the commentary of Cardinal Cajetan on that teaching.

When we speak of the speculative and the practical intellect, St. Thomas points out, we are not speaking of two different powers, but of the same power looked at from different points of view. For it is accidental to that power which is the intellect that it be ordained or that it not be ordained to some operation. And it is this ordination, this direction, this purpose that distinguishes the speculative from the practical intellect. For the speculative in-

[2] Part of what follows is adapted from Herbert Johnston, "The Social and the Moral Sciences," *The Catholic Educational Review*, 55, 7, 8, 9 (October, November, December, 1957). Reprinted by permission.

tellect does not direct what it apprehends to any operation, but solely to the consideration of truth; whereas the practical intellect directs what it apprehends to an operation. The speculative and the practical intellect, then, differ according to the *end* involved; they remain, however, two aspects of one power.[3]

The speculative intellect seeks truth as its end; the practical intellect seeks truth as ordained to operation: to doing or making. And since the matter involved must be proportioned to the end, the subject matter of the practical sciences must be those things which can be done or made by our operations and the knowledge of which can be ordained to operation as its end, whereas the subject matter of the speculative sciences must be those things which are not done or made by our operations and the knowledge of which cannot be ordained to operation as its end.[4]

It will follow that some knowledge is speculative only, some is practical only, and some partakes of both orders. For knowledge can be called speculative in three ways. First, on the part of the *things known,* which are not operable (cannot be done or made) by the knower; for example, human knowledge of natural or divine things, things which cannot be made by men but must be known as they are given. Second, as to the *mode of knowing;* for example, a knowledge of a house obtained by defining and dividing and considering the universals predicated of it (the sort of knowledge which would enable one to describe a house and to say what it is, but which would not enable one to build a house); for this is to consider operable things in a speculative mode and

---

[3] St. Thomas Aquinas, *Summa Theologiae,* I, 79, 11, c.
[4] St. Thomas, *In Librum Boetii De Trinitate,* V, 1, c. Cf. *In II Metaph.,* lect. 2, Cathala ed. No. 290; *In III De Anima,* lect. 15, Pirotta ed. No. 820. For a commentary on these passages, see Yves Simon, *Critique de la Connaissance Morale* (Paris: Desclée de Brouwer, 1934), pp. 9–11, 61–63, 68, 72–73.

not as they are operable. Third, as to the *end;* for the practical intellect ordains its knowledge to the end of operation, whereas the end of the speculative intellect is the consideration of truth. Therefore knowledge which is speculative by reason of the thing known is speculative only; but that which is speculative either according to its mode or according to its end is in one respect speculative and in another respect practical.[5]

Two comments should be made on this text. The first is that, as we shall see at greater length below, all knowledge, even that which partakes in some measure of both the speculative and the practical orders, can be reduced ultimately to one or the other; all knowledge is in the long run either speculative or practical.

The second is the point that Cardinal Cajetan makes in his commentary on the text paraphrased above, the distinction between the end of the knower and the end of the knowledge. If a builder, for example, considers how to build a house but does not on this occasion intend to put his knowledge into practice, his knowledge may be said to be speculative from its end on the part of the knower only, not on the part of the knowledge itself. For the knowledge of how to build a house is practical in itself, whether or not any particular person intends to put that knowledge to use.[6] The intention of the knower is accidental to the knowledge itself. Mathematics, for example, is of its very nature speculative knowledge of what is, even though the personal intention or end of someone who studies it may be to keep books or to build bridges. Metaphysics is, as knowledge, speculative, even though some people earn a living by teaching it. And moral science is practical in itself, because its conclusions are directive of human actions, even though a particular student of moral science may have no intention of guiding his own life by it. Here we are concerned with establishing the

[5] St. Thomas, *Summa Theologiae,* I, 14, 16, c.
[6] *Comm.* Card. Caiet. in I, 14, 16, par. III. (See Leonine edition of *Opera Omnia* of St. Thomas Aquinas.)

relations among various disciplines, and hence with the *finis scientiae,* the end of the knowledge, and not with the *finis scientis,* the end of the knower.[7]

Four Types of Knowledge

On the basis of the texts considered above, it should be possible to distinguish four types of knowledge, the first two of which can be reduced to speculative knowledge and the last two to practical knowledge.

First, there is purely speculative knowledge, that of a non-operable object, that is, of something that we cannot do or make. This type of knowledge yields conclusions whose copula is *is* or *will be.*[8] Such knowledge is not of itself directed to any further end. Examples of this type of knowledge would be the sciences of mathematics and metaphysics.

Second, there is speculative knowledge of an operable object, of something that we can do or make. In spite of its object, this knowledge remains speculative in its mode and its end, and is ultimately to be characterized as speculative rather than as practical knowledge. This type of knowledge also yields conclusions whose copula is *is* or *will be.* St. Thomas's example is the study of a house in order to obtain a descriptive definition of it as opposed to the (practical) study of a house as an architect studies it, that is, in order to know how a house *is to be* built. A similar example would be that of art appreciation. Again, in the article referred

---

[7] *Ibid.,* in I, 79, 11, par. II.

[8] It is important to observe that a conclusion whose copula is *will be,* that is, a predictive conclusion, is not by that fact a practical conclusion. The difference between *is* and *will be* as the copula of a conclusion is merely a difference in tense. The statement is still a statement describing a fact, not a statement prescribing what *is to be* or *should be* or *ought to be* done or made. It is this latter type of copula that marks the conclusion in which it occurs as practical.

to in note 2 above, it was maintained that the social sciences, taken in themselves and so far as they are autonomous sciences, fall within this category of knowledge and constitute speculative knowledge of an operable object, that is, of the actions of men in the institution and operation or the establishment and preservation of such human societies as the domestic, the political, and the economic. This second type of knowledge is also exemplified by studies of the laws of a particular state which pertain to education, or of the structure and functioning of a school system, or of a psychology of learning.

Third, there is remotely practical knowledge, that is, knowledge of an operable object for the purpose of remotely directing operation. This type of knowledge yields conclusions whose copula is *is to be, should be,* or *ought to be* done, and is ultimately to be characterized as practical rather than as speculative knowledge. Its speculative and scientific element comes from the fact that its conclusions are applied to objects that are in some degree universal, as moral science concludes to the rightness or wrongness of species or types or kinds of act, not to the rightness or wrongness of individual acts. It is also being maintained that when the social sciences and other speculative studies are incorporated into the wider context of moral science and so fall within this category of knowledge, they then become identified with moral science itself, and thus constitute practical knowledge.

Fourth, there is immediately practical knowledge. This is knowledge of an operable object for the purpose of immediately directing operation; further, this type of knowledge applies its conclusions to action. These conclusions, of course, are in terms of what *is to be* done, and are applied to singular actions considered here and now. The example of this type of practical knowledge is prudence. There is, of course, no science involved here.[9]

[9] See Edmund Dolan, "Resolution and Composition," *Laval Théologique et Philosophique,* 6 (1950), 9–62, espec. 17, note 2. Some implications of the existence of both specu-

Perhaps a schema would make this outline easier to grasp:

Type of knowledge	Examples	Conclusion
Purely speculative	Mathematics, metaphysics	Copula of conclusion is *is* or *will be*
Speculative consideration of an operable object	Description of house, art appreciation, social sciences, psychology	Same as above
Remotely practical	Moral philosophy, architecture (remotely directs operation)	Copula of conclusion is *is to be, should be,* or *ought to be*
Immediately practical	Prudence (immediately directs operation)	Same as above

The examples given of the second type of knowledge are being called speculative in spite of the fact that many of those who investigate them do so with very practical purposes in mind; for example, a legislator may study economic theory so as to vote more intelligently on proposed fiscal laws, or a teacher may study psychology of learning so as to make his teaching more effective. But this purpose pertains to the intention of the knower and does not affect the nature of the knowledge itself. It refers to what we have called above the *finis scientis,* the end of the knower, rather than to the *finis scientiae,* the end of the knowledge taken in itself. And our concern is with the kind of knowledge that these dis-

---

lative and practical intellectual functions are developed in John W. Donohue, S.J., "From a Philosophy of Man: Reflections on Intelligence as a Dyadic Function," *Educational Theory,* 9, 3 (July, 1959), 140–151, 155.

ciplines constitute, not with the personal convictions of those who pursue them. For these convictions—that good laws and good teaching are important, and that they do not just happen—have merely suggested to the student in question his field of investigation; they have not at all determined his findings.

Likewise, the examples given of the second type of knowledge are being called speculative in spite of the further fact that they investigate human actions and their results. It is true that no properly human act, taken individually, can be morally indifferent; but it is possible to study those acts under a formality other than that of their moral goodness or badness. To discover what men have done in certain circumstances, and to try to find some sort of pattern in their actions, is quite possible without any judgment about whether they should have done what they did. There can, then, be a speculative study of human and social events and realities, in itself avoiding any value judgments, and yet in no way denying the moral character of every properly human act or the existence of a practical moral science to which such a study would be subordinate, and in which its conclusions, originally speculative, would be taken over and used in a new and practical context.[10]

Moral science itself falls within the third classification as remotely practical knowledge. Its conclusions—for example, "Lying is a type of act that is not in conformity with man's rational nature, and hence evil, and hence not *to be done"*—are only *remotely* practical because they deal with a *type* of act, with action taken universally. But they remain *essentially* practical because they are of their very nature directive of action.[11]

[10] For a longer and more detailed treatment of the relation between the second and the third types of knowledge, see the article referred to in note 2 above.

[11] St. Thomas, *In I Ethic.*, lect. 3, Spiazzi ed. No. 40; *ibid.*, lect. 1, No. 1–2; *Summa Theologiae,* I, 79, 11, ad 1. Cf. Simon, *op. cit.*, pp. 78, 91–93, 103.

From Speculative Study to a Practical Decision

Using the same examples of the legislator studying economics or the teacher studying psychology, let us see how the thing would work. One of the areas of economic study is economic theory or general economics. On the macroeconomic level, which studies the whole economic system, efforts are made to predict more or less accurately the size of the national income from a study of private and public investment intentions. From the experience of previous years the economist might have reached the conclusion that "an annual capital investment of so many dollars, other factors remaining equal, *does* maintain national income at such a figure." This generalization arose from observation, and holds, obviously, only for the most part. This is an example of the first function of economics—analysis, or pure economics. The conclusion, or law, falls within the second division of knowledge, and constitutes speculative knowledge of an operable object. The second function of economics—prediction, or applied economics—would be based on this conclusion, and would be formulated somewhat as follows: "If annual capital investment is so much, then, other things being equal, national income *will be* maintained at such a level." Again, we have speculative knowledge of an operable object; the only thing changed is the tense of the copula of the conclusion. Finally, and as a continuation of applied economics, the prediction could be expressed as a *hypothetical* directive of action: "*If* you want to maintain national income at such a level, then, among other things, you *should* pass these fiscal laws encouraging investment."

In spite of the *should,* the statement remains speculative, for the practical directive of action is only hypothetical. The legislator-turned-economist has not made a statement about an end or a good or a value. He has obtained knowledge which, along with much other such knowledge, he can use as a means of reaching an end that he has selected on other than economic grounds, an end about which economic theory, taken precisely as such, has said nothing.

The transition from the speculative to the practical order, from the second to the third type of knowledge, occurs when this purely hypothetical directive loses its hypothetical character and becomes incorporated in a judgment in the area of social ethics, an area which runs from the most general normative judgments about society to the policy statements just above the prudential level. In the present example, the conclusion in question would be stated as a policy directive, for example, "This government's fiscal policy should encourage investment." Finally, on the level of practice, which is the prudential level of the individual act to be done, the particular legislator would decide: "I should vote for this tax measure here and now proposed."

In the second example—that of the teacher studying psychology—observation and generalization would yield some such conclusion as, "Students learn better when personally interested." As a prediction, this statement would read, "If students are personally interested, they will learn better." The hypothetical directive based on this prediction would be, *"If* you want students to learn better, you *should* try to interest them personally in what is going to be studied." Up to this point one remains in the speculative order, in the second type of knowledge. When, on the basis of this knowledge, the teacher formulates the policy directive, "Teachers should try to get their students personally interested in the topic at hand," he has left the speculative order and entered that branch of social ethics which is philosophy of education. Finally, he reaches the fourth type of knowledge with the prudential judgment, "Here and now I shall introduce this topic in this way."

PHILOSOPHY OF EDUCATION: A BRANCH OF SOCIAL ETHICS

Philosophy of education is one of many branches of social ethics, which in turn is the application to various societies of moral philosophy, or ethics. Moral philosophy establishes knowledge of the end of man and of the species or kinds of act by which he may reach that end. The part of moral philosophy which directs the individual person to his end was called "monastics" by Aristotle and St. Thomas. Man, however, is a social being by his very nature, and hence needs the cooperation of other men in various societies to achieve the conditions of life proper to him and best allowing him to reach his final end. That branch of moral philosophy called "social ethics" establishes knowledge of the kinds of society proper to man and of the general means of his organizing and preserving those societies. Hence there will be a philosophy of the state (the supreme discipline in this order, because the civil society is an ultimate end for man in the temporal order and not merely a means), a philosophy of the economy, a philosophy of the family, a philosophy of the educational system (as a whole and in its parts), and a philosophy of any other society contributing to the good of man in the natural order. Such knowledge is remotely practical, and within this context such disciplines as the social sciences and psychology lose their original formality and nature and become identified with social philosophy, with their conclusions oriented to the practical end of establishing and preserving those societies. Yet taken in themselves before any incorporation into social ethics, these disciplines remain speculative in character; and they must be developed and studied as the speculative disciplines that they originally are before they can perform the work demanded of them as later included in the context of social ethics.

Schematically arranged, the foregoing classifications would appear as shown on page 13.

In order to constitute the first three examples of social ethics given above, there would be necessary at least some knowledge of the conclusions both of general ethics and of the social sciences, and, as well, as extensive and secure a grasp as possible of the reasons lying behind those conclusions. Incidentally, this is why neither the moralist nor the social scientist is competent, on the

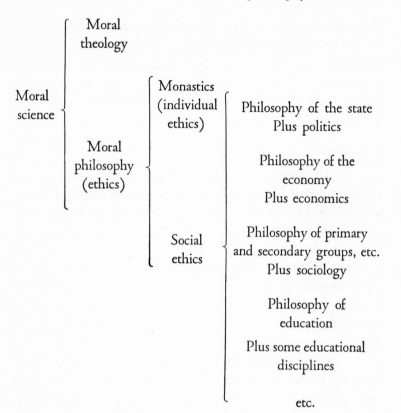

basis of his specialty alone, to prescribe for the social order; both areas of knowledge are involved in social ethics, and expertness in one of them does not make unnecessary as much expertness as possible in the other. In the same way and for the same reason, in order to constitute the last example of social ethics given above, there would be necessary at least some knowledge of the conclusions both of general ethics and of some of the educational disciplines, and, again, of the reasons lying behind those conclusions. It is true that a good many of the conclusions concerned are already widely accepted as true. Yet unless the reasons *why* they are true are also understood, the knowledge of them remains on the level of opinion or of faith rather than on that of science. In this course we shall take for granted at least some degree of such knowledge on the part of the student; and the next chapter will summarize a few of the conclusions of general ethics—at least as I see them—which are fundamental to all that follows, so that there may be no mistake about just what it is that is being taken for granted.

Educational Disciplines

As was mentioned above, some knowledge of certain educational disciplines is also necessary for the scientific construction of a philosophy of education. The most basic of these—and, perhaps along with the history of education, the only ones which could themselves be called sciences—are the experimental and the philosophical psychologies of learning. The former deals with such topics as readiness to learn, the rate of learning, the transfer of learning, and the acquiring of attitudes; the latter would consider principally the human cognitive powers and their interaction in the learning process.[12] Other studies are concerned largely with supplying and organizing factual information that is indispensable, or nearly so, for the functions of teaching or administration. A course devoted to one of these, as described in a university bulletin of information, deals with "the structure of the American school system, public and private, with attention given to the units of the system, their interrelations, their legal basis, their financial support, and the qualifications and duties of administrators." Another, as described, is devoted to "an analysis of the basic principles, types, and methods of educational and vocational guidance." Because some knowledge of these speculative disciplines is prerequisite to the development of a philosophy of education, at least some of the

[12] There is an immense literature in the field of the experimental psychology of learning. The only adequate work that I know devoted to the elaboration of a philosophical psychology of learning is Tad W. Guzie, S.J., *The Analogy of Learning* (New York: Sheed & Ward, Inc., 1960).

14

courses devoted to them should ordinarily be taught before or at the same time as the course in philosophy of education.

With this last discipline we enter the practical order, and from this point the student is learning to apply what he has previously studied to making or doing, to art or prudence. Within the classroom he himself can be taught and can learn the arts of teaching, of administering, of constructing a curriculum, and perhaps others, and all of these at the various educational levels. Such functions as counseling, on the other hand, do not seem to be arts, since they involve no construction. Stemming principally from psychologies of learning and philosophy of education, as well as from certain generalizations drawn from counseling experiences, they appear to be practical sciences, though ones much closer to the level of the prudential decisions of daily practice than is philosophy of education itself. Finally, there come certain combined knowledges, such as those involved in learning how to construct and interpret tests, and how to obtain and use occupational information.

Again, a schema may be helpful in summing up the foregoing development:

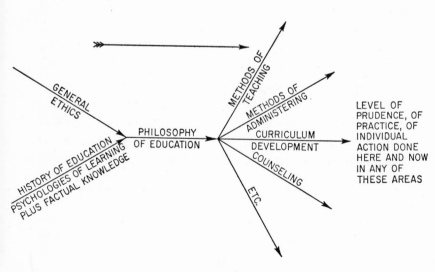

PHILOSOPHY OF EDUCATION, PRUDENCE, AND CONSCIENCE [13]

Ultimately all these practical disciplines point to and have their completion in a particular decision and action by an individual person such as a teacher, an administrator, or a counselor. One of the roots of such a decision is a conviction about the conclusions reached in a philosophy of education, a conviction about what a classroom or a school or a school system is and what it is supposed to be doing. Obviously, this does not mean that no one can reach a particular educational decision and translate it into action without first having been exposed to a formal course in philosophy of education. For it is highly probable that all who are professionally engaged in education, and most of those who are not, have developed, from whatever sources, their own philosophy of education. Indeed, since the first sputnik it would have been difficult to avoid doing so. What it does mean is that formal instruction in and formal study of a philosophy of education will allow such particular decisions and actions—along with other and more particular knowledges—to flow from a reasoned and scientific body of conclusions about how to establish and conserve an educational society and how to direct it to its proper goals.

For all those, then, who are engaged in the process of education in any way, the practical importance of such a study can hardly be exaggerated. Yet even a thorough knowledge of a true philosophy of education can never guarantee that the immediate decisions based in part upon it will themselves always be the correct decisions.[14] For the philosophy of education is a science, since its conclusions are demonstrated and have a certain degree of necessity

[13] This section is adapted from Herbert Johnston, *Business Ethics,* 2d ed. rev. (New York: Pitman Publishing Corporation, 1961), pp. 25–31. Reprinted by permission.

[14] The dangers inherent in the failure to distinguish suffi-

and universality. It is this last characteristic that causes the difficulty. Conclusions that can be called scientific must be universal in character. The physicist, for example, is concerned with and concludes to the general law governing the expansion of metal under heat, not the performance of any particular piece of metal; the psychologist of learning is seeking to establish general laws of learning, and is interested in individual observations and experiments only so far as they can lead him to these general conclusions. Since philosophy of education is part of social ethics, it is concerned with human acts; and as a science its conclusions will pertain to actions taken as universal, not to particular, concrete actions. Those conclusions will relate to what the school should do and should not do in the total educational process, not to the decision whether driver training shall be included in the curriculum next year; they will relate to whether the teaching of sacred doctrine should stress primarily the intellectual or the moral, not to the decision on just how to introduce tomorrow's lesson. The difficulty is that human actions are always concrete, individual events done by this person at this time; whereas the conclusions of a philosophy of education are in general terms. There is a gap here that must be bridged, but a gap that the science of the philosophy of education is incapable of bridging by itself.

It is well to know what the school should do and why, but one administrator is worrying about whether, in very concrete and perhaps complex circumstances, to include driver education in next year's curriculum—a unique event. It is well to have a conviction

---

ciently between educational philosophy and educational practice are sharply pointed out by Everett J. Kircher, "Philosophy of Education—Directive Doctrine or Liberal Discipline?" *Educational Theory*, 5, 4 (October, 1955), 220–229. Cf. Philip G. Smith, "The Relation of Philosophy to Education as a Discipline," *Educational Administration and Supervision*, 46, 1 (January, 1960), 41–51.

about whether the teaching of sacred doctrine should be directed primarily to the development of understanding or to the influencing of conduct, but one teacher is wondering, again in concrete circumstances, how to go about teaching tomorrow's class—another unique event.

The administrator and the teacher are not alone in their difficulties. Everyone faces much the same sort of problem and faces it often—and, ultimately, alone. For each man must reach his decisions himself; each man must live his own life. Personal experience enters here, and the ability to profit by it. There are no easy grades given out in the school of hard knocks, and there is no substitute for maturity. All of us develop, to a greater or less extent, an ability to cope with situations, to weigh circumstances and arrive at a more or less reasonable decision about what we should do in them. That ability is the virtue called prudence, and it largely makes the difference between a happy and an unhappy life.[15]

Prudence as a Virtue

Prudence is both an intellectual and a moral virtue. It is a moral virtue because it leads to decisions in the moral order and requires, as a prerequisite, the right ordering of the will. That is, you have to want the right end before you can possibly reason successfully about the means of attaining it. If the teacher ought to be preparing tomorrow's class but decides instead to grant a free period because he can't be bothered making the preparation, there is not much chance that he will introduce properly a lesson that he is not willing to teach at all. Before you have the least chance

[15] On this virtue, see Josef Pieper, *Prudence* (New York: Pantheon Books, a Division of Random House, Inc., 1959); Charles J. O'Neil, "Prudence, the Incommunicable Wisdom," in R. E. Brennan, O.P. (ed.), *Essays in Thomism* (New York: Sheed & Ward, Inc., 1942), pp. 187–204.

of deciding on and taking the right means to an end, you must first have your will fixed on the end. That is why prudence is a moral virtue, because it demands as a prerequisite the rectitude of the will.

Supposing the will to be rightly ordered, however, it is still necessary to reason, and often very carefully, about the means to be taken to reach that end. You must know not only where you are going but also where you are, and as much as possible of the ground that lies between. The ability to weigh, to consider, and to come to a reasonable conclusion—the ability to pick one's way across often difficult ground to the right goal—is the virtue of prudence. Prudence is an intellectual virtue because it perfects the intellect to reason correctly about particular actions to be done. As a supernatural virtue it is, like any other, a direct gift of God. As a natural virtue it is, like any other, developed by continual practice. And the conclusion of the process of more or less prudent reasoning about what to do is the judgment called conscience, the decision that, considering both the end and the circumstances, this particular act is right and should be done.

Here, then, is the bridge between the universal proposition with which the science called philosophy of education concludes and the particular proposition resulting from the judgment which is conscience. The judgment of conscience is most practical, being concerned with this individual, concrete act. But the prudential reasoning that leads to conscience has to start somewhere; before general knowledge can be applied to given circumstances there must first exist some general knowledge. The sources of such knowledge are many, but one of them is that body of conclusions built up by philosophy of education. In order to reach a decision about including driver education it is not enough to know what the specific function of a school is and why; yet no reasonable decision can be reached unless it is known what the specific function of a school is and why.

A number of difficulties here present themselves. Suppose that two authors or two consultants, presumably expert authorities in philosophy of education, give contradictory answers to the administrator's question about including driver education. What is he to do then? Just what he must always do—use his best judgment and make up his own mind. The fact of the contradictory answers does not mean that the study of philosophy of education is necessarily a waste of time. These answers may have arisen from either of two causes. First, and more basic, the authors or consultants may espouse differing philosophies of education based on differing convictions about the nature and end of man or the nature and end of such agencies of education as the school. What the administrator can do in these circumstances is to evaluate these positions in the light of his own philosophy of education and then reach the best decision he can based on his own convictions. Second, the experts may be in fundamental agreement on a philosophy of education but disagree in the application of its conclusions concerning the function of the school to the administrator's particular problem. For within the contingent order of prudence, of reasoning about individual circumstances and actions to be done, there is no possibility of scientific necessity and demonstration. There are right and wrong decisions, and they are certainly right or wrong; but that certainty is often much less easy for us to see because it is more wrapped up in a sometimes confusing welter of facts and fancies. Again, though, the conclusions reached in a philosophy of education provide a starting point, though no more than that, for the reasoning required in the order of prudence. And without such a starting point, even a sure beginning from a sure principle would be impossible, and a correct conclusion would become largely a matter of chance. Philosophy of education is remotely but really practical, and the consultants in question, even though they disagree in their philosophies of education or on a particular point of application, might, through their discussion of the whole problem and what lies behind it, help the administrator to clarify his own convictions as a starting point toward reaching his own decision on his particular problem.

Certainty in the Practical Order

Ultimately, only he can reach it, and often in fear and trembling. For if there is no demonstration and no necessity about the operation of prudence and the judgment of conscience, how can he be sure what course of action to follow? The answer is that, even when the problem is difficult, he can always be sure practically, though he cannot always be sure speculatively. It is simply impossible always to know with certainty that this particular course of action, and not some other one, is the right one in the existing circumstances. For, among other difficulties, we hardly ever know all the pertinent circumstances.

From the point of view of the speculative order, the order of what is, the administrator may not know for a long time what decision he should have made, and he may never know with anything approaching certainty. But in the practical order, the order of what is to be done, he can assess the situation as well as possible, apply what general knowledge he has or can get to reasoning about that situation as carefully as he can, and reach a decision. He may be in doubt at the very moment that he is making or carrying out that decision, but the doubt is about the material correctness of his conscience and about the speculative rightness of his action. He need have no doubt about the formal correctness of his conscience and about the goodness of his action in the practical order. For though the rightness of the speculative intellect comes from its conformity to things as they are, the rightness of the practical intellect comes from its conformity to a rightly ordered will. And the object of the will is the good as known or as knowable. As long as the administrator (or the teacher, or anyone else) has done what is possible in the existing circumstances to get whatever knowledge is available to him and to apply it as carefully as he can, he has done all that can be expected of a human being. Whatever may be the outcome of his action, he is morally or practically right. And it is possible for him to be certain that he is morally right.

Neither the administrator nor we ourselves should look for a speculative certainty that is impossible in the contingent order. Yet we need not for that reason despair of finding a practical certainty; and in that endless search we may, in our own particular field, obtain a good deal of assistance from the study of philosophy of education.

PHILOSOPHY AND THEOLOGY OF EDUCATION

The last section of this chapter will be devoted to a consideration of the very possibility of a philosophy of education as distinct from a theology of education. The problem is directly raised by Father Donlan in the following terms: "No philosophy can make an adequate statement of Catholic education. Catholic educators can claim no complete philosophy of Catholic education because no such thing exists. There is only a theology of Catholic education." [16]

In this passage the repetition of the adjective Catholic and the general context suggest that the author is here taking "education" in the sense of that lifelong process of development which is identical with the course of a human life itself and which has the same supernatural end. It is this same meaning of education that Pope

[16] Thomas C. Donlan, O.P., *Theology and Education* (Dubuque: Wm. C. Brown Co., 1952), p. 18, note 5. Reprinted by permission of the copyright holder, The Priory Press, Dubuque, Iowa. Cf. Edward A. Fitzpatrick, *Exploring a Theology of Education* (Milwaukee: The Bruce Publishing Company, 1950).

Pius XI seems to have had in mind when he said, "Christian education takes in the whole aggregate of human life. . . ." [17]

Yet even if one takes education in this sense (and there are also narrower but still legitimate meanings of the term), a philosophy of education remains a possibility. For, understood in this signification, the end of education is the same as the end of life itself, and the philosophy of education becomes identical with that aspect of moral philosophy called monastics.[18] One may, with Maritain, hold that there is a Christian moral philosophy, distinct from theology, which, while remaining philosophy, takes account of man's existential condition as fallen and redeemed and the subject of supernatural grace.[19] Or one may hold that monastics is the science of man's natural ultimate end known by reason, though pointing to and demanding completion in moral theology.[20] Whichever of these views one supports, there is still a philosophy and not only a theology of man's actions as directed to his end, and there is still a philosophy and not only a theology of education.

Throughout this book, however, the term education is not being taken primarily in the sense of the lifelong process that points to the individual person's ultimate supernatural end, though this

[17] *Christian Education of Youth* (Washington, D.C.: National Catholic Welfare Conference, 1936), p. 36.

[18] See above, pp. 12–13.

[19] See Jacques Maritain, *An Essay on Christian Philosophy* (New York: Philosophical Library, Inc., 1955), espec. pp. 61–108; and *Science and Wisdom* (London: Geoffrey Bles, Ltd., 1940), pp. 79–81, 107–127, 161–167, 174–205.

[20] See John A. Oesterle, *Ethics* (Englewood Cliffs, N.J.: Prentice-Hall, Inc., 1957), pp. vii–viii, 10–12, 250–256. A brief application of this position to philosophy of education is made by Mortimer J. Adler, "In Defense of the Philosophy of Education," in Nelson B. Henry (ed.), *Philosophies of Education*, part I, The 41st Yearbook of the N.S.S.E. (Chicago: The University of Chicago Press, 1942), pp. 220–221.

most important meaning of the term is neither ignored nor rejected. Education is here being taken, specifically though not exclusively, to refer to those formal educational institutions which are the classroom or the school or the school system. This will apply to Catholic schools as well as to others, for Catholic schools remain schools. In this sense, a philosophy of education, including a philosophy of Catholic education, will not be identical with monastics, looking directly to the perfection of the person in view of *his* end. Rather, it will be a branch of social ethics, concerned immediately with the direction of the educational society, on whatever level, to *its* proper end. And though this educational society must, if it is to function as it should, take account of the ultimate supernatural end of the persons to be educated in schools, yet the end of that society itself is a temporal end, and the body of knowledge which directs it to that end is a philosophy and not theology. As a parallel example, the civil society is made up of persons whose ultimate end is a supernatural one, to be attained only by the aid of divine grace; further, a sound civil society will take this fact into account and will indirectly assist its members to attain this final goal. Yet the end of the civil society itself is the *temporal* common good of the body of citizens as a whole, and it is directed to that end by that branch of social ethics which is *philosophy* of politics. So also, that discipline concerned with the direction of the educational society to its end, including a Catholic educational society, the discipline dealt with in this book, is *philosophy* of education.

For those holding this position, it will follow that "There is, in the proper sense of the terms, no Catholic philosophy of education." Vincent Edward Smith, *The School Examined: Its Aim and Content* (Milwaukee: The Bruce Publishing Company, 1960), p. viii. This is not the same position as Father Donlan's; the relations of the words philosophy, education, and Catholic make the difference.

QUESTIONS

1. What is the relation between philosophy of education and psychology of education?
2. Why are philosophy and education so closely related?
3. Would a philosophy of education for Catholic schools differ from one for public schools? Why or why not?
4. Is a philosophy of education something personal and peculiar to each of us?
5. "While a man is studying in medical school he doesn't get lectures on medical ethics; if he does, they are window dressing; but, working along with other people, he acquires a certain identification with them. He finds himself a member of a corps; he is imbued with a certain *esprit de corps;* he has a certain kind of morale; unconsciously he soaks in a medical ethos." [21] Evaluate this statement. What bearing does it have on any of the issues discussed in this chapter?
6. "To think is to develop a plan, to believe. And to believe is to be willing to act. At this stage, man holds views concerning both what is and what ought to be. But he also runs into a baffling problem. How may thinking be exercised so that he feels himself to have a reasonable control over what is and a reasonable certainty about what ought to be." [22] Evaluate this statement. What bearing does it have on any of the issues discussed in this chapter?

[21] Gail Kennedy in Brand Blanshard (ed.), *Education in the Age of Science* (New York: Basic Books, Inc., Publishers, and The American Academy of Arts and Sciences, 1959), p. 48. Reprinted by permission.

[22] Reprinted by permission of Dodd, Mead & Company,

7. Instead of making philosophy of education a separate course, why not teach students philosophy in a more general way and let them combine this with their professional instruction in education?

---

chapter two

༈

The Nature of Man

The first question to be considered in such an undertaking as this is the nature of the one to be educated. If a man is considered a rational and responsible being, capable of achieving truth and of directing his own life, his education will, at least in its general lines, take one direction. If he is seen as merely another biological organism, a rather complex member of the animal world and subject to all its limitations and determinations, his education will take a different direction. If the final goal of a man is thought to be a supernatural and eternal union with God, this conviction will have a tremendous bearing on his education both inside and outside the school. If, on the contrary, some form of human society is regarded as his highest end, then his education will be modified accordingly. Any kind of education, whether formal or informal, involves the development of a human being in some way. But it must be the development of something that is already there to begin with. So we design a man's education according to our convictions about his nature and ultimate destiny.

As Maritain has expressed it: [1]

> It is clear that the primary aim [of education] is determined by human nature. The question, "What is man?" is the unavoidable preamble to any philosophy of education. It has two implications: first, a philosophic or "ontological" implication, dealing with human nature in its essential being; second, a scientific or "empiriological" implication, dealing with human nature in the phenomenal characteristics that lie open to our modern sciences of observation and measurement. These two implications are in no way incompatible; they complement each other.

Robert Ulich has warned against asking "empiriological" investigations to answer "ontological" questions about the nature of man: [2]

> Nor can experimental psychology be the teacher's exclusive guide for human understanding. Only parts of the totality and depth of the person are accessible to the scientific method

[1] Jacques Maritain, "Thomist Views on Education," in Nelson B. Henry (ed.), *Modern Philosophies and Education,* part I, 54th Yearbook of the N.S.S.E. (Chicago: The University of Chicago Press, 1955), p. 63. Copyright 1955 by the University of Chicago. Reprinted by permission. For a brief history of educational psychology, see Cyril Burt, "The Impact of Psychology upon Education," in George Z. F. Bereday and Joseph A. Lauwerys (eds.), *Education and Philosophy* (New York: Harcourt, Brace & World, Inc., 1957), pp. 163–180. For a much broader picture, see J. P. Chaplin and T. S. Krawiek, *Systems and Theories of Psychology* (New York: Holt, Rinehart and Winston, Inc., 1960).

[2] Robert Ulich, "Comments on Ralph Harper's Essay," *Modern Philosophies and Education,* pp. 255–256. Copy-

as it is generally understood in the departments of psychology and education.... Man is not only a cross section of "behavior patterns"; he reaches into an ontological sphere, however veiled this sphere may be to our intellects.... That says nothing against the attempt to catch as many forms of human reaction and experience into the network of experimental proof as possible. It only says something against false claims of completeness.

SPECIFIC DIFFERENCE BETWEEN MAN AND BRUTE

What sort of being are we trying to educate? [3]   In general, we know what things are from watching what they do, reasoning that if they act thus and not so it must be because they are thus and not so.   Among many other things that a man does, he feeds himself, he grows, he reproduces his kind, he sees and hears, he imagines and remembers, he wants some of the things that he sees, he is angry and he is joyful.   If he does these things, it is obviously because he has the power to do them; and a being with such powers belongs to that biological group called animals.

Abstract Knowledge

A man does more than this, however.   From knowing individual men, he attains the general notion man, and uses it as we are now doing; from counting particular things, he achieves the notion of number, and learns to count without using his fingers; from observing concrete actions through which one man gives an-

right 1955 by the University of Chicago.   Reprinted by permission.
    [3] The following five paragraphs are adapted from Herbert Johnston, *Business Ethics,* 2d ed. rev. (New York: Pitman Publishing Corporation, 1961), pp. 4–6.   Reprinted by permission.

other what is coming to him, he reaches the concept of justice and of virtue. In each instance he starts with the concrete, particular things of the physical universe, but does not end there. From these things he draws general, universal knowledge, called "abstract knowledge" from the Latin verb meaning "to draw from." And this abstract knowledge is new, is different, is irreducible to the particular things and images from which it was drawn. For no arithmetical sum of images of individual men will yield the abstract notion man; the more images you combine, the more confused the composite image becomes, whereas the general concept is quite clear and intelligible. Again, the binomial theorem requires much more than the manipulation of individual images; and the binomial theorem exists.

Abstract knowledge, then, is knowledge which, though originating in something known by the senses, ends in something known by the intellect, something which is different in kind and not only in degree from the sensible objects from which it is drawn. If men possess general knowledge, they evidently have the power of abstracting that sort of knowledge. And if men have knowledge which is independent of its sensory origins, as abstract knowledge is, then it would seem a safe inference that the power by which this knowledge is obtained (called the intellect in Aristotelian and Thomistic terminology) can operate independently of any particular physical organ, such as the brain. For if it used a physical organ, as the sense powers do, its knowledge would be restricted to particular things, as sense knowledge is. Not that there would be any intellectual knowledge if there were no sense knowledge; but, although the senses supply the raw material of intellectual knowledge, they do not enter intrinsically into its constitution.

On the basis of what he does, then, a man is seen to be an animal with intellectual knowledge, and hence with a nature different in kind and not only in degree from that of those animals which do not have such knowledge. For, again, to find out what a thing is, you watch what it does.

An important feature of the general knowledge that a man can have is knowledge of the good. This is not to say that all men, or perhaps any men, know completely in what the good consists, or that there is any general agreement about its nature. But the notion is at least intelligible, even to those who despair of its real existence. And knowing even this of the good, men can and do judge that this or that particular good is not *the* good, that the possession of any concrete good would not leave them forever satisfied and desiring nothing more. And as long as they can see this difference, as long as they can make this contrast, as long as they can see that no wealth, no person, no fame will mean complete and eternal happiness, they are free in the face of particular goods, free to take them or to leave them alone. By his very nature, a man necessarily wills the ultimate good: he cannot desire not to be happy, however perverse his notion of happiness may become. For that very reason, however, he does not necessarily will any particular good, but freely chooses this as opposed to that, because he can see that neither of them is the final good. This is not to say that such choice is always easy; it is merely to say that it is possible. A man's freedom, then, is rooted in his intellectuality, in his power of abstract knowledge.

Language and the Arts

Indeed, the whole picture of human achievement, marred as it so often is by folly and by malice, points to human capabilities unknown to the other animals, to intellectual and moral capacities that cry out for the development which is education. Perhaps the most obvious example is that of language. Brutes make sounds that seem to express emotion. Men use language to signify ideas and their relations; their concepts and judgments are expressed in terms and propositions, and their language has a formal grammar and syntax. This element of formal construction indicates an intellectual grasp not only of abstract concepts or ideas but of their connection in a larger whole whose parts are no longer isolated. Man's world is a cosmos, not a chaos, and his language expresses this fact. The lack of any developed language in the other animals points to a lack of any developed intellectual grasp of reality; the basic reason that brutes do not speak is that they have nothing to say.

In the realm of language it is not only the possession of grammar and syntax that marks man off as unique in the animal world; it is also the capacity to produce and appreciate what we call literature. In whatever form—drama, novel, lyric, epic—the great writers have caught something of the constant and the universal in human nature and human life and have expressed it in concrete and telling terms. And they have been able to do so because human beings have the stuff of greatness in them, the capacity for both heights and depths unknown to the brutes. There are some great animal stories, but they are stories less of the individual animal or even of the species than of the whole intelligible world of nature as it comes from and is guided by the finger of God; they are really stories of divine providence. Further, it is men who write stories about animals, not animals who write stories about men.

So it is with that particular kind of story which we call history. As with science, this undertaking involves much more than a mere chronicling of individual events; it involves an attempt to get behind the surface phenomena and to identify and understand an intelligible causal pattern in human affairs somewhat as the natural sciences attempt to see order in physical occurrences.

So it is, too, with arts other than the literary. In such useful arts as carpentry and tailoring, men show an ability, also unique in the animal world, to grasp complex relations of cause and effect and to select some from among many possible means to an end previously decided on. In such fine arts as painting and sculpture and the dance, a further reach of intelligence is manifested. For in these arts something is made, is seen as good, which is not directed to a utilitarian end, which is not a useful good directed to the satisfaction of bodily needs. Here, as in literature, we have a striving for the beautiful seen as good in itself, worth having for its own sake. Here, again, are frontiers specifically human, far beyond any animal reach.

A Moral and Religious Capacity

The specific difference between men and brutes is most evident, perhaps, in the moral and religious capacities of the former. However much men may differ about what they consider morally right and morally wrong, they agree that the distinction exists and is meaningful. Any man will, on occasion, praise or blame another man's conduct, but will not make this judgment of anything else. When he says that he has a good neighbor and that he has a good hunting dog, he is not using good in the same sense. And when men practice a religion; when they worship a divine power, in whatever form; especially when some few of them reach heights of mystical intuition, they are in the presence of an experience completely alien to any that is possible to the other animals, bound as these are by the limits of space and time.

Men do have the same basic physiological and psychological equipment as the other animals for the simple reason that they too are animals, and this equipment is quite worthy of being developed and cultivated. Motor skills and muscular abilities are important in many phases of an ordinary human life, and are worth developing for that practical purpose. But men also have powers that the other animals do not have, powers of intellect and of will that open to men a whole world of knowledge and of love that is closed to the beings which do not have these powers. Here,

33

then, is the area of specifically human education, the possibility of a development that is open only to men. If the educational process is to take account of the nature of the persons to be educated, here will be the area of its principal focus. The aim of education, whether formal or informal, is to make a man in the sense of developing as much as possible those powers, and the virtues that perfect them, which are precisely the ones that make him human in the first place. It is a question of actualizing potentialities, of making ever more human the beings who are to be educated. And unless we see them as human to start with, unless we recognize those potentialities as distinctively and irreducibly human, we shall not be very likely to develop the persons and their powers in any truly human way.

THE END OF MAN AND THE MEANS TO THE END

In the latter part of Chapter one,[4] it was stated that the term "education" is not being taken primarily in the sense of the life-long process that points to the individual person's ultimate supernatural end, but rather to refer to those formal educational institutions which are the classroom or the school or the school system; it was also said, however, that this educational society must, if it is to function as it should, take account of the ultimate supernatural end of the persons to be educated in schools. Even though the process of schooling has, directly, a temporal end, the subjects of that schooling have an ultimate end which is beyond the temporal. Education in the sense of schooling is a distinct function with its own end and its own means; but it is also part of education in the wider sense that is identical with all the influences and events of a human life and that has the same end. For this reason,

[4] See the section on Philosophy and Theology of Education.

those who study philosophy of education so that they may better direct formal educational institutions to their natural end should be conscious, among other truths, of two related ones. The first is the fact that they are not directly engaged in education in its ultimate meaning, that the end of the school or of the classroom is not the end of life. The second is the complementary fact that their students have a supernatural end beyond the natural one for which schools directly and specifically, though not exclusively, are intended to prepare them. Schools can do their best work when those who teach in them and administer them know not only the nature but also the destiny of the human beings whom they are educating. They can then see their own work, distinct as it may be, in its proper context.

Briefly, the end of man, an end which can be neither known without revelation nor achieved without supernatural, divine grace, is to enjoy the knowledge of the essence of God for eternity. This goal is infinitely above the limited capabilities of human beings; yet God has supernaturalized human actions so that they may become means of achieving men's supernatural last end. Works, as well as faith, are meritorious because of the grace of God. As we shall see in greater detail in Chapter three, the immediate internal source of these actions is human powers strengthened for their operations by virtues. The source of supernaturally meritorious acts can only be supernatural virtues, infused into men by God rather than acquired, as the natural virtues are, by repeated human acts.

The end of man, then, is the knowledge of God; the means to that end are human actions; and the internal sources of those actions are the virtues. Education in its widest sense is the process that aims at this end by these means; the agents immediately concerned are God and the human person, with the Church as the divinely instituted society Whose specific task is to assist men to reach their supernatural end. Education in the sense of schooling

35

is a part of education in this wide sense, and must never proceed as though it were a completely autonomous whole, even though it does have its own natural goal. For, first, the specific end of the school, the intellectual development of its students, is but one phase of the education of human beings, whose last end is supernatural. And, second, the school inevitably has a tremendous influence on the development of the moral as well as of the intellectual virtues, and, where it cooperates with the Church, in the acquisition of the supernatural as well as of the natural moral virtues.

HUMAN EDUCATION DEVELOPS HUMAN POWERS

This discussion has to some extent anticipated Chapters three and four, in which the virtues and the various agencies of education will be discussed at greater length. Our immediate task is, in view of the established nature and end of man, to find out what precise contribution that educational institution which is the school can be expected to make to his development. What must be kept in mind is that the direct, specific end of the school is a natural one, worthy of pursuit for itself, and with its own means; and also that the end of the school is not the same as the end of life.

The school, as has been said, cannot wisely ignore the end of life. Though this is not its specific purpose, the church-related school can and should provide for the regular practice of religion on the part of its students. In Catholic schools this is usually looked after by the provision of opportunities for assistance at daily Mass, reception of the sacraments, an annual retreat, and a generally religious atmosphere. Further, and this does refer to its specific purpose, the church-related school can furnish instruction in sacred doctrine as the most important of its intellectual functions. In both of these areas, the secular school cannot make the same provisions; it has, though, the obligation of not interfering with the believing student's practice of his religion and not weakening his theological convictions. Further, it will be argued below,[5] the state has the obligation to make religious instruction possible for those who wish it.

The teaching of the intellectual disciplines, and, where possible, that most important discipline which is sacred doctrine, is the specific work of the school, of any school, and is the function which justifies the existence of the school as such. This work is accomplished particularly in the classroom, the laboratory, and the library. Even here there will inevitably be some degree of moral influence on the student, though it is indirect and informal. Further, since the school as a whole is a broader and more inclusive educational agency than the classroom, part of the operation proper to it will be the direct and conscious effort to help the student develop his moral virtues. In part this goal can be achieved through the intellectual function of the school, through the concept of his own nature that the student there receives; you cannot consistently demand moral responsibility of a being who, as you explain him to himself, is simply another biological unit. In part this goal can be achieved directly through the experiences which the student has in the school and the demands that are made on him, and which can lead to the further development of perseverance, honesty, justice, courage, and most of the other moral virtues.

Closely related to this function of the school, and one that is also specifically human, is that of developing social awareness and some of the social graces in its students. Precisely because he has intellectual knowledge and moral responsibility, man is naturally a social animal, not in the way that ants or bees are social, but in a peculiar human way. Though a man is a man before he is any-

[5] See in Chapter four the section on The State.

thing else, before he is a member of any society, yet it is only in various societies that he will be able best to develop his capacities, especially his specifically human capacities. To become better men and to lead more human lives we all need the experience of living socially. Societies will be more or less successful, and thus will be of more or less benefit to their members, to the degree that those members develop the knowledge and the willingness that will enable them to cooperate in achieving, so far as they do, the goals of those societies. Both the knowledge of what societies are and the willingness to work for their success must be developed; the school can play an effective part in such development, both inside and outside the classroom.

Finally, since men are animals, though animals of a unique sort, they have certain physical powers that also deserve development if the notion of educating the whole man has any validity. Such motor skills as writing are obviously indispensable for any real intellectual achievement. An extension of this ability to include typing can also be justified as a useful tool for further learning. And physical training of almost any kind, whether aimed at participation in organized sports or not, is, in itself, an admirable thing, for it is better to have a healthy body than not to have one. Since it is a human being that goes to school, and not just an intellect or a will, any power that a human being possesses can lay some claim to consideration. It remains true, however, that there are other educational agencies, and that the specific, though not the exclusive, function of the school as a school is an intellectual one.

TRANSFER OF TRAINING

One of the perennial and highly controversial problems in the field of education, and one related to the question of the nature of man, is that of the transfer of training. Distinguishing this notion from those of mental discipline and formal discipline, Kolesnik points out that the conviction that transfer of training occurs lies behind all formal schooling: [6]

Of the three concepts in question, transfer of training is generally regarded today as the broadest. It refers to the application of knowledge, skills, habits, attitudes or ideals acquired in one situation—such as the physics laboratory—to another situation for which they had not been specifically learned—such as the kitchen, the farm, the machine shop or the algebra class. Whereas the possibility of transfer was once denied, it is now generally accepted as a sound principle that under certain conditions and to a certain extent transfer can and does take place. Except for some psychologists and educationists, perhaps, no one has ever doubted this. The very notion of formal education seems to assume it. Indeed, if the knowledge, skills and ideals acquired in the classroom could not be carried over and made to function outside the classroom, it is doubtful that the time, money and energy being expended on schooling could be justified.

[6] Walter B. Kolesnik, *Mental Discipline in Modern Education* (Madison: University of Wisconsin Press, 1958), p. 5. Reprinted with permission of the copyright owners, the Regents of the University of Wisconsin. See also William A. Kelly, *Educational Psychology*, 4th ed. rev. (Milwaukee: The Bruce Publishing Company, 1956), pp. 324, 338, 349; W. D. Commins and Barry Fagin, *Principles of Educational Psychology*, 2d ed. (New York: The Ronald Press Company, 1954), p. 588; Lester D. Crow and Alice Crow, *Educational Psychology*, rev. ed. (New York: American Book Company, 1958), pp. 324, 330, 339–341; Henry E. Garrett, *Great Experiments in Psychology* (New York: Appleton-Century-Crofts, Inc., 1941), pp. 239–257; Lloyd G. Humphreys, "Transfer of Training in General Education," *The Journal of General Education*, 5 (1951), 210–216, reprinted in Lester D. Crow and Alice Crow (eds.), *Readings in Educational Psychology* (Ames, Iowa: Littlefield, Adams and Co., 1956), pp. 306–316; Jaime Castiello, S.J., "The Psychology of Habit

39

Further, it might be added, the conviction that transfer of training occurs lies behind education in another of its meanings, behind all the conscious and organized efforts of the family, the church, the state, and other societies to educate their members, as well as behind the work of the school. Concerning all these societies, but particularly the last, it can be said that: [7]

> From the viewpoint of the educational psychologist the problem of the transfer of learning reduces to the following questions: How and to what extent does learning one thing facilitate the learning of something else? To what extent does school learning carry over to situations outside the classroom? What conditions are necessary or helpful for the occurrence of these two kinds of transfer?

The problem of the transfer of training is central to the whole educational process. The position that one takes on this problem will depend principally on his philosophical convictions concerning the nature of man and the human cognitive and volitional powers. The pedagogical implementation of that position will depend principally on the empirical findings of educational psychologists. Further, the position taken on transfer will be probably the most important influence behind one's convictions on curriculum development. For what a student should be taught will depend on what he is and how he learns, as well as and even before it will depend on the accidental features of his present situation.

What a human being is we have already seen, however briefly, in the earlier part of this chapter. What his curriculum should be will be touched on, also briefly, later in this book. How he learns, and the psychological aspects of the transfer of training, at least so far as sensorimotor and intellectual processes are concerned,

---

in St. Thomas Aquinas," *The Modern Schoolman*, 14 (1936), 8–12.

[7] Commins and Fagin, *op. cit.*, pp. 588–589. Reprinted by permission of The Ronald Press Company.

lie beyond the professional competence of this writer and must be left to educational psychologists. Since, however, such things as attitudes and ideals are also involved in the transfer of training, and since these lie to some extent within the field of the moral philosopher, there may be some point in examining this aspect of the question.

Transfer in the Moral Order

Does such transfer exist in the moral order? It depends on what one takes the question to mean. It is not usually understood as asking whether a man who develops to some degree the virtue of temperance will also, and by that very fact, develop the virtue of justice. It is usually understood as asking whether a man who develops the virtue of temperance in one set of circumstances will also exercise that virtue in another set of circumstances. Actually, however, the question usually seems to be whether the original set of circumstances will really develop the virtue of temperance in the first place; what people are really asking, it would seem, is not so much whether moral training can be transferred, as whether moral training can be achieved at all in whatever particular way is under discussion.

In explaining why the state is of moral as well as material benefit to its members, St. Thomas Aquinas, following Aristotle, long ago pointed out that if a situation arises in which a father is physically incapable of disciplining his rebellious sons, he can, in an organized society, appeal to the guardians of public order.[8] And he is not referring simply to the fact that these public officers will restore order in a disordered situation, important as that fact is. He is also referring to the influence of such restoration on the young men in question. He is saying, in more modern language, that juvenile delinquents will not only be deterred from crime by the

[8] St. Thomas, *In I Ethic.*, lect. 1, Spiazzi ed. No. 4.

threat of police action, but will also be morally improved. Forced obedience, the hypothesis runs, will in time generate voluntary obedience, will develop the virtue of obedience. The question that seems to be at issue in most discussions of the transfer of moral training is actually that of the possibility of the development of moral virtue by whatever means is in question—in this example, by the threat of coercion.

If virtue is developed by repeated actions—and on the natural level it is so developed—then repeated acts of obedience to authority, even if the original reason is ignoble, should make it continually easier to obey, should make it seem ever more natural to obey. These repeated acts, even if originally forced, should, in short, develop the virtue of obedience in those who through self-will or faulty home training or both are lacking in that virtue.

Can Virtue Be Legislated?

This is the theory lying behind social legislation. Far from believing that "You can't legislate morality," those who support such social legislation as The Fair Employment Practices Act or school integration laws maintain that legislation is one of the forms of education and that social legislation will produce better men as well as better situations. And it is certainly true that law is a matter of reason before it is a matter of will, that it issues primarily from the reason of a legislator and is a form of explanation to those to whom it applies of what they should do in order to achieve their common good.[9]

On the level of the civil authority, the theory seems to have

[9] Among others, Robert M. Hutchins has put this point forcefully: "The importance of law is not that it is coercive, but that it is pedagogical. The way to begin the rule of law, therefore, is to begin it and to rely on its educational force." "The Nurture of Human Life," Center for the Study of Democratic Institutions, *Bulletin* (March, 1961), p. 3.

a large amount of justification. When they were first proposed, laws regulating child labor, safety conditions in dangerous occupations, minimum wages, and other such things were opposed as placing impossible burdens on the economy. They were at first obeyed only because of the legal sanctions attached to disobedience. Yet no one would today even suggest a return to the conditions existing before such legislation. There may be many reasons for such a changed attitude toward the rights of working people; one of them would clearly seem to be that the business world followed the legal directives, found that the economy somehow survived under these directives, got used to working in such conditions, and gradually came to accept the situation as normal and right. Such a development constitutes real progress in the virtue of justice, and that development can largely be put down to the influence of social legislation. Experience would indicate that, at least in this meaning, you can legislate virtue.

Certainly, most societies take the possibility for granted and attempt to do so. The Church insists on her members' obeying ecclesiastical law not only for the sake of the law but also for the sake of the members. That law is designed to make better men as well as to get certain things done. Parents lay down certain rules for their children to obey primarily in order to develop a sense of responsibility in the children, to help them to grow up and reach the condition in which they may run their own lives without further rules from their parents. The basic idea is not just to get the dishes done or the grass cut or even to get the children off the street and out of harm's way at a reasonable hour, though these results are not unimportant. The basic idea is that repetition of these actions, even though there is a certain amount of coercion involved, is designed to lead to a greater degree of maturity, to a heightened sense of responsibility in the children. And it is a pretty general experience that responsibility developed during adolescence will carry over into adult life.

Coercion and Rebellion

Is this the way, though, to develop responsibility in the first place? Sometimes it works and sometimes it doesn't. Certainly, to let people of any age do exactly as they please is an open invitation both to social chaos and to the deterioration of character; it is not good for any of us to be answerable to no one but ourselves. Yet it is also possible to make discipline so strict and coercion so severe as to invite rebellion. Captain Bligh was interested in developing strict and unquestioning obedience in his crew; the way in which he went about it produced mutiny on the *Bounty* instead. Clericalism has led to previously loyal Catholics leaving the Church. Parents who are unreasonably strict have driven their children to leave home and, as a gesture of defiance, to live as they know their parents would not wish them to.

The fact that coercion ordinarily reaches a point, varying with the individual person, at which it produces rebellion does not invalidate the claim that moral virtue can be developed by the repeated performance of good acts. What it means is that prudence must be exercised in applying sanctions and that the natural human inclination to exercise the freedom of choice cannot be entirely ignored. It is this delicate balance that must be maintained in every attempt to develop the moral virtues in others. Should parochial school authorities require their students to attend Mass daily? Should parents insist that their children take the pledge before they are of legal age? Should Federal courts insist that school integration be undertaken immediately? There is no easy answer to these and similar questions. But what is at issue and in question is not really whether moral virtues can be developed by repeated action, even when a certain degree of coercion is involved. What is really at issue is whether, in this particular instance, the coercion that will have to be used may not defeat its own purpose—that of eventually leading to a voluntary acceptance of the rule in question. The problem of the transfer of training in the moral order is actually the problem of the exercise of prudence in a given situation.

This whole matter of the transfer of training suggests the subject of the following chapter, the nature and development of the virtues.

QUESTIONS

1. Is an honor system the answer to the problem of cheating?
2. Is student government a reliable way to train character? At all levels? At any levels?

chapter three

✦✦✦

The Virtues

HABITS IN GENERAL

Everyone engaged in any phase of the educational process, like everyone engaged in any other conscious and deliberate activity, is trying to accomplish something. The goals at which he is aiming may be unformulated and indefinite in his mind, or they may be expressed at wearying and repetitive length in a book on the philosophy of education; but the goals are there, or the educator would not be engaged in trying to reach them. And whatever relative place he may give it in his hierarchy of values, probably every educator sees himself as, among other things, helping the person to be educated improve his ability to know or to do something, or both. The educator may be a parent consciously giving his child an example of responsible living; he may be a school-

47

teacher explaining fractions to his students; he may be a weapons instructor showing a recruit how to sight a machine gun. In each of these instances the educator knows from observation that the person whom he is trying to influence has certain powers, both to know and to do, and is confident, on the basis of his experience, that the operation of these powers can be made better. The parent has observed that his child shows the ability to judge actions in moral terms, and, within the limits common to men, to exercise a free choice of what actions he will perform; he wants him to develop an increasing sureness in choosing and performing actions that they both regard as morally right. The teacher has observed that the members of his class show at least some ability to see the relations among quantitative parts and to reason from cause to effect; he wants them to develop an increasing competence in their intellectual handling of these relationships. The weapons instructor has observed that the recruit shows an ability to understand and remember and follow instructions; he wants him to become able to sight a machine gun rapidly and accurately.

The Powers Open to Habituation

If the operation of a power is to be improved—and not just for one action but in a stable and relatively permanent manner— the power must be susceptible of this kind of improvement, called "habituation." The teacher does not try to increase the basic intellectual capacity of his students, for he knows that this cannot be done; he tries to get each student to heighten his ability to use his power of knowing within its natural limits. The weapons instructor does not try to increase the recruit's basic sharpness of vision, for seeing one thing leaves no permanent impression enabling him to see other things better; he tries to get the recruit to focus on some things to the exclusion of others and thus to bring his naturally limited power of vision to bear on this particular task with increasing effectiveness. Native intellectual capacity, so far at least as the agent intellect [1] is concerned, is an example of what is technically known as active operational potency; sight is an example of passive operational potency. Active operational potency cannot receive a habit; that is, it cannot be informed by a stable perfecting quality which is a principle or source of act, because it is already a principle of act by its very nature. The agent intellect is always at the height of its power. Passive operational potency cannot receive a habit, in the strict Thomistic sense of *habitus,* because the quality which it receives from its actuating principle (the thing seen) does not *inform* the potency but remains only while the operation in question is being performed; it belongs to that species of quality which is a passion rather than a habit. After you look at something, your power of vision, your ability to see other things, has not increased.[2]

Between active and passive operational potency there stand the specifically human powers which are the intellect (the possible intellect, not the agent intellect) and the will (the rational ap-

[1] In the Aristotelian and Thomistic theory of knowledge, the agent intellect is that power which, through abstraction from sense images, and perhaps directly from things themselves, makes intellectual knowledge possible. See St. Thomas, *Summa Theologiae,* I, 79, 3–4; 85, 1. See also Herman R. Reith, C.S.C., *An Introduction to Philosophical Psychology* (Englewood Cliffs, N.J.: Prentice-Hall, Inc., 1956), part III, sec. A, espec. pp. 165–169; Robert Edward Brennan, O.P., *Thomistic Psychology* (New York: The Macmillan Company, 1941), chap. 7, espec. pp. 179–195.

[2] St. Thomas approaches the subject of habit from a metaphysical rather than a psychological point of view. See *In IX Metaph.; De Virtutibus in Communi,* espec. art. 1; *Summa Theologiae,* I-II, qu. 49–64. An excellent secondary source on this subject is Vernon J. Bourke, "The Role of Habitus in the Thomistic Metaphysics of Potency and Act," in R. E. Brennan, O.P. (ed.), *Essays in Thomism* (New York: Sheed & Ward, Inc., 1942), pp. 103–109.

petite), and, to a lesser extent, those powers which, though not specifically human, come to some extent under the control of intellect and will. These latter powers are the sense appetites, the imagination and the memory, and, at the bottom of the scale, the nervous and the muscular systems. All these powers differ from purely active potency in that, in order to serve as a principle or source of act, they must be actuated by an active principle; the possible intellect, for example, must have an intelligible object present to it before the act of knowing can occur. These powers differ from purely passive potency in that they are not restricted to only one sort of operation, as is the power of sight, for example, but may be used well or badly; through the operation of the will, for instance, one may develop either the virtue of justice or the vice of injustice. Further, they differ from purely passive potency in that they receive not just a passion, as does the power of sight in the example that we have been using, but a form that remains after the operation in question has ceased and that makes further operation of the same kind easier; a man who habitually pays his bills is more likely to repay the money he borrowed from you than one who usually dodges his bills, and the difference is a difference in the men and not just a matter of mathematical probabilities.

As examples of powers open to habituation we have been using the intellect and the will. In a reduced meaning of the term "habit" or "virtue," other powers are also capable of perfection by those qualities which are virtues. The following schemata are intended to outline the powers of the soul and the virtues by which some of them may be perfected. The aim is to set in context the notions which will be discussed in the following pages.

Even though most of the powers outlined below involve bodily activity, they are properly powers of the soul, or vital powers, because they are the source of operations which are peculiar to living things, to organisms endowed with a principle of life, that is, a soul. If you plant an acorn in the ground, and if the conditions are right, you will eventually have an oak. If you plant a stone in the ground

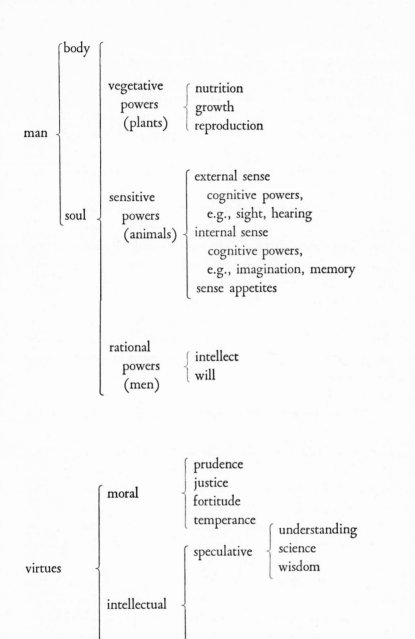

man
- body
- soul
  - vegetative powers (plants)
    - nutrition
    - growth
    - reproduction
  - sensitive powers (animals)
    - external sense cognitive powers, e.g., sight, hearing
    - internal sense cognitive powers, e.g., imagination, memory
    - sense appetites
  - rational powers (men)
    - intellect
    - will

virtues
- moral
  - prudence
  - justice
  - fortitude
  - temperance
- intellectual
  - speculative
    - understanding
    - science
    - wisdom
  - practical
    - art
    - prudence

beside the acorn, you will never have anything but a stone in the ground. The stone will not grow because it is not alive; the acorn will grow because it is alive. There are many terms for that principle through which living things are alive and perform vital operations; the philosophical term for this principle is the soul. It is for this reason that the powers that living things exhibit, even though most of them involve bodily functions, can be called powers of the soul.

How does one know what these powers are? The means that all of us constantly use are those of observation and inference. How did we know that the acorn was alive and the stone not alive? Because the acorn did something—grew into a tree—and the stone did not. This seems to be the way in which we reach all conclusions of this sort. In order to find out, to whatever extent is possible, what something is, we watch what it does. Then we infer that if it does this sort of thing, for example, grows, it must have the power to do so. Last, if we are interested in a further inference, we can reason that if it exhibits such and such powers, it is such a kind of being.

We see, for example, some things that show evidence of life by growing, by nourishing themselves in the process, and by reproducing themselves. Unlike stones, to take our previous example, things such as acorns do not have to have something added by way of an extrinsic source in order to increase in quantity; they grow by a principle intrinsic to themselves. They do so by absorbing chemical elements from their environment and changing them into living tissue. Further, they reproduce their kind through another vital process. These things we call plants.

Again, we see some other things, which we call animals, that do all that plants do and, in addition, exhibit some form of consciousness, a phenomenon irreducible to the physiological events that are connected with it. The higher animals show evidence of having five external sense cognitive powers, by means of which they become conscious of objects and events immediately present to them. They also show evidence of possessing memory and imagination, as well as some form of instinct. These are called internal sense cognitive powers because they do not have any organ on the surface of the body. In addition, animals evidently have an attraction to or an aversion from some of the things that they are conscious of; they give evidence, in other words, of sense appetites and emotions.

Finally come men, whose powers of intellect and will, it was argued in the preceding chapter, serve to mark them off as different in kind from the other animals. Our task here is to find out, by the same kind of psychological approach, which powers that men show evidence of possessing are capable of being habituated. Certainly that power which is the intellect is the subject of various virtues, such as the arts and the sciences. A student who has, we say, learned geometry, has developed a quality, an intellectual virtue, which enables him, first, to become to some extent a geometrician and, second, to reason with some degree of efficiency in the field of geometry. And so with the other sciences and with the arts. That power which is the will can acquire the same sort of perfection, through the development, for example, of the virtue of justice by which we are led to respect the rights of others and to give them what is owing to them. When we come to the sense appetites, we find that virtues are also able to be developed, but in a somewhat less perfect way. Fortitude and temperance are real virtues, perfecting the sense appetites so that we can pursue bodily goods in a reasonable way and can face firmly the obstacles that make it difficult for us to do what is right. Yet these powers are never more than imperfectly under the control of the intellect and the will, and hence the virtues developed in them are less perfectly virtues than are those of the rational powers. When it comes to the powers called imagination and memory, there is some doubt about the extent to which virtues can be developed.

These powers should, theoretically, be open to habituation to the extent that they can be controlled by the intellect and the will. The actual extent, if any, to which they are so open to habituation can best be determined by further work in experimental psychology. Observation would indicate that this is as far as we can go in developing virtues. The power of sight, for example, does not seem to acquire any increased ability to operate by being used extensively. Powers of concentration can be increased, but this does not seem to be a perfection of the sense power itself. Finally, on the vegetative level it should be quite evident that no virtues can be developed; no personal effort, for example, will bring the process of growth under rational control.

Once more, then, we can say that, in the strictest sense of the term, only the specifically human powers of intellect and will, which are rational in themselves, are the subject of virtues. In a reduced meaning the sense appetites can be said to be the subject of habits so far as they fall within the control of reason and will. With a further reduction in meaning, one can say that even the internal sense cognitive powers of memory and imagination can receive habits so far as "these powers are moved to operation by the command of reason." [3] Last, neural and muscular patterns can also be built up through repeated operations; these resemble habits, in the meaning in which we are using the term, but are not accurately so called. [4]

A schema would present the situation thus:

Intellect and will: rational by their nature; they develop habits in the most proper meaning of the term.

Sense appetites: to some extent under the control of reason and will; they develop habits in a less proper meaning.

Internal sense cognitive powers: still less under the control of

[3] St. Thomas, *Summa Theologiae,* I-II, 50, 3, ad 3. Cf. *ibid.,* 56, 5, c.

[4] *Ibid.,* 50, 3, ad 3.

reason and will; they develop habits in an even more reduced meaning.

Bodily powers: controlled by reason and will until their operation becomes automatic; they develop what may be called
patterns or skills or techniques.

Properly speaking, habits are qualities inhering in the soul by
way of the powers that they perfect; these qualities produce stable,
relatively permanent accidental changes that constitute in their
possessor what is literally a "second nature." Men perform human
acts by means of their powers, among others, of intellect, will,
sense appetites, memory, and imagination. If these powers can be
improved by qualities inhering in them as forms, that is, by good
habits or virtues, those men will perform their human acts more
easily, efficiently, and surely. And since any end, including man's
last end, must be achieved by means of human acts, the development of good habits will necessarily be a primary aim of the educational process on any of its various levels.

Habits and Skills

Throughout this section we have been speaking of habits in
a strictly technical sense, and have maintained that they can inhere
primarily in the specifically human powers of intellect and will and
secondarily in those powers into whose operation reason and will
enter in a particular way. These habits, then, unlike muscular or
neural patterns, are not at all automatic or unconscious; they do
make subsequent actions easier and more certain, but not by re-
ducing them to a mechanical level. You do not become prudent
unconsciously; you do not learn to weigh possible courses of action,
to judge that one of them provides the best means to the desired
end, and to carry out the decision arrived at, without considerable
thought. And no matter how prudent you may become, you
never exercise the virtue without thinking, and thinking carefully.
Courage, again, does not involve becoming insensitive to fear or

hardship; it involves feeling fear or laziness and going ahead and doing the right thing anyway. No matter how long you have been getting up early in the morning you never, I have been told, reach the point at which you can do it without effort. Habits taken in this proper sense (and we are, of course, interested in the possibility of developing good habits, or virtues) make it easier to act as we should, but the actions springing from these virtues are always done at the conscious level as fully human acts. In this book the word "habit" will consistently be used in that technical sense.

Many of our actions, however, are really automatic. Some of them are always automatic—for example, digestion; and some of them become automatic after learning—for example, typewriting. These actions are sometimes called reflex actions, and, at least in many of their aspects, do not involve consciousness. We must certainly be conscious and even very careful when, for instance, we are driving a car; but we are not really skillful and accomplished drivers until we can do most of the required actions without having to stop and think about each one. Other examples, from innumerable possible ones, are swimming, skating, operating an adding machine, running a punch press. Let us call these acquired abilities "patterns" or "skills" or "techniques," and let us not confuse them with habits in the technical sense of the word.[5]

After we first make mental judgments about what should be done and how it should be done, we develop patterns or skills by controlled repetition. Initial attempts at, say, learning typewriting will usually be halting and difficult. But correct practice, conscientiously repeated day after day, will gradually develop the needed skill, until striking the correct key, shifting for capitals, and all the other motions that make an expert typist (though never an absolutely perfect one) will become easy to perform and largely automatic. Chiefly because of their importance for daily living,

[5] Cf. p. 51 above.

skills as well as habits are legitimate and even indispensable aims of education in most of its meaning.

NATURAL AND SUPERNATURAL VIRTUES

Since this is a book in philosophy rather than in theology, it will be concerned directly with the natural rather than the supernatural order, and hence with the natural rather than the supernatural virtues. Yet it is important for us to keep in mind the existence and the importance of the supernatural virtues even though we cannot, by our own efforts, develop them either in our students or in ourselves. Natural virtues are those which we develop and practice in order to perfect our human nature. Our last end, however, is beyond the reach of that nature if it is left unaided; hence, it will need to be strengthened, if we are to have any chance of reaching that end, by good habits which are also beyond human nature, that is, by supernatural virtues. These virtues cannot at all be acquired by human effort; they must be directly infused into us gratuitously by God.[6]

Examples of these would be the theological virtues of faith, hope, and charity, none of which can be developed by purely human effort. Further examples would be the infused cardinal virtues of prudence, justice, fortitude, and temperance. There are also, of course, the natural cardinal virtues which concern the same subject matter and perfect the same powers and have the same names as the supernatural cardinal virtues. Yet the latter are specifically different from the naturally acquired virtues—different in kind and not just in degree—for the supernatural virtues dispose us toward an end that exceeds infinitely the capacity of human nature. A man who stops smoking because he is afraid of cancer or because he wants to develop his character is practicing the natural virtue of temperance, and will increase that virtue in him-

[6] St. Thomas, *Summa Theologiae,* I-II, 51, 4, c.

self by maintaining his abstinence; his immediate reason is his health or his self-command, both of them natural goods. A man who gives up smoking as an act of reparation for past sins is practicing the supernatural virtue of temperance, which can be increased in him only by a continuation of divine grace; his immediate reason springs from his love of God, a supernatural motive.[7]

Nevertheless, natural and supernatural virtues are not unrelated; and a person who has not, to continue the example, developed by his own efforts the natural virtue of temperance to a considerable degree would be unable to practice perfectly the infused virtue of the same name. For the supernatural order, the order of grace, is built upon the natural, not upon its ruins.

This is why a regular, conscious, and determined effort on our part to build up the natural virtues in ourselves and to help our students or others under our care build up the natural virtues in themselves may have indirect results even in the supernatural order. This is not to say that our own actions can in any way cause in us the supernatural virtues, which are the effect of divine grace alone. But the acquisition of natural virtue can at least dispose us favorably to the reception of supernatural virtue.

Since natural virtue is acquired through one's own repeated actions, one of the best ways of gradually building up these virtues will be through the imitation of the lives of good persons. The ancients were fond of pointing out the value to be derived from watching and imitating the best and wisest men. In every time and in every land, national heroes have been held up before youth for their admiration and emulation. For the better development of the spiritual life, both in ourselves and in our students, the study and imitation of the lives of the saints and of the life of Christ Himself are the traditional and the tested means of encouraging the sanctity that leads to ultimate and eternal success and happiness.

[7] *Ibid.*, 63, 4, c.

The most telling example, however, the one most likely to have a deep and lasting influence on our students' lives, is the one which they receive directly rather than vicariously, from life rather than from books, from deeds rather than from words. This fact puts a truly awesome responsibility on all those whose actions the young observe, and observe with frightening clarity—on parents, on priests, on school administrators, on teachers—to live and act in such a manner that those under their care will be themselves led to cultivate good habits rather than bad ones, virtues rather than vices. This responsibility will be spelled out at greater length in the following chapter; its importance simply cannot be exaggerated.

MORAL VIRTUES

The intellectual virtues, which will be discussed in the following section, are those which enable us to *know* what is true and to *know* how to do and to make things. For the good life, however, we must not only know but actually do what is right. The good habits which perfect our human powers so that we can do what is right—that is, perform the actions that will lead us to those ends which we actually have, including our last end—are called moral virtues.[8] There are many such virtues, because there are many areas in which we are required to act well. Traditionally, though, the most important and inclusive of the moral virtues have been called the cardinal virtues: prudence, justice, fortitude, and temperance. It will be maintained throughout this book that the specific task of the school, and especially of the classroom within

[8] See Sister Mary William Hollenbach, S.S.N.D., *The Nature of the Intellectual and Moral Virtues and Their Various Relationships* (Notre Dame, Ind.: unpublished dissertation, 1959). Many parts of this dissertation are applicable to philosophy of education.

59

the school, is the development in students of the intellectual virtues. Yet our students are human persons, not walking intellects; and the school, like every other educational agency, has to some degree the task of helping those students develop the moral as well as the intellectual virtues.

As was mentioned above,[9] the first of the cardinal virtues, which is prudence, is also and primarily an intellectual virtue, because it improves our ability to reason to a sound conclusion about what we should do in any given circumstances. It is a moral virtue as well, however, because it leads to decisions in the moral order, and also because it requires that our will be rightly directed in the first place. That is, we have to want the right end before we can possibly reason successfully about the means of attaining it. The student who attends college primarily for social reasons is not likely to get as much out of his experience, intellectually speaking, as one who attends college primarily for the sake of learning. If his will is fixed on the wrong end, he will be unlikely to decide on and take the means that will lead him to the right end. Prudence is a moral as well as an intellectual virtue.

The second of the cardinal virtues, justice, is one that perfects our will so as to enable us consistently to give to other persons or groups what is owing to them, or what they have a right to expect. To respect the rights of others is to do them justice. A student is practicing justice when he replaces a book which he borrowed and then lost. His father is practicing justice when he reports his full income to the government. His teacher is practicing justice when he prepares his classes as carefully as he possibly can. The school authorities are practicing justice when they decide scholarship winners on the strict and exclusive basis of academic achievement.

Fortitude, or courage, is a virtue that perfects one of our sense appetites so that we will go ahead and do what we should do even

[9] See in Chapter one the section on Philosophy of Education, Prudence, and Conscience.

in the face of difficulty or danger. Martyrs show fortitude in undergoing torture and death rather than deny their faith. Soldiers show fortitude in facing probable death for the good of their country. Students and teachers show fortitude in getting down to work when tired minds and bodies are crying out for them to put their feet up. Administrators show fortitude in expelling failing students whose wealthy parents, they know from sad experience, will be down on them with every kind of pressure.

Temperance is a virtue that perfects our other sense appetite so that we exercise a reasonable restraint in our pursuit of such particular goods of the body as money, drink, and sex. The previous example of the man who gave up smoking illustrates the operation of the virtue of temperance. Those who surrender present ease in order to study are exercising the virtue of temperance as well as that of fortitude. They are also performing an act of justice by fulfilling their obligations to others. And in view of the requirements of the life of study and, in particular, of tomorrow's assignment, studying is also the prudent thing to do in the circumstances.

This last example does not mean that all the cardinal moral virtues are really one and the same. They differ according to their objects, for it is not the same thing to observe someone else's rights and to face difficulty firmly.[10] They also differ according to the power which they perfect, for prudence is a quality inhering in and perfecting the possible intellect, justice is in the will, fortitude is in the irascible appetite, and temperance is in the concupiscible appetite. These virtues are specifically distinct. Yet they are also related in that one operation, one action, may require and involve all of them, as in the example of study given above.[11] They are also related in that prudence, being what Aristotle called the architectonic virtue, in a sense governs and directs them all, for

[10] St. Thomas, *Summa Theologiae*, I-II, 54, 2; 60, 1.
[11] *Ibid.*, 65, 1.

any morally virtuous act is also by definition a prudent act, and without prudence none of the other moral virtues can exist.[12]

Taken on the natural level, these moral virtues, like any other natural virtues, are developed by repeated action. The more often we reason successfully about what to do in a given situation, the more often we respect the rights of others, the more often we face a difficult situation squarely, the more often we use moderation in enjoying sense pleasures, the less difficult such behavior becomes in the future. Both virtues and vices are gradually built up by our repeated actions, and both become progressively harder to break. This does not mean that they determine our actions so that we can no longer choose freely, or that they make our properly human actions automatic, but that they make choice in one direction rather than in another much easier and more likely. And on such choice depends the success or failure of our lives as a whole, and also the lives of those on whom we exercise an influence.[13]

INTELLECTUAL VIRTUES

In view of the overriding importance of our last end, an end that will be reached or missed on the basis of human acts whose

[12] For an excellent account of the relation of the moral virtues among themselves, see Josef Pieper, "On the Christian Idea of Man," *The Review of Politics,* 11, 1 (January, 1949), 3–16, reprinted in M. A. Fitzsimons, Thomas T. McAvoy, and Frank O'Malley (eds.), *The Image of Man* (Notre Dame, Ind.: University of Notre Dame Press, 1959), pp. 20–32. See also Pieper's *Fortitude and Temperance* (New York: Pantheon Books, a Division of Random House, Inc., 1954), *Justice* (New York: Pantheon Books, a Division of Random House, Inc., 1955), and *Prudence* (New York: Pantheon Books, a Division of Random House, Inc., 1959).

[13] St. Thomas explains (*Summa Theologiae,* I-II, 53, 3, c) that both moral and intellectual virtues can be diminished or even lost entirely through not being used.

principles or sources are virtues, the development of the moral virtues both in ourselves and in our students would seem to be the most important task in the world, for if we fail here we fail altogether. On the other hand, though, there is a sense in which the speculative intellectual virtues are superior to the moral virtues, for they have, taken in themselves, a more noble object, which is universal truth.[14] And even if we concentrate on the sense in which the moral virtues are superior, the intellectual virtues remain worthy of development as perfections of the power through which, ultimately, men are distinguished from brutes. To know the truth is a properly human operation. Indeed, it is *the* properly human operation, and is a kind of foretaste of the Beatific Vision.[15] To develop the ability to know the truth, and to help others to do so, is, as the following chapter will attempt to spell out, a work of sufficient dignity and intrinsic importance to merit the best efforts of a whole life. To develop the ability to know the truth, whether in the speculative or in the practical order, is to develop the intellectual virtues, just as to develop the ability to do good is to develop the moral virtues. And if, as will be maintained, the specific though not the exclusive aim of a teacher as such is to help his students strengthen their intellectual powers by the increase of intellectual virtues, it would be well for us to find out, at least in a general way, what these intellectual virtues are.

The Speculative Intellect: Understanding, Science, and Wisdom

The virtues of the speculative intellect, those good qualities which perfect the intellect for its work of knowing the truth about reality, are traditionally called understanding, science, and wisdom. The virtues of the practical intellect, those good qualities which

[14] St. Thomas, *ibid.*, 66, 3, c. A related point is that, whereas the journey through this life to our last end requires morally good acts, the last end itself is an intellectual operation.
[15] *Ibid.*, ad 1.

perfect the intellect for its work of knowing how to make and to do things well, are called, respectively, art and prudence.[16]

The beginning of all knowledge, called principles (*principia*), is some self-evident propositions, known in themselves without any reasoning. An example would be, "A thing cannot both be and not be in the same respect," or, more particularly, "A whole is greater than any of its parts," or "Two quantities equal to the same third quantity are equal to each other." To say that these propositions are self-evident is not to say that their truth is innate, inborn, in the human mind. Some experience of reality, some acquired knowledge of the meaning of the terms involved, a consciousness of existence, a grasp of the meaning of whole and part and equal are required before the propositions can even become intelligible. But once the meaning of these terms is known from experience, the truth of the propositions is grasped immediately and without any intermediary step of reasoning, for the predicate of the proposition is seen to belong necessarily to the subject. It should be mentioned that for someone to see such a relationship it is not necessary for him to be able to state the principle explicitly; a child who cannot formulate the proposition, "A whole is greater than any of its parts," will still know the difference between a whole pie and a piece of pie.

The quality, the good habit, which perfects the intellect to see the truth of such propositions is called understanding. Is any conscious and deliberate development of this virtue possible, and, if so, can the school make any contribution to such development? Only, it would seem, by its regular work of teaching. For if someone is to see a proposition as self-evident, he must see that

[16] *Ibid.*, 57, 2–5. A useful commentary on this general topic is Joseph Luke Lennon, O.P., *The Role of the Intellectual Virtues in Education According to the Philosophy of St. Thomas Aquinas* (Notre Dame, Ind.: unpublished dissertation, 1950).

the predicate belongs necessarily to the subject. And that requires knowledge of the meaning and of the implications of the meaning of the subject. The proposition "God is" is self-evident to one who knows that God's essence is His existence, but not to one who does not. Here the virtue of understanding could be developed by teaching concerning the nature of God. Again, "We hold these truths to be self-evident, that all men are created equal. . . ." Are they? They are, but you cannot know that they are unless you know quite a bit about what men are. Here the virtue of understanding could be developed by teaching concerning the nature of man. And so on. The virtue of understanding can be developed and increased, but only by the ordinary work of teaching which will make clearer the meaning and the implications of the various terms which enter into the formation of propositions. What is self-evident to the man who knows will always be anything but that to the man who does not know.

Most propositions, however, are not self-evident; their truth must be reached, if reached at all, by hard reasoning. This is one of the prices that we pay for being men rather than angels. The human intellect is a power of a soul that is the life principle of a body; all our intellectual knowledge, as a consequence, must be abstracted from sense knowledge; and sense knowledge depends for its very existence on the operation of bodily organs. Our intellectual knowledge, then, our knowledge in general and universal terms, is won only with difficulty, and can lead to further intellectual knowledge, to conclusions derived from principles, only at the expense of frequently involved reasoning going from one step to the next. The triumphant Q.E.D. is not reached easily, but it can be reached. There is no royal road to learning, but there is a road. Those qualities, developed by practice, which enable us to reason more surely and efficiently from principles (beginnings) to conclusions (terms or end points), are the virtues of science and wisdom. These virtues resemble each other in that both of them perfect the intellect for its operation of reasoning from principles to conclusions, of seeing conclusions as necessarily implied in their principles or causes. They differ in that science concerns reasoning to conclusions from principles that are ultimate only in a given order of reality, such as the mathematical or the physical or the biological; whereas wisdom concerns reasoning to conclusions from principles that are ultimate absolutely. There are, then, as many sciences as there are kinds or fields of knowable truth, though there is much difference of opinion as to just what these fields are and how they are related. Since, however, the ultimate cause of all reality is one, there is only one wisdom; in the natural order it is called metaphysics and, in the supernatural order, sacred theology. Let us look first at the intellectual virtue called "science," to see what it is in itself and how the school can contribute to its development.

Science and What It Is Not

In the meaning which Aristotle and St. Thomas attach to the term, science is certain knowledge through causes, knowledge of conclusions as related to principles. Knowledge of individual facts is not scientific knowledge, no matter how true and how important the facts in question may be. To know that this particular line is four inches long is not to have scientific knowledge; to know that the square on the hypotenuse of a right triangle is equal to the sum of the squares on the legs, and to know why, is to have scientific knowledge. It is to see why, given the self-evident principles of Euclidean geometry (axioms, postulates, and definitions), the conclusion is true, must be true, and must always be true. Necessity and universality characterize the conclusion. Further, the conclusion was reached through reasoning rather than through an inspired guess; science involves seeing *why* the conclusion is true. Another example: To know that this particular beaker of water breaks down into 2 parts of hydrogen to 1 of oxygen is not to have scientific knowledge; to know that hydrogen and oxygen, united in a proportion of 2 to 1, will form water, and to know why (in terms of the atomic structure of these elements), is to have scientific knowledge.

Most perfectly, science involves reasoning to conclusions which have an absolute universality and necessity and in such a way as to afford a complete causal explanation. We have relatively little knowledge of this sort. Less perfectly, but still properly, we can speak of scientific knowledge in such basically inductive disciplines as chemistry. Here the necessity of the conclusions is a merely hypothetical one, for there is no intrinsic necessity in the present order of creation, since God could have made the world other than He did. Further, the causal relationship of conclusion to principle is not entirely clear, for we know only *that* a certain atomic structure invariably acts in a certain way, not why it does. We can say why hydrogen and oxygen unite in a certain way; the cause is their atomic structure. And this knowledge constitutes a real explanation. But we cannot say why such an atomic structure invariably causes such a union. This knowledge does not constitute a full explanation. Yet there is still, in such disciplines as chemistry, a knowledge through causes, and a knowledge involving some degree of universality and of necessity. At what point the attribution of the term "science" to our knowledge becomes not only imperfect but improper is a matter of dispute, a decision which involves a certain degree of arbitrariness, as it also does with such terms as art and teaching. Do what are called the social sciences constitute properly scientific knowledge? Is history a science? The position taken in this book will be that the term science can be applied to bodies of knowledge, to series of conclusions, in a diminishing but still proper sense, first, as long as there is any degree of universality that abstracts from singular examples taken one by one, even if the occurrence in question can be expected only "usually" or "for the most part"; second, and related to the first, as long as there is even that degree of "necessity" achieved by the operation of laws of probability; and, third, as long as some causal connection, some *why,* is established between the conclusions and the observed facts that served ultimately as principles.

In this view sacred theology and the philosophical, mathematical, and natural sciences are certainly scientific. So, too, though in a reduced sense, are those disciplines included under the general heading of the social sciences. The statement that in an open market, supply and demand tend toward equilibrium is a generalization abstracted inductively from many particular examples observed. Its necessity is not at all that of the natural sciences, for the individual examples that served as the basis for the universal conclusion are themselves not necessitated but are acts of free choice by persons in the market; nevertheless there is that degree of constancy assured by a propensity of human nature that exhibits itself on the average or "for the most part," though not in every instance. Finally, there is a relation established between the conclusion, which is the economic law, and the cause, which is human nature. Another example would be the conclusion that the separation of legislative and executive powers reduces the possibility of dictatorship, or that general economic conditions have a measurable effect on the incidence of white-collar crime. The difference between the degree of universality and necessity achieved by the conclusions of the natural sciences and the conclusions of the social sciences lies ultimately in the fact that human nature allows free choice and physical nature does not. Yet in both cases there is a nature, something stable and constant, that makes possible generalizations of at least some degree of necessity if the induction is based on a sufficient enumeration of particulars, a sufficient number of examples, and that makes possible the establishment of a relation of cause and effect.

I do not have either the competence or the courage to debate the question of the scientific nature of history, though I have never been able to understand arguments against including it among the social sciences. Certainly, history is more than chronology; it involves the establishing of causal relationships. But do historical conclusions involve any universality or necessity? Conclusions established historically can themselves become principles leading to more general conclusions; an example of the latter would be the famous dictum that power tends to corrupt.[17] Do conclusions of this type belong to history or to philosophy of history? Should either history or philosophy of history be considered a social science? [18] These issues must be left to the professionals in the field. The way in which they are resolved, however, will make a considerable difference to the manner in which the discipline in question (and, indeed, any discipline) is taught. Behind pedagogy lies, among other things, epistemology.

Wisdom and Communication

The third of the virtues of the speculative intellect is wisdom. As stated above, wisdom comprises sacred theology and metaphysics, the latter culminating in natural theology, that knowledge which men can have of God as the cause of the natural order. Wisdom is also scientific, for it improves the intellect in its operation of reasoning from principles to conclusions. But the principles involved here are those which are ultimate absolutely, and not only

[17] Acton-Creighton Correspondence, in Lord Acton, *Essays on Freedom and Power* (New York: Meridian Books, Inc., 1957), p. 335.

[18] An interesting anthology devoted largely to the discussion of these and related issues is Hans Meyerhoff (ed.), *The Philosophy of History in Our Time* (Garden City, N.Y.: Anchor Books, Doubleday & Company, Inc., 1959). Cf. Folke Dovring, *History as a Social Science: An Essay on the Nature and Purpose of Historical Studies* (The Hague: Martinus Nijhoff, 1960).

in a given order of reality. To develop the good habit of looking at reality under the divisions of essence and existence or of potency and act, of looking at whatever one comes to know in relation to God as its beginning and its end, is to learn to look beyond the proximate causes of the particular sciences to the ultimate cause of reality. It is to begin the task of achieving, to whatever degree it is given to men to achieve it, the virtue of wisdom. Not that wisdom can be given to youth, neatly packaged, by an undergraduate course, whatever its title, nor, on the other hand, that it is inaccessible to any who have not been exposed to such a course. But the school can do something by way of a beginning, a beginning which gradual maturity, much more knowledge, and the habit of reflection may bring to some real development.

Precisely because wisdom strengthens the ability to see reality as a whole in relation to its ultimate cause, whereas particular sciences strengthen the ability to see segments of reality in relation to the ultimate causes only of those segments, wisdom can rightly be said to judge and to put order into all other knowledges; for in the last analysis all truth is fully intelligible only in relation to its ultimate cause. This fact should give pause to those experts in particular sciences who are fond of considering the proximate causes with which they deal to be the ultimate causes of the whole of reality, and who blithely trespass on the fields of metaphysics and of theology with a cavalier disregard for the requirement of competence in these areas. This is scientism rather than science. The same fact should also give pause to those experts in metaphysics or in theology who consider that some knowledge of the ultimate cause of reality absolves them from the effort of trying to understand the proximate causes of various areas of the same reality, and who just as blithely trespass on the fields of the particular sciences with no appreciation of the methods of investigation appropriate to them. This is theologism rather than theology, philosophism (if such a term may be allowed) rather than philosophy.

A great deal of the tragic insufficiency of communication between theologians and philosophers on the one hand and mathematical and natural and social scientists on the other (and, indeed, among all specialists) can be reduced to this cause, and also to a common but mistaken conclusion drawn from it, often almost unconsciously. The metaphysician or theologian is right in taking a dim view of the positivism which arbitrarily reduces all science to positive science and refuses the name of science to any other kind of knowledge. Yet he is wrong if he also takes a dim view of the positivist in question, who may be a man of considerable ability when he sticks to his own field, or of the whole of the particular science which the positivist represents. Such condemnation stems from the same mistake as that made by the positivist who is being condemned, the failure to distinguish between science and scientism. The social scientist is right in taking a dim view of a social philosopher's utopian schemes for reforming a social order whose complexities he lacks the professional equipment to understand, and who mistakenly considers any attempt at constituting a purely observational social science to be another form of positivism. Yet he is wrong if he also takes a dim view of the philosopher in question or of the whole of the discipline which he represents. When particular scientists come to see that competence in one area of reality does not by itself confer competence to make judgments concerning reality as a whole and to answer the ultimate questions concerning its nature; and when those who have made some beginning in the acquisition of speculative wisdom come to see that knowledge of ultimate causes does not by itself confer knowledge of proximate causes, that some knowledge of the whole can yet leave knowledge of the parts very vague; then perhaps the representatives of both these areas will come to realize that they may be able to learn something from each other.

Further, the intellectual difficulty involved is compounded by another one, which may perhaps be called psychological. A good deal of the difficulty of communication here spoken of can be reduced to simple human resentment. Scholars are still human beings, and it would be asking too much to expect them to be above pride of place and above personal and professional jealousy, much of it distressingly petty. No one likes to have someone else tell him how to do his job; still less does he like having someone else tell him, and usually in no uncertain terms, that he really doesn't have a job worth doing. No one likes to have it implied, still less to have it explicitly stated, that a merely common-sense approach to his field is quite sufficient and that properly scientific method is required only in another field. Such attitudes breed personal antagonism; they turn what should be scholarly discussions into acrimonious disputes; and they add an emotional reason for the tighter closing of minds that, more than any others, should not be closed. On all sides, a little less personal pride and a little more personal consideration would do a good deal to remove irrelevant but very real obstacles to understanding among representatives of various disciplines.

A final point: The vice called intellectual pride seems to be an occupational hazard of those engaged in the intellectual life, a life to which all teachers are called by their very profession. Pride of intellect is a bad thing, but it is at least more defensible than pride of place, for it is pride in something essentially human. Those who devote considerable effort to eradicating intellectual pride would be well advised to attack the pride rather than the intellect. The distinction is not always made.

The Practical Intellect: Art and Prudence

The virtues of the practical intellect are art and prudence. Art is described by St. Thomas as *recta ratio factibilium,* which may be rendered as correct reasoning about how to make things. Today we usually think of the term art as applicable to the fine arts, as we usually think of the term science as applicable to the natural sciences. Art applies, however, to anything that men make, whether it is a painting, a table, a cake, a poem, or a reasoned argument. Whenever a person forms in his mind an idea which he intends to express in some medium, reasons about the steps to be taken, and then, normally, expresses the idea, he is using his intellect strengthened by the quality which is art. Like any other virtue, art is developed by repeated acts. Like any other virtue, art builds on already existing natural aptitudes, which will vary with the person possessing them.

There are a number of possible ways of classifying the arts, though, as was mentioned above,[19] exclusive reliance on any one of them seems to involve some degree of arbitrariness. In one classification [20] those arts are called "liberal" arts which guide the making of things by the mind, for the mind, and in the mind. Examples would be logic, grammar, composition, and, at least traditionally, such mathematical arts as arithmetic and geometry. In logic a process of reasoning such as a syllogism is constructed by the mind according to the rules of valid argumentation; its purpose is the knowledge to which it leads; and the whole construct remains within the intellect of the one who constructs it, and, if it is outwardly expressed, in the minds of those who follow it. In geometry a series of figures is constructed by the mind and their properties explored; the purpose of this construction is also the knowledge to which it leads; and the whole construct remains within the intellect of the one who constructs it and of those who

[19] See p. 67.
[20] See Bernard I. Mullahy, C.S.C., "The Nature of the Liberal Arts," *The New Scholasticism*, 23, 4 (October, 1949), 361–386, espec. 384–386. For another study, see Benedict M. Ashley, O.P., *The Arts of Learning and Communication* (Dubuque: The Priory Press, 1958). See also Pierre H. Conway, O.P., and Benedict M. Ashley, O.P., *The Liberal Arts in St. Thomas Aquinas* (Washington, D.C.: The Thomist Press, 1959).

grasp it intellectually (the drawings made of these figures on paper or blackboard are not mathematical entities but physical representations, never quite exact, which aid the intellect by enlisting the support of the imagination).

In this same classification those arts are called "fine" arts which guide the making of things by the mind and for the mind, but not in the mind. Examples would be painting, sculpture, poetry, and the writing of novels and plays. A picture is painted according to an idea in the artist's mind; its purpose is the communication of that idea to the viewer through, ordinarily, both his intellect and his sensibility; but its medium is something external to both artist and viewer. And so with the others. Incidentally, it is being taken for granted here that the purpose of any work of art, as here referred to, is the purpose intrinsic to the work of art itself, not any extrinsic though laudable purpose of the artist, such as making a living through the sale of the work of art.

Further, those arts are called "useful" arts which guide the making of things by the mind but neither for the mind nor in the mind. Examples would be the making of cakes, of guns, of automobiles, and of chairs. To make a chair, you must definitely know what you are doing, and order your actions according to a plan intellectually conceived; the purpose of the chair is that someone may use it to sit in; and the medium in which your idea is expressed is a material one external to the mind.

A good many of the arts overlap these divisions, at least in some of their expressions. Architecture is a useful art in that it leads to the construction of a building whose purpose is to shelter human beings; but it is also a fine art in that it aims at such a construction as will appear beautiful to those who see it. An automobile is certainly constructed of physical materials for a quite utilitarian purpose; but a good deal of effort goes into designing models whose appearance as well as mechanical performance will be pleasing. Again, music is in one sense a liberal art allied to mathematics, and in another sense it is a fine art. More will be said about the various arts in Chapter six, when their place in the work of different educational agencies will be considered.

It should be pointed out that the perfection of the virtue of art lies in the thing made, not in the maker. A bad man may be a good poet; and to speak of a man as a good pickpocket makes sense. So a man may be a bad man and a good artist. And a good artist may ordain a well-made work of art to a personal end which is evil, as a witness at a trial may fabricate a false but convincing story that will convict the defendant, whom he hates, of a crime he has not committed. Further, a good artist may fear that what he is called upon to make will, of its very nature, or because of the probable intentions of those for whom he is to make it, be used for morally wrong ends; it is the consideration of such a possibility that worries more than one of the scientists and engineers engaged in work on atomic and hydrogen bombs. Situations such as these involve the virtue of prudence as well as that of art, the virtue which is a moral as well as an intellectual one.

Prudence is traditionally described as *recta ratio agibilium*, which may be rendered as correct reasoning about how to do things. Prudence is wisdom in the practical order. Unlike art, its perfection lies not in the thing made but in the agent himself. Since every act of making something is also itself a human act, it is possible, as we have seen, to perform an act which is artistically good but morally bad, that is, imprudent. For a man to act prudently, he must first will the right end and must then reason successfully about what to do in order to achieve that end. Because prudence presupposes the rectitude of the rational appetite, the will, it is a moral virtue; art does not require such rectitude. Because prudence also demands successful reasoning about the means to an end, it is an intellectual virtue. The stages in the operation of prudence involve considering the various possible means to the intended end, judging that one of them is best, and directing that the right choice be made.[21]

It is possible to be prudent in some particular respect without being prudent absolutely. A businessman, for example, may be able to weigh carefully the circumstances involved in his business activity and to reach sound decisions concerning what he should do to achieve the ends proper to his situation, and may yet be a man who habitually leads a bad life. The same may be said of a person in any occupation, so far as concerns the achievement of the limited ends of that occupation. A person is said to be prudent absolutely, however, when his will is fixed on attaining the final end of his life, and when he habitually reasons correctly about the means to that end and carries his decisions into practice.[22]

Because both art and prudence, the virtues of the practical intellect, concern the singular and contingent rather than the universal and necessary order, they cannot involve the sort of demonstration that is proper to science, and hence cannot be taught in the same demonstrative fashion. And because prudence is a moral as well as an intellectual virtue, involving the rectitude of the will, it cannot, strictly speaking, be taught at all. Nevertheless, a great deal can be done, by all educational institutions, to promote the conditions in which the virtue of prudence is likely to be developed. What those institutions are, and what is the proper function of each, will be the theme of the next chapter.

[21] Cf. Vernon J. Bourke, *Ethics* (New York: The Macmillan Company, 1951), pp. 235–241.
[22] See St. Thomas, *Summa Theologiae,* I-II, 57, 3–5; 66, 3; II-II, 47, 4; 169, 2, ad 4. See also John A. Oesterle, *Ethics* (Englewood Cliffs, N.J.: Prentice-Hall, Inc., 1957), pp. 185–192.

QUESTIONS

1. How does one inculcate such moral virtues as thoughtfulness, gratitude, and respect for property?
2. Which should be most emphasized: knowledge, attitudes, or skills?
3. Has a student a moral obligation to develop his intelligence and increase his knowledge?
4. Should the elementary school stress chiefly the development of memory and the secondary school the development of reasoning? How much reasoning can be expected from high school students?
5. "The greatest contribution that procuring an education makes is the discipline you have to enforce on yourself." Discuss.

chapter four

The Aims and Agencies

of Education

EDUCATION AS A POTENTIAL WHOLE

Education is something that happens to human persons, and only
to them. It is the development of their powers—the actualizing
of their potentialities—so that they may be something more than
they were and, as a result, may do something more than they did.
Good education is the development, in those powers capable of it,
of intellectual and moral virtues; bad education is the development
of intellectual and moral vices. Good education means the development of the ability to arrive at true rather than false historical
judgments, to construct intelligible rather than unintelligible para-

graphs, to appreciate the beautiful rather than the ugly, to swim rather than to sink in the water, to will that justice rather than injustice prevail in human relationships, to love all men as equally children of God. Education is personal growth. Good education is growth in the direction demanded by the nature and the destiny of the human person.

Reference has already been made, however, especially in Chapter two, to the fact that the term "education" has a number of meanings. Just as it is absolutely fundamental for those engaged in the process of education to know as much as possible about the nature and the destiny of the human persons whom they are educating, so it is absolutely fundamental for them to know as much as possible about the different meanings of education and the relations of those meanings. Parents and professional teachers, for example, are both engaged in educating young people, and even the same young people; yet the educational work of parents is not the same as the educational work of teachers. A great deal of confusion arises from the failure to distinguish adequately the various meanings of education, the aims proper to education in each of its meanings, and the educational agencies engaged in pursuing those aims.[1]

Education is a whole made up of parts, and its relation to its parts constitutes it as the kind of whole it is. In technical language, education is a potential whole rather than a universal or an integral whole. A universal whole is one which is present in each of its parts in its total essence and in its total power, as in the relation of genus to species. Thus "animal" is a universal whole of which man and horse are parts in the sense that each is essentially an animal and in the sense that the entire notion of animality functions or is exercised in both men and horses. At the other

[1] This point has been made by Willis D. Nutting, *Schools and the Means of Education* (Notre Dame, Ind.: Fides Publishers Association, 1959).

end of the scale is an integral whole, which is one that is not present in any of its parts either in its total essence or in its total power. Thus a house is an integral whole of which wall and roof are parts in such a way that neither one of them is a house and the notion of house is not exercised or realized in either one. Between these two comes the potential whole, which is present in each of its parts according to its total essence but not according to its total power. Thus the human soul is a potential whole of which the nutritive and the sensitive powers are parts in the sense that the whole human soul is present in and functions in each part; on the other hand, the total power of the human soul does not function in the operation of each part; for example, the sensitive power does not function in the operation of nutrition and the intellectual power does not function in either nutrition or sensation.[2] Another example of a potential whole would be that of political government in relation to its executive, legislative, and judicial powers. Each one of these parts is essentially governmental, each exists by the same authority as that by which the government as a whole exists, and to exercise any one of the functions is truly to govern. Yet the functions are not the same, and the notion of government is not exhausted in any one of them. These branches or parts represent different powers of the same potential whole which is government.

Moral, Intellectual, and Physical Education

Education is a whole made up of parts, and it will be important to see what kind of whole it is and what relation it has to its parts.

[2] St. Thomas, *Summa Theologiae,* I, 77, 1, ad 1. Cf. *ibid.,* I, 76, 8, c; II-II, 48, 1, c; III, 90, 3, c. See Thomas C. Donlan, O.P., *Theology and Education* (Dubuque: Wm. C. Brown Co., 1952), pp. 12–13, for a clear analysis of the same text and its application to education. See also *The Curriculum of a Catholic Liberal College* (Notre Dame, Ind., 1953),

Since education is the development of human powers, the parts of education should, it would appear, correspond to the kinds of human power to be developed. There are many human powers, which it would seem possible to classify broadly as moral, intellectual, and physical. There are certainly important areas of human growth, such as the emotional and the social, which are not specifically included in this classification; yet perhaps they can be reduced to some combination of these three and considered as implicitly contained in them. For both emotional and social development, to take the examples mentioned, involve some application or other of each of the three basic types of human power: physical, intellectual, and moral. Emotional stability, for example, is promoted by such factors as good physical health, the intellectual habit of looking objectively at the realities outside oneself, and the humility needed to accept these realities as they are and not to try to use them simply as means to one's individual ends. The social graces are likewise promoted by the feeling of confidence that comes with good health, by intellectual knowledge and appreciation of the indispensability of various societies for human life, and by the genuine respect and consideration for other people that ultimately lie behind good manners and civilized conduct. Basically, then, there seem to be three parts of that whole which is education, and such particular educational aims as, for example, mental health, the ability to get along with other people, and religious devotion, are so many combinations and applications of these three basic parts of education. Nevertheless, these last examples and other educational aims are sufficiently distinctive to be spoken of and treated separately even though they do not in themselves constitute fundamental parts of education.

If the parts of education are physical, intellectual, and moral,

pp. 32–33; Vincent Edward Smith, *The School Examined: Its Aim and Content* (Milwaukee: The Bruce Publishing Company, 1960), pp. 269–271.

what kind of whole do these constitute? It cannot be an integral whole, for each of these parts is itself truly education, involving the development of human powers. Neither can it be a universal whole, related to its parts as genus to species, for the whole notion of education does not function, is not exercised, is not exhausted in each of these parts. Education is rather a potential whole, present in each of its parts according to its total essence but not according to its total power, related to its parts as the soul to its powers or the government to its branches. Each of the parts of education is truly education, as each of the branches of government is truly government. But to pass laws, to execute laws, and to judge in accordance with laws are not the same operation, and to confuse them does not do the cause of government any good. To educate morally, to educate intellectually, and to educate physically are not the same operation either, and to confuse them does not do the cause of education any good.

The parts of education are related because the powers to be perfected by education are powers of the same human person. Yet the powers are distinct, and the person can grow and develop only through the growth of his powers. It is true that the whole man comes to school, as he comes anywhere else; but he cannot be educated as a whole. The whole man comes anywhere because he is one substance, and he could not come in any other way. Yet the man, while a substantial whole, is a whole composed of body and soul and exhibiting a good many distinct powers. It is only by way of perfecting his powers, of actualizing his potentialities, that he can develop and become more a man than he was. Such development, such growth, is precisely education. Since a man can grow only through the growth of his powers, and since his physical, intellectual, and moral powers are distinct, the parts of his education will also be distinct. Once more, the whole man is to be educated; but he cannot be educated as a whole.

Failure to grasp this fact leads to confusion among the various

83

agencies of education and the goals proper to each; especially, it leads in practice to asking the school to shoulder the whole burden of education, to the inevitable neglect of its proper work. For example: [3]

> Human improvement, the true end of education, is total improvement. It cannot successfully concentrate on one phase of the life of the individual to the neglect of other phases, because human personality is a unitary thing which cannot be dissected and divided. . . . Therefore our physical health, our economic well-being, our social and civic relations, our cultural development, all are bound up in the most intimate manner with our moral and spiritual progress. To educate the child, consequently, means to promote his growth in all these spheres. To neglect any one of them means to stunt his growth in all.

It would be convenient if each of the parts of education could be assigned to a particular educational agency which would then pursue its course and perform its function independently of the others. Unfortunately, the situation is not that simple. The home, for example, is interested in all three fundamental parts of education because of the relationship of parents to children; so also is the civil society, though for somewhat different reasons; and so also, and again for somewhat different reasons, is the Church. Further, because it is the whole man and not simply an intellect that comes to school, what he does and what he does not do in the school are bound to have some influence on his moral and physical as well as on his intellectual development. In spite of this double source of overlapping, however, education remains a potential whole, and it should be possible to distinguish various meanings of

[3] Rt. Rev. George Johnson, "Education for Life," in Sister Mary Joan, O.P., and Sister Mary Nona, O.P., *Guiding Growth in Christian Social Living* (Washington, D.C.: The Catholic University of America Press, 1946), vol. III, p. 4. Reprinted by permission.

the term and the specific aim of each of the principal agencies of education.[4]

Four Meanings of Education

The first and broadest meaning of the term education is that which equates it with growth induced by the total experience of a lifetime. This meaning of education is taken from the point of view of the learner, whether he learns by his own discovery or through the example or instruction of other people. The learner, of course, is the principal agent in any kind of education, for unless he does the learning there is no education going on. We do not, however, ordinarily speak of agencies of education in this sense, but rather reserve the term agencies for education looked at from the point of view of teaching, whether by institutions or by persons. We can, though, speak of an aim of education in this first sense of the term. And since this education is something that each of us is engaged in achieving throughout his life, its aim or goal will be the same as the ultimate aim or goal or end of human life, that is, the eternal vision of the essence of God. In this sense, education is life, and its end is the end of life.

The other meanings commonly assigned to education are taken from the point of view of the teaching rather than of the learning process. One of these, and the second meaning of the term, involves the work of societies other than the school in influencing their members and other persons. The principal educational agencies of this kind are the Church, the state, and the family. The Church is the supernatural society founded by God for the purpose of assisting men to reach their final end; the state can be taken as the civil society itself, a society natural to men in the

[4] A consideration of this topic and of most of those dealt with in the rest of this book will be found in Edward J. Power, *Education for American Democracy* (New York: McGraw-Hill Book Company, Inc., 1958).

sense that they need to unite with others so that all may have the conditions of a properly human life; the family or domestic society is natural to men in the sense that it supplies their most immediate vital needs. These are the three fundamental human societies, required by men for human living as no others are, and hence with rights and obligations in the field of education that no others have. There are, however, innumerable other societies that quite legitimately enter the field of education as they deliberately attempt to influence and to form the ideas and the attitudes of their members and of others. Examples would be labor unions and professional societies of all kinds, fraternal associations, veterans' groups, and societies for the preservation or the abolition of everything imaginable. If education is the development, for good or for ill, of the moral, mental, or physical powers of human persons, then all these societies are engaged in education in the form of teaching so that their members and the others to whom they appeal may be engaged in education in the form of learning.

A third meaning of the term education is usually reserved for the work of the school. This work can be distinguished from the educational efforts of other societies in that it is the sole function proper to that particular society, it is generally confined to the comparatively young, and it is carried on in a more formal and organized way. Schooling requires separate classification because of the ways in which the school differs as an educational agency from the family, the state, the Church, and other societies which are also interested in education. Nevertheless, though the school is different from these other societies and possesses its own autonomy, it is related primarily to the family and secondarily to the Church and the state as their instrument in the overall education of persons.[5]

[5] It has been pointed out that in the encyclical *Christian Education of Youth* Pope Pius XI spoke of education in a much wider meaning than schooling. See Neil G. McClus-

The fourth and narrowest meaning of education is that which is applicable to the work of the classroom within the school, a work which, directly, is exclusively intellectual. It is true that the school exists ultimately for the classroom; yet that educational agency which is the school aims directly at the cultivation of its students' moral and physical as well as intellectual powers. The classroom is narrower than the school in its educational aims and functions.

Though other classifications could no doubt be justified, these four meanings of education, while related, seem sufficiently distinct to require separate enumeration and consideration. Their relationships are complex and difficult and will doubtless always remain so. Yet the greatest effort must constantly be made to clarify those relationships as completely as possible, for it is confusion about the different meanings of education that is at the bottom of most of the confusion about the functions proper to the various agencies of education and about the curriculum through which those functions should be carried out.

VARIOUS EDUCATIONAL AGENCIES AND THE SPECIFIC TASK OF EACH

As we saw earlier, the first meaning of education is taken from the point of view of the learner and does not involve a consideration of any agency of education as such. Education in this sense is life; and each person must, in the last analysis, live his own life, learn his own lessons, and bring his personal adventure to a happy or to a tragic conclusion.

With the second meaning of education we come to a consideration of the educational process from the point of view of

key, S.J., *Catholic Viewpoint on Education* (Garden City, N.Y.: Hanover House, Doubleday & Company, Inc., 1959), pp. 70, 77–80; Donlan, *op. cit., passim.*

agencies other than the school. The first of these agencies which we shall consider is the Church.

The Church

As a supernatural society, the Church has for the end of its educational work the salvation of its members. Through the normal channels of grace, such as the Mass and the sacraments, these members receive the infused, supernatural virtues which are one of the means of that salvation. With the same end in view, the Church, as the guardian and interpreter of the deposit of faith, teaches men what God has revealed about Himself and His creation, and also teaches men how God wishes them to live in order to attain salvation.

The Church performs each of these functions principally through Her priests and in church buildings. Yet She also founds and maintains schools in order, among other things, to continue to serve Her members in these ways. Mass and the sacraments will be more readily available to students of a day school built beside a parish church and to students of a residential school with chapels in the residence halls and priests available at all times than to students of a secular institution. Sacred doctrine—knowledge of what God has revealed—will be more thoroughly taught as a regular school subject than through a Sunday sermon or a diocesan weekly paper. This will apply both to the speculative and to the practical or moral branch of sacred doctrine. In addition, that intangible but very real thing which is a religious atmosphere is a powerful incentive to putting moral knowledge into practice and to living the sort of life that will lead to salvation.

Negatively, the school can also assist in the work of salvation by seeing to it that its students are taught nothing that would be contrary to faith or harmful to morals. In connection with this last point, it is true that the school is an autonomous educational agency with its own end and its own means; yet this autonomy is on the natural and the temporal level and should not be allowed to interfere with the student's attaining his supernatural and eternal destiny. Since She is charged with assisting all men to reach salvation, the Church has the abstract right to protect all students from damage to their faith or morals. Concretely, however, the Church has the power to exercise this right only in those schools which She establishes and maintains. Censorship is a difficult, delicate, and dangerous business; it is also a necessary one.

A final point, and one which will be enlarged on later: It may be that the ultimate reason why the Church encourages schools has to do, directly or indirectly, with Her task of leading men to their supernatural last end. Yet the school remains a school and not a church, a separate educational agency whose distinct and specific though not exclusive end is the enlargement of human knowledge and the cultivation of the human intellect. The teacher who regularly uses his class in social studies or biology or anything else for pious little homilies on Christian living is not advancing the work of the Church; he is rather confusing one educational agency with another to the detriment of both. He is also cheating the student, who paid someone's money to be taught social studies or biology, not to be preached at.

The State

Unlike the Church, the state or civil society has a natural rather than a supernatural end: the temporal common good of all its members. In very general terms, the work of the government, which is the organ of the civil society, is to maintain the continuity of the political process and to provide external and internal security, peace, and order, within which conditions the citizens may live a truly human life in common. The end of the state is the common weal, and the attainment of any reasonable degree of the common weal depends, especially in a democracy, on the physical, moral, and intellectual qualities of the citizens. It follows that the state has a right to require that, both in public and in private schools, definite efforts be made to develop these qualities in students so far as they affect the attainment of the end of the state.

Thus it is that the civil authority, at whatever level it directs the work of schools, may require that a certain amount of physical education and health instruction be included at some place or places in the school curriculum. Since a healthy body of citizens is a national asset, the state may insist that the school—in which the future citizen spends so much of his time during most of his formative years—play some reasonable part in his physical development. Yet this does not mean that the state may, for example, force the school to become the organizing agent that dragoons its students into semimilitary organizations devoted to the whipping up of nationalistic fervor. For, in the first place, the school has a real if limited autonomy, with a nature and an end proper to it; ultimately the school is an intellectual institution, though it is also many other things. In the second place, the school is directly the auxiliary of the family, not of the state; the state establishes and supports schools to enable the educational responsibilities of the family to be carried out more successfully than they could be without that assistance. The family remains prior to the state in nature and probably in time; the government remains the servant and not the master of the people; and using the schools directly for its own ends is a usurpation by the state of an authority it does not possess.[6]

For the same reasons, the state is rightly concerned about the moral development of its citizens, especially in a democracy, for a group of people who are overwhelmingly selfish and irresponsible will not succeed in governing themselves. Once more, the goal

[6] On this subject, see Thomas Dubay, S.M., *Philosophy of the State as Educator* (Milwaukee: The Bruce Publishing Company, 1959).

of the state is limited to the temporal common good; it is not charged with obtaining the eternal salvation of its members. This is why the law of the land is interested in the prevention of crime rather than of sin, in the establishment of order rather than of sanctity. As charged with securing the conditions of a good human life, the state should, though with great caution, protect its members from such demoralizing influences as pornographic literature. Positively, however, its efforts to inculcate virtue should be restricted to the natural level of the civil law. The state might reasonably require of the school that it do what it can, without violating any student's conscience, to increase the virtue of patriotism in its students through such means as a daily pledge to the flag and a reading of the biographies of the nation's heroes. For every nation has produced men of whom it can rightfully be proud; and when the school leads its students to know and to admire these men it is performing a legitimate and an important educational function.

Something along this line is probably as far as the state should go in what it requires of the schools in the way of moral education. A totalitarian state, of course, teaches its own religious doctrine and enforces its own morality, for it sees itself as the beginning and the end of human life. But a state which recognizes the dignity of its citizens and their human rights, especially the right to freedom of conscience—a state which does not claim to be the ultimate goal of human existence and the source of all truth and goodness—cannot itself espouse and teach any particular religious doctrine or a moral code based directly on such doctrine. Even apart from the fact of religious pluralism among its citizens, the very nature of the state as a temporal and natural society would preclude its teaching Lutheran or Methodist religious doctrine or enforcing Catholic or Jewish religious practice.

When we speak of practice we are still in the moral order, in the order of doing, and are concerned principally with the moral virtue of religion.   When we speak of doctrine we are in the intellectual order, in the order of knowing, and are concerned principally with the intellectual virtue that we have been calling sacred doctrine—a science which in its upper reaches is that wisdom which is theology.   In the rest of this section we shall be considering the relation of the state to the school as an agency no longer of moral but of intellectual education.

First, a word on the rights of the state and on the demands that it may reasonably make on the school intellectually.   It may and indeed should keep a constant though reasonable pressure on all schools to maintain a high level of intellectual instruction.   For the higher the general level of knowledge and of culture, the more successfully will any group of people govern themselves; an educated citizenry is essential, at least to a democracy, though alone it is not enough.   The state may also rightly require that schools provide instruction in certain particular subjects such as civics and national or state history, a knowledge of which is especially helpful in carrying out the duties of citizenship.   Students need greater, though not exclusive, emphasis on the history of their own country for the simple reason that they are living in it; they are, however, entitled to have the history presented accurately, not as a form of nationalistic propaganda.

Second, a word on the obligations of the state to the school as an agency of intellectual education.   We have seen why the state, as a natural rather than a supernatural society, may not teach any particular religious doctrine or enforce any particular religious practice.   Yet this fact does not entail the consequence that the state should ban religious instruction from publicly supported schools or that it should merely tolerate and not support religiously affiliated schools.   For the school from which religious teaching is banned is in fact an irreligious school, teaching its students indirectly but powerfully that religious conviction is simply irrelevant to the studies pursued in the school.   This statement is not meant to reflect on the able and dedicated teachers in public schools, the example of whose devotion to their vocation acts as a powerful influence for the development of moral virtue in their students. It is directed to the intellectual rather than the moral order. It means that we teach by what we exclude as well as by what we include, and that the exclusion of sacred doctrine from the course of studies says to the student that it does not belong in a course of studies, that it has no relevance to the intellectual life. The state cannot itself teach any religious doctrine or enforce any religious practice; yet neither can the state, especially a democratic one, afford to have its students irreligiously educated.[7] For the democratic ideal was,

[7] See Etienne Gilson, *The Breakdown of Morals and Christian Education* (pamphlet; Rochester, N.Y.: St. John Fisher College, 1960); Leo R. Ward, C.S.C., *Religion in All the Schools* (Notre Dame, Ind.: Fides Publishers, 1960). There seems to be a growing realization of the importance of and the need for some kind and degree of religious instruction within public education for those who wish it, especially with a view to the development of moral values. See, for example, A. L. Sebaly (ed.), *Teacher Education and Religion* (Oneonta, N.Y.: The American Association of Colleges for Teacher Education, 1959); *Training for Moral and Ethical Values and Citizenship Training* (Detroit: Brady School, n.d.); Claude V. Courter, "Teaching of Moral and Spiritual Values in the Cincinnati Public Schools," *Religious Education,* 51 (July–August, 1956), 271–272; Erma Pixley, "A Brief Sketch of the Development of Moral and Spiritual Values in the Los Angeles City Schools," *ibid.,* 272–275; Ellis Hartford, *Moral Values in Public Education: Lessons from the Kentucky Experience* (New York: Harper & Row, Publishers, 1958); Howard Hong (ed.), *Integration in the Christian Liberal Arts College* (Northfield, Minn.: St. Olaf College Press, 1956), p. 91; Theodore Brameld, *Education for the Emerging Age* (New York: Harper & Row, Publishers, 1961), pp. 166–173. For historical material, see Neil Gerard McCluskey, S.J., *Public Schools and Moral Education* (New York: Columbia Uni-

historically, born of the Christian belief in a redeeming God and will die with that belief. If men are not children of God and have not an eternal destiny, then they are simply members of one more biological species engaged in the great game of survival; and there are no reasons beyond transitory sentimental ones why they should dedicate themselves to any cause, such as the political common good, beyond their own gratifications. Neither is there any solid reason why the state should recognize anything resembling human rights in its citizens, now become its subjects, or regard them as anything but means to its own ends.

And yet, disturbing as this prospect is, the ultimate reason why the state should foster instruction in sacred doctrine for those who wish it within both public and private education is not that such a course offers the best prospect for the survival of a free society, though it does. The ultimate reason is that the state has no right to do anything else. For, in establishing and maintaining a school system the state is not acting in its own name and creating what is essentially a state agency. It is acting in the name of the third great educational society, the family, and is very reasonably acting as an auxiliary to the home in a task which belongs to the domestic society essentially but which the latter usually lacks the means to bring to anything like completion.

On the natural level education is primarily the responsibility of the family simply because of the relation which exists, in fact, between parents and children. In cooperation with the creative

---

versity Press, 1958); William Kailer Dunn, *What Happened to Religious Education?* (Baltimore: The Johns Hopkins Press, 1958). For an inclusive survey and explanation of the place of the Catholic school in contemporary America, see Mc-Cluskey, *Catholic Viewpoint on Education;* Jerome G. Kerwin, *Catholic Viewpoint on Church and State* (Garden City, N.Y.: Hanover House, Doubleday & Company, Inc., 1960), chap. 4.

act of God, parents bring children into existence. Since that existence is a human existence, it is primarily the responsibility of the parents to see to it that their children have the opportunity of becoming as fully human as possible, of developing their powers—physical, mental, and moral—to the fullest possible extent. In brief, the education of their children is primarily the responsibility of parents.

With responsibilities go rights. If someone is to be obligated to achieve a certain task, to reach a certain goal, he must obviously have access to the means of doing so. You cannot reasonably require a man to travel 500 miles in a day and then insist that he walk; you cannot reasonably require a student to complete an assignment when he cannot possibly reach the books he needs. Neither can you reasonably require parents to educate their children—and the nature of the relationship demands that they educate them—unless they have within their reach the means of doing so. It is the claim to access to these means which constitutes the parents' right to direct the education of their children. And because the relationship on which it is based is the natural relationship of parenthood, the parental right to educate children is a natural right.

This fact means that the family is the first educating agency, in nature as well as in time, and that it has rights in the educational process that no other agency has given it and that, hence, no other agency may take from it. The government, for example, that would force its citizens to send their children to state schools exclusively would be violating the prior natural right of the parents to direct their children's education.[8] In the same way and for the

[8] There are educationists who seem unworried by such a prospect. See John L. Childs in Brand Blanshard (ed.), *Education in the Age of Science* (New York: Basic Books, Inc., Publishers, 1959), pp. 78–79. On the other hand: "The fundamental theory of liberty upon which all governments in

same reason, the church officials who would deny parents any effective voice in decisions concerning the church-related school would be violating the same natural right.

This fact does not, however, mean that the family is the only educational agency or that its rights are unlimited. A right is a claim on the means that *will* get you to an end that you *do* have; it is not a blank check to do as you please. The rights of parents in the education of their children is a right to educate them, not to fail to do so, and to educate them in truth and goodness, not in falsehood and vice. This is why the state quite reasonably imposes a minimum school-leaving age, insists that certain intellectual standards be met in the schools, and, in extreme cases, takes children away from parents who are seriously neglecting their upbringing. This is why the Church quite reasonably insists that parents use every available means for their children's education in religious doctrine and practice, though Her sanctions are of a different character from those of the state.

The school is an educational society in the natural order, not in the supernatural. Its end is intellectual development, not salvation. Any school, then—public or private, religiously affiliated or not—exists to aid parents in a part of the educational process that the parents cannot carry out as well themselves. Every school, precisely because it is a school, is directly an agent of the family, not of either the state or the church. Church-affiliated schools,

---

this Union repose excludes any general powers of the State to standardize its children by forcing them to accept instruction from public teachers only. The child is not the mere creature of the State; those who nurture him and direct his destiny have the right, coupled with the high duty, to recognize and prepare him for additional obligations." *Pierce v. Society of Sisters,* 268 U.S. 510 (1925). To quote from the Pierce case (Mr. Justice McReynolds) on this point is not to quote selectively, for this position was not questioned in such later cases as Cochran, Everson, McCollum, and Zorach.

for example Catholic schools, exist for the same reason for which any schools exist, namely, for the transmission of knowledge and the development of the ability to use it and to gain more. For the believer, sacred doctrine is the most important knowledge that exists. Catholic sacred doctrine, from catechism to theology, would have to be taught, whether in a public or in a Catholic school, under the auspices of Catholic ecclesiastical authorities, for sacred doctrine begins with an act of faith—a belief that certain data have been divinely revealed—and its development as sacred doctrine must be carried on under Church auspices to ensure that such development remains faithful to the original belief. But the development, as sacred doctrine, is an intellectual one, and finds its place in a school for the same reason that any other doctrine finds a place in a school. The Catholic school is still a school; it exists, directly, for the teaching of religious doctrine as intellectual knowledge, not for the developing of religious practice. The Church, like the state, establishes schools to assist parents in what is primarily their task.

This is a doctrinal rather than a historical statement, a description of what the situation ideally is or should be, not of what it historically has been or is. The American Catholic school, for example, has become what it is largely for religious reasons,[9] and the American public school has become what it is largely for social and political reasons. The statement made above attempts to prescind from historical circumstances.

At first glance it would appear that the obligation of the state to the family would be ideally discharged by the provision for instruction in sacred doctrine by competent teachers within the public school system. For some parents this would be true. For

[9] See Leo R. Ward, *New Life in Catholic Schools* (St. Louis: B. Herder Book Co., 1958), p. 9. Cf. Edward J. Power, *A History of Catholic Higher Education in the United States* (Milwaukee: The Bruce Publishing Company, 1958).

97

other parents, however, it would not be true. Realizing that many studies, such as literature and history, give rise because of their very nature to problems having theological overtones, they might quite properly require that teachers of these subjects be competent, through some training in sacred doctrine as well as in the particular related subjects, to handle the problems involved. Realizing also that sacred doctrine is the only knowledge in the light of which all other knowledges can ultimately be integrated in the human mind—since God is the ultimate cause of all reality—they might quite properly require that, for strictly intellectual reasons, the teachers of their children be competent to make some attempt at drawing all particular knowledges, all arts and sciences, into that unity which is the beginning of speculative wisdom. On either count the state has the duty to maintain, on the same basis on which it maintains public schools for those who wish them, religiously affiliated schools for those who wish them.

One standard objection to this position is that it would result in the destruction of the public school system and the bringing into being of innumerable schools serving innumerable splinter groups throughout the country. In view of the fact that many parents, for many reasons, prefer having their children educated in public schools, the first fear seems quite unfounded. So far as the second is concerned, the establishment of church-related schools would, of course, have to take into account the economic facts of life. It would be impossible to establish such schools except in circumstances in which a sufficient number of students of a particular religious conviction made the project economically feasible. Because of their geographical location, some parents would inevitably have to be content with something less than what they considered the ideal situation.

Another standard objection is that church-related schools are divisive and undemocratic. They are certainly divisive, but so also are existing differences in color, in ethnic origin, in political affiliations, in economic interests, in social standing, and in a hundred other thngs. These differences do not make it impossible for citizens to cooperate on the political level, to unite for the achievement of the goals of a democratic society, while differing on other points. There can be unity without uniformity. Differences on other points are no danger to a democratic society but only to a totalitarian society, a society which sees the state as the end of human existence. A pluralistic society, based on the conviction that *e pluribus* there can be *unum,* will not fear but will rather welcome as both a sign and a condition of liberty the existence within a political unity of many differences of other kinds. The church-related school is not undemocratic; it is untotalitarian.

To sum up: Parents have the primary obligation to educate their children and hence the primary right to choose the means of doing so. The state, like the Church, is in the field of school education primarily to help the family and is the educational agent of the family. Parents who wish instruction in sacred doctrine for their children should have the help of the state in this as in other forms of education. To provide this help is not to confuse Church and state, since the state acts for the family, not for the Church, and does not itself espouse any religious doctrine. To refuse this help is to deny to the parents who wish it the public assistance in education to which they have a right as citizens.

The Home

Within the home, however, the family carries out many educational functions by and for itself. In the area of physical development the home has the task of providing such necessities as food, clothing, shelter, and medical care so that the child may become and remain as healthy as his basic constitution allows. Also under this heading would come instruction in such skills as getting into and out of overshoes and handling a toothbrush. Insistence on the regular observance of the practice of brushing teeth and getting enough sleep would also involve the development of the moral virtue of obedience and a certain increase in intellectual knowledge. Once again, it is the same person who possesses many powers, and it is rare that an educational operation has an influence on the person through one power only. Almost always, and from the very nature of the situation, the whole man is being educated; yet it remains true that the powers through which he is educated are different powers and the virtues that perfect them are different virtues.

Among those virtues that the home is charged with helping its members develop are the moral virtues, the nature of which was briefly discussed in the preceding chapter. Ultimately each of us must develop or fail to develop his own virtues; no one can be virtuous for us. Yet parents can do a great deal, because of their situation, to influence their children morally, and have a heavy obligation to do so. Again, only God can infuse supernatural virtues, and only the Church can offer Mass and dispense the sacraments that are the normal channels of grace. But parents can do a great deal to make their children open to the infusion of supernatural virtues by seeing to it, for example, that they assist at Mass and receive the sacraments regularly. They can also help their children develop the natural virtues, which are both good in themselves and ordinarily the bases upon which the supernatural life of grace is built. Parental influence here is not absolutely determining, for each human being remains free to make or mar himself; but it is probably stronger than any other influence. The means available are precept, backed by sanctions, and example, especially the latter. Through the use of these means parents exercise a tremendous influence over the likelihood of their children's developing the virtues of justice—including that part of it which is religion—of loyalty, honesty, unselfishness, temperance, perseverance, and all those others that make what we call a man or woman of character and that are the indispensable means of achieving ultimate success in life.

Closely related to these physical and moral parts of education is the matter of mental health and emotional stability. Physical health is an evident advantage here; some of the psychoses, at least, have a physiological origin. So, too, is a strong development of the moral virtues, through which the emotions may the better be brought under the control of the intellect and the will. The home can contribute perhaps more than any other educational agency to emotional stability. It can do so, first of all, through ensuring, so far as is possible, the physical health of the children. Further, in the home alone is there possible that intangible but very real atmosphere of warmth and trust and affection that makes children feel secure and wanted and a real part of a real society. As anyone knows who has more than casually visited an orphanage, children need love almost as much as they need food, and they cannot find that kind of love outside their own homes. If the family fails in this most important part of the task of developing human beings, the job will forever remain undone, for no other educational agency can do it.

Along with love, however, parents will contribute to their children's mental health by not spoiling them, by insisting on their fulfilling certain family responsibilities. For in this way, too, children are made to feel that they belong to the family group, and are given firsthand experience at contributing to as well as benefiting from the common good of a society which is a whole of which they are parts. The children whose parents spoil them, for whom family life is all take and no give, are robbed of the tremendous experience of sharing in the achievement of a common good— one of the most satisfying experiences that life offers. For these parents tell their children, through what they do, that everything and everyone exists as a means for the gratification of the children's desires. The children thus tend to acquire a distorted vision of reality, and to lose the ability to see things as they are, objectively, because they habitually see things only in relation to themselves, subjectively. The abrupt encounter with a reality that is other than their home education led them to expect may prove a severe emotional shock. Whatever degree of personal happiness is possible in this world is achieved as a by-product of pursuing some other and greater good, or it is not achieved at all. Children to whom all is given and from whom nothing is required have no opportunity of learning what it means to take into account the good of other people and to get their minds off themselves. They have little chance of achieving that maturity, based ultimately on humility, that enables them to see reality as it is and to see their own rather small place in it. And without that maturity there is a constant and serious risk of the development of a warped personality, the risk of a frenetic pursuit of personal happiness by ways that make its achievement impossible. This is not the road to emotional balance and mental health.

Much the same factors enter into the development of the social graces, an area in which, again, the home is or should be the principal agent of education. A good deal of this kind of education involves the imparting of knowledge: which fork to use and what kind of invitation to send out. And this knowledge is not unimportant or trivial, for we are by nature social beings who can live properly human lives only in the society of others, and anything that makes that civil intercourse run more smoothly is a human gain. Physical health, too, enters into this situation to some degree, in that it tends to impart a feeling of confidence that, if not overdone, contributes to ease of bearing and conduct.

Basically, however, sociability is a matter of moral virtues, and especially of those that also contribute to emotional health. The gentleman is ultimately the charitable man and the just man and the humble man, who respects other people's rights and recognizes their human value and dignity as equal to his own. Here, too, the home is the first and probably the most important teacher. Spoiled and selfish children, centered almost entirely on themselves, tend to lose the sense of the reality of other persons to the point at which they do not really care whether anyone else lives or dies, is happy or unhappy, except so far as they are themselves affected. They gradually become incapable of true friendship or of true love, of gratitude or loyalty or affection. Wrapped in the awful loneliness of the selfish, they become incapable of true social life and hence of a truly human life. And in this area the hard surface polish of sophistication is not an adequate substitute. The externally correct but basically selfish man of the world is still a hollow man; a truly social life is impossible for him because he is unwilling to give to as well as to take from any society. The beginning of this fatal selfishness lies usually in the home, and one of the most important of the forms of education that the family can provide is the kind of example and discipline designed to impress on children the reality of other people and to prepare them for a real part in social life.

Intellectual education also begins in the home, but, perhaps more than any other, must be carried forward outside the home. Parents can teach small children a great deal by reading to them and telling them stories and by answering questions as carefully as possible. Most important of all, perhaps, they can try to arouse some sense of the wonder of creation and of the excitement of coming to know it. Later, whether or not they are themselves well educated in the formal sense, they can show a respect for learning and try to inculcate this attitude in their children. Most parents, however, have neither the time nor the technical competence to carry forward their children's intellectual education. This is a job for professionals, and for professionals who spend their whole time at it. Out of this need was born that institution which is the school.[10]

THE SCHOOL

By the very nature of the situation, the school is an auxiliary of the home, called into being by parents to aid them in fulfilling one of their parental responsibilities. And regardless of who, in historical fact, founds and maintains a particular school or system of schools, the school remains an agent of the family, with the exception of such special schools as seminaries and national military colleges. In the ordinary school the Church and the state may quite reasonably insist on certain means being used to ensure the students' education with a view to their membership in the city of God and the city of man. Yet these are features of the students' education that their parents should have made a point of including anyway, and are merely the expression of these other educational agencies' legitimate interest and rights in the development of human beings who are also members of various societies. The school remains ultimately an auxiliary of the family, and, within such limits as those indicated above, is answerable to the family.

The school, however, is not the family nor simply an extension of the family; it is another educational agency with a character and a limited but real autonomy of its own. As an agent of the family it acts in the interests of the family; but it acts on its own initiative and its own judgment in view precisely of the expert knowledge which led to its becoming such an agent. This situation makes for a somewhat delicate relationship between the family and the school. Education is ultimately a responsibility of the parents, and they have a right to decide on the means to be em-

[10] For an analysis of the relation of the school to other educational agencies, see Arthur Bestor in Brand Blanshard (ed.), *Education in the Age of Science*, pp. 57–71.

ployed. But once they employ that means which is the school, they must allow it to function as what it is and may not reasonably impose on it tasks for which, as an institution, it is not fitted. Though parents have the right to set broad policies in regard to the kind of education they want for their children, and do not at all surrender or transfer their rights to the school, yet they must allow the professionals to do their professional work without undue hindrance or obstruction.

Just where the line is to be drawn between these two educational agencies is a matter requiring a great deal of tact and prudence, often more than is actually displayed. In general, it might be said that the parents may choose the type of school to which they wish to send their children (though this is not, in fact, always possible), may insist that they not be harmed morally or intellectually, but must leave the precise details such as length of class period and method of teaching to those who presumably know what they are doing. The somewhat shadowy nature of this dividing line gives rise to inevitable and recurring tensions. Tensions, however, are a part of life, and one can learn to live with them. The unfortunate temptation is to try to eliminate the tension by eliminating one of the opposing factors. This is like eliminating either the warp or the woof; you also eliminate the cloth. Both parents and school administrators have been known to claim an inordinate degree of authority for themselves in an effort to eliminate the influence of the other, and hence eliminate the tension. They succeed in their attempt only at the expense of the educational process. In this situation the one who really suffers is the student, for whose benefit the whole educational apparatus theoretically exists.

The Agency of Intellectual Education

The school was instituted primarily to assist the family in its task of educating its children intellectually; it is basically an agency of intellectual education, and exists for the sake of what goes on in its classrooms, laboratories, and libraries. This fact is sometimes forgotten by those who have charge of certain extraclass activities and by administrators. The school play is supposed to be the natural expression of a study of the drama; it is not supposed to be a piece of year-end advertising achieved by demanding time from the participants that they should have spent in the classroom or doing homework. The same can be said of the piano recital, sometimes polished by having the students practice one piece for a month when they should have been learning music. And so of the yearbook, and a dozen other projects, each good as a natural by-product of intellectual instruction, but grossly wasteful of student and teacher time and disruptive of school life when allowed to get out of hand and when regarded as the product rather than as the by-product. The basic fault, of course, does not lie with the teacher in charge of the project, for those who should know better mistakenly judge him and his work on the basis of such public presentations. As long as his recognition and advancement depend on the kind of show he can put on, then he is going to give most of his attention to putting on a show rather than to teaching. It is understandable that the public should tend to judge in this way; but it is neither understandable nor excusable that the administrators of schools, on whom depend the promotion and pay of teachers, should so forget the nature of what they are administering as to judge in the same way.

Another point that administrators could well keep in mind is that they exist to administer an institution which in turn exists for what goes on in the classroom. School policy and practice should always be set with a view to advancing intellectual instruction, not with a view to the greater convenience of the administration. The exercise of power is necessary, but it is also somewhat dangerous, and has been known to give people ideas about themselves. The Pope glories in the title of servant of the servants of

God; the statesman calls himself and acts the part of the public servant; the good school administrator will realize that he exists for the school and that the school exists ultimately for the intellectual instruction of its students, and he will try to keep the tail from wagging the dog.

The development of the intellectual virtues in its students is the specific reason for which the school exists; it is this goal which makes the school the kind of thing it is. But it is not the only reason for which the school exists, since schooling inevitably involves the other parts of education as well. This is especially true of the residential school, in which students live as well as study, absent for fairly long periods from their homes and parishes. In such circumstances the school simply must make an effort to substitute to some extent for both the home and the church, and accordingly it becomes directly involved in more parts of education than the intellectual. Even such a school, however, remains a school, and is ultimately to be justified on intellectual grounds. The more familiar day school is also, though to a smaller extent, involved directly in other kinds of education than the intellectual for the good reason that it is in a peculiarly advantageous position to supply the means of such development, and sometimes also for the reason that attention must be given to these other kinds of education before much can be done for the intellect. Yet all these other activities, proper as they are to the school, are not what specifies it as a school, and should not be allowed to interfere with the work of intellectual instruction.

Athletics

In the matter of the physical part of education, the residential school must evidently take over some of the work that is ordinarily done at home by prescribing reasonable hours of sleep, providing ready access to medical service, and so on. It should also supply what it can afford in the way of athletic equipment, for participation in sports, whether organized or not, is a convenient and enjoyable means of getting needed exercise. Programs of intercollegiate athletics cannot be justified on these grounds, for they provide exercise for only a small number of students; but the indirect benefits to the school in improved student morale and, on the college level, the added income, which any school can put to good use, would seem to justify such a program. The dangers of athleticism are well known and are very real; but they are also avoidable.

A day school has a less compelling reason to provide all its students with opportunities for sports, for they can presumably play in their own neighborhood after school hours. But high schools and even grade schools would seem to be acting reasonably in supporting interschool organized sports, chiefly, perhaps, for emotional rather than physical reasons. Again, school morale is usually helped, and school morale is not unimportant. Further, those who do succeed in making the various teams have the really healthy experience of success at something that not everyone succeeds at, the experience of doing something well. There is always the danger of a swelled head or twisted values, as well as of a swelled ankle or twisted knee, but there is probably some danger in almost any undertaking. It is, one hopes, more than nostalgia that makes school athletics look, on the whole, good.

Physical education, again, is not the specific function of the school as a school; but even day schools on the elementary level should provide some facilities for physical exercise, because the neglect of this part of education during the whole of a school day would constitute a handicap that even after-school play could hardly make up.

Moral Development

Neither is moral education the specific function of the school as such; but for much the same reasons it cannot be left entirely to the home and the church. Indeed, it is an infinitely greater loss to the student to have his moral and spiritual education neglected, for this kind of education pertains directly to his ultimate end. The church can directly reach its members for only a small part of their day or week; and even the home sends its children off to school for a considerable part of their waking hours. During this time the process of the student's moral formation does not go into a temporary deep freeze; inevitably it continues, and the school that has charge of the student during those often-critical hours has the direct responsibility to see to it that such moral formation continues along the lines of virtue rather than of vice.[11]

Negatively, each school should take the obvious precaution of carefully screening its applicants for teaching positions so as to exclude those whose known personal convictions or personal conduct would be likely to do moral damage to students. Concerning conduct, the relics of puritanism in our society are perhaps likely to make the demands unreasonable, rather than the opposite. A teacher's real devotion to his work need not preclude his being allowed to breathe a little on his own time, and even a mild addiction to stogies, bourbon, and poker should hardly be equated with corrupting the morals of the youth. If it is so equated, the teacher concerned would be well advised to move to a neighborhood some distance from the school in which he teaches. Concerning convictions, the situation is more difficult. A religiously affiliated school could not be expected to condone teaching calculated to undermine the very religious beliefs and practices which it was officially encouraging. For example, a teacher who, in his course on the family, came out strongly in favor of divorce and artificial birth control could not reasonably expect to hold a position in a

[11] See Jacques Maritain, "Moral Education," *A College Goes to School* (Notre Dame, Ind.: St. Mary's College, 1945), pp. 3–25; Mortimer J. Adler, "Character and Intelligence," *ibid.*, pp. 75–87.

Catholic school. In secular schools, however, the question of academic freedom is more complicated. Finally, schools have the responsibility of so supervising their extraclass activities that no moral damage is likely to result for the students.

Positively, the school with the heaviest obligation for the moral development of its students will be the religiously affiliated residential school, which to a considerable extent will have to substitute for both the home and the church. A Catholic school of this sort, for example, could reasonably be expected to make available to its students opportunities for daily assistance at Mass and regular reception of the sacraments, at least one retreat or mission a year, membership in at least some Catholic Action groups, such special devotions as the October recitation of the rosary, and access to a priest at almost any time for the discussion of personal problems that have spiritual implications. In fact, the Catholic residential school often supplies opportunities for moral and spiritual development that make it, in that respect, a more-than-adequate substitute for home and parish.

The day school need do less because it does not have to substitute for these other educational agencies. But it can assist them greatly in their work through close cooperation. The parish grade school, for example, physically close to the parish church, is able to arrange for daily Mass for its students, regular confessions in the church, preparation for sacraments, and many other religious practices. Such a school can cooperate with the home (and sometimes, unfortunately, must substitute for it) in seeing to it that the students know the standard prayers and recite them daily. On the level of high school and college it should be possible to leave a great deal more to the individual student, who by this time has presumably made some progress in the development of the moral virtues and in the practice of his religious duties.

Both the residential and the day school can do a great deal for the moral education of their students by the provision of a religious atmosphere. The crucifix on the wall, the prayer at the beginning of class, the religious garb of at least some of the teachers, the frequent and matter-of-fact references to God and the life of grace—all these and other factors are calculated to increase in the student the moral virtues and especially that of religion. The atmosphere that surrounds us is imperceptible except upon reflection; but it is one of the most powerful of all influences on our moral convictions and our sense of values.

Because of the variety of religious beliefs represented among its student body, the public school cannot directly concern itself with the virtue of religion or with religious practices. As indicated above, however,[12] this does not mean that the public school need be irreligious in the sense of forbidding any religious instruction under its auspices. Still less does it mean—and this fact, unlike the preceding one, is almost universally recognized—that the publicly supported school should entirely neglect the moral development of its students. On the purely natural level this school ordinarily and quite properly does a great deal to develop in its students such virtues as patriotism, industry, honesty, perseverance, concern for the good of others, and many more. The nobility of the teacher's task is that he is a maker of men and not just of things; and most teachers are as anxious to make men morally better as to make them intellectually better. Character as well as knowledge is ordinarily taken for granted as a goal of the school.

Traditionally, there are two ways of influencing people to develop moral virtues—precept and example. Of these it is likely that the latter is the more effective. Children tend to imitate what they see their elders doing rather than what they hear them saying. And students of all ages are likely to be influenced much more than is generally realized by the policies and the practices of the school which they attend. Indeed, students, being young, are

[12] See in this chapter the section on The State.

prone to be impatient with and critical of authority and official-dom, and are likely to be unduly critical of whatever their school does. All the more reason for the school to be doubly careful of its conduct so that it may not only be above reproach in its practices but may be so obviously above reproach that it is an example for good even to those who are looking for the worst. The school which, however good its intentions, is careless in this re-spect, is teaching its students that moral virtue is for the classroom rather than for the world, for the child rather than for the adult, for the word rather than for the deed.

The basic moral lesson that the student draws from his school's general conduct is that of honesty or dishonesty. The school which is, as its policies and practices indicate, devoted to reality before appearance, to substance before shadow, to performance before reputation—this school is giving its students a shining example of the exercise of moral virtue in the midst of all the stresses and strains of the workaday world into which they are going. The school that quietly does its job instead of talking about it, the school that is truly devoted to scholarship and not just to the reputation for scholarship, the school that is still a school and not a business—this school will not only do superbly well the intel-lectual work proper to a school, but will also set before its observant students a shining example of integrity and of devotion to duty and of basic honesty that will serve to counteract the general influ-ence of a world that is indeed worldly.

Mental Health

What the school can and should do in the way of promoting emotional stability and mental health in its students will probably depend on the situation of the school in question—its size, the age of its students, and whether it is a residential or a day school. In general, schools will probably do most for their students' emo-tional stability by providing a reasonable balance of academic, athletic, and social activities, with the emphasis on the first to such an extent that students will not have time to worry too much about events in the other two. Yet personal problems do arise, especially for students of high school and college age, and the school may not simply ignore them. One reason it may not do so is that students with emotional difficulties cannot concentrate on the primary work of the school. But beyond this the school, without going overboard and confusing itself with a clinic, can usefully supplement the work of the home in this area.

For countless years the older and more experienced have been giving counsel and guidance to the younger and less experienced. Among these have been teachers, whose work brings them into daily and intimate contact with younger people. This sort of guidance, of course, is needed by all young people, and not only by those who are disturbed by special difficulties. Yet even these have frequently been helped by teachers whose understanding, kindness, and prudence have eased many an emotional problem. Specialization, however, has advantages in this field as in most others, and schools which can afford it, at least on the secondary and college level, would be well advised to secure the services of one or more such specialists. Unfortunately, some of the most important of the qualities of a counselor, such as kindness, patience, and prudence, are moral qualities that cannot be directly taught or learned in a school; there is no such thing as specialization in these areas. Yet there is such a thing as specialization in the intellectual knowledge needed for guidance and counseling. School authorities can do little more than choose someone for this important task on the basis of respectable training in this field plus what appear to be the moral qualities also demanded. Experience and observation should gradually indicate whether this estimate of the person concerned has been accurate.

When a student appears with a problem that seems to be deeper in its causes and circumstances than appears at the conscious level, the teacher or the counselor will be well advised to urge the student and his parents to seek competent medical assistance. Unfortunately, the field of psychiatry is still a young one within the wider area of medicine and is even more susceptible than most other areas to differences in both theory and practice. Indeed, it is not unknown for psychiatrists, perhaps those especially who lean heavily on a Continental background, to put ideas, and damaging ideas, into the conscious mind of their patient while actually trying to draw out what is in the patient's unconscious mind. The results are certainly damaging to the very mental health that the psychiatrist is trying to improve and may be morally damaging as well. In the face of such an uncertain situation it is not enough for the school or the family to call on any psychiatrist who happens to be geographically near at hand; it is also necessary to exercise a good deal more caution than would be needed before calling in a general practitioner. Perhaps the advice of the family's personal physician would be helpful. For the Catholic school or the Catholic family it might be well to seek out a psychiatric hospital operated under Catholic auspices, or to ask for a suggestion from any local Catholic hospital. Such recommendation would at least make unlikely the possibility of definite damage being done the patient through well-intentioned but disastrous therapy based on an inadequate view of human nature.[13]

Social Activities

The school also has a certain responsibility for the social development of its students. Part of this development will come from the very nature of the situation, from the association of many

[13] For suggestions concerning this and related situations, see George Hagmaier, C.S.P., and Robert W. Gleason, S.J., *Counselling the Catholic: Modern Techniques and Emotional Conflicts* (New York: Sheed & Ward, Inc., 1959), espec. chaps. 8 and 13. See also Charles Arthur Curran, *Counseling*

students in one place for one general purpose. Over and above this the school can and should do something positive to assist the home in this sort of education. The school can help by demanding civilized dress and behavior from its students. It can also help by promoting, within the limits imposed by its primary dedication to intellectual education, clubs and social events that will get students used to working together for the achievement of a limited but real common good. For school is more than books, though it is principally books, and school days should contain more than study, though they should contain principally study. Before the years bring adult responsibilities there should be some room for fun, for enjoyment in the company of other carefree youngsters, for the stuff that memories are made of. Social activities must not be allowed to run away with the school; but they do have a place.

THE CLASSROOM

Because it is an educational auxiliary of the family and because it has charge of the student for so many of his waking hours, the school must to some extent be directly concerned with all the parts of that potential whole which is education, just as the home itself must be. But among these parts there is one that specifies the school, that makes it what it is, that marks it off from the home and the church and any other educational agency. The specific goal of the school is the development of the intellectual virtues in its students; it is this end which constitutes it as a school and not as something else. The unity of a society is not a substantial unity, but rather a unity of order, of the order of its parts to the same end and, as a result, to each other. It is, then, the common end or the common good which specifies each society, which makes it the kind of society it is. In this order the final cause is also

in Catholic Life and Education (New York: The Macmillan Company, 1952).

the formal cause. What specifies that society which is the school is also its end or goal, the achievement of the intellectual part of education.

Education in Its Fourth Meaning

Other educational agencies also teach, but they do so in a different context. The church, the state, the family, and other societies engage in some form of instruction as one of their ordinary functions and not as a mere incidental. Yet this function cannot be said to specify them, to constitute the goal for whose achievement they exist. It does, however, specify the school as the kind of society it is. The intellectual development of its students is not the only aim of the school; but it is the aim for which the school as an institution was brought into being and whose pursuit explains and justifies its continued existence. And because the formal means by which the school carries on intellectual instruction is classroom teaching, the heart of the school will be the classroom, with the library and the laboratory as extensions.

The business of the teacher in the classroom is to teach, and to teach the subject matter that is supposed to be taught at that time. The three indispensable qualifications of any teacher are a knowledge of the subject to be taught, a knowledge of how to teach it, and the desire to teach. With these qualifications, and with a subject matter that presumably has some intellectual content, the one job that the teacher directly has in the classroom is to teach. Education in its fourth meaning is his task, and if the teacher and the classroom fail in this task there is no other educational agency to fill the gap; the job of teaching will then simply not be done.

It is a question of relating ends and means, whole and parts. Education, again, is a whole made up of potential parts, each of which is truly education but is not the whole of education. The classroom is the classroom; it is not the home or the church or the state or the whole school, and if it attempts to take over the work of these other educational agencies it will succeed only in confusing the issue and failing to do the work which it alone is capable of doing. Schooling is not the only part of education, and, considering the final end of men, it is not the most important part. But it is a real part, and it makes its own demands. The intellectual virtues are not the only virtues, and, in ways, not the most important virtues. But they are virtues, and they perfect a power; if they are not developed, that power which is the intellect will not be perfected. As we have seen,[14] there are ways in which the intellectual virtues can be said to be superior to the moral virtues and other ways in which the moral virtues can be said to be superior to the intellectual virtues. Yet even looked at in the second way, as inferior to the moral virtues, the intellectual virtues are still real and are still qualities perfecting the power by which man is first said to be made to the image of God.

Why are these qualities worth developing? On the natural level, simply because it is better to know than not to know, to be able to think than not to be able to think. Knowledge, as Newman put it for all time, is its own end, worth having for what it is. The man who knows is, in that respect, a better—because a fuller and more human—man than the man who does not know. An end may be a real end without being the absolutely ultimate end, and it may be an end which is more than simply a means to a further end. To be physically healthy is a good thing, and we ask the physician to keep us in good health rather than to guide us to our eternal destiny. To play games well is a good thing, and we ask the football coach to teach his charges to block and tackle. To know is also a good thing, and teachers have the job of bringing their students to learn and to keep on learning. If the intellectual part of education is not important enough to do, we should close

[14] See in Chapter three the section on Intellectual Virtues.

the schools and leave education to the other agencies. If it is important enough to do, we should devote classroom teaching to that end, and, directly, to no other. The teacher whose real ambition is to be a missionary should join the mission band, not clutter up the classroom.

This is not to say that the teacher's sole and exclusive job is intellectual; in the very nature of the case it could not be. For example, his personality and his attitudes will inevitably have a powerful moral influence on his students. What it does mean is that what he consciously and directly does should be either intellectual instruction or something that will make intellectual instruction possible. When children come to school without enough food or enough clothes they are in no condition to learn successfully, and the teacher will have to take whatever steps are possible to see to it that the situation is improved. The same will hold for students who have real emotional problems or physical handicaps. Where any means exist for the removal of these conditions the teacher should see to it that the means are used. As a human being the teacher is interested in his students' welfare simply because they are other persons, and persons with whom he has a certain relationship; but strictly as a teacher he is interested in his students' welfare because it affects their ability to learn. Outside the classroom the teacher may function as unofficial but often very successful counselor, and may be guide, philosopher, and friend; inside the classroom he is not counselor but teacher, aiming directly at intellectual instruction and at nothing else.[15]

If someone is asked to do a certain job, it is only reasonable for him to suppose that he will be given a chance to get it done. If a teacher's job in the classroom is to teach, he should not have to waste time and energy selling chocolate milk, collecting money for the adoption of pagan babies, or balancing accounts after the

[15] On these points, see also Smith, *op. cit.,* pp. 33–38.

sale of Christmas cards. Chocolate milk is a good thing for children, but if their parents want them to have it during school hours, the parents should arrange for one of their number to be on hand to carry out the arrangements that make it possible. It is better for pagan babies to be baptized and to be reared as Christians than for them to remain pagan, but the arithmetic period is supposed to be devoted to arithmetic, not to pagan babies. It is necessary for such schools as parochial schools, unjustly denied any share of the school taxes that the members of the parish pay, to have recourse to such projects as the sale of Christmas cards to raise money for library books and maps and other teaching aids. But it should not be necessary to burden the individual teacher with the task of keeping the books for the operation or to steal time from his proper task of academic instruction. Directly, the classroom has only one reason for existence, and in that respect it is unique among the agencies of education. It remains, of course, part of the school, and a convenient unit for the carrying forward of certain school activities which transcend the classroom; it was for such situations, however, that the home-room period was invented, and the situations should be confined to that period, at least as far as is humanly possible.[16]

The Moral Influence of Competent Teaching

Mention was made earlier of the moral influence of the teacher on his students. Such influence is inevitable, simply from the impact of one personality on another. But it remains true that the

[16] For a set of directives designed by a diocesan superintendent of schools to cope with this situation, see *Our Sunday Visitor,* The Fort Wayne Diocesan Edition (September 7, 1958), p. 1 A. Cf. *Our Sunday Visitor,* Fort Wayne–South Bend Diocesan Edition (September 3, 1961), p. 3 A. For criteria useful in judging the appropriateness of these activities, see Harold C. Hand, *Principles of Public Secondary Education* (New York: Harcourt, Brace & World, Inc., 1958), p. 27.

function of the classroom teacher precisely as such is to teach, and to let the moral influence look after itself. Experience says that his moral influence will be greatest and best if he does exactly that and sticks to his business. One of the greatest contributions that his students can make to society after they leave school is to do thoroughly, competently, and conscientiously the work that it is given to them to do. The daily example of a teacher who does exactly that is one of the most powerful and one of the most needed moral influences to which they can be subject. The teacher who gives an immediate example of justice by teaching arithmetic in the arithmetic period, and by teaching it with the competence that comes only from adequate preparation, is doing far more for the students' moral life than he could by exhortation. In the moral order, example is much more efficacious than precept. Personally, I have always been somewhat suspicious of teachers who were reputed to inspire their students. A legitimate question is, "Inspire them to what?" The word originally, we are told, had something to do with breath, and in practice it often stays quite close to its original meaning, largely because it does not demand the labor of preparation. The only inspiration at which a classroom teacher should aim is inspiration to learn; the only love which he is supposed to be developing is love of learning. And he cannot possibly develop that love in others if he does not have it himself.

The teacher can do a great deal for the moral formation of his students, and he can do it best by paying no direct attention to it. Morally speaking, we teach by what we are and by what we do— and by what we really are, not by what we unsuccessfully try to kid other people into thinking we are. That teacher will best develop honesty in his students who is himself honest and simple and unpretentious, who grades papers with strict impartiality, who stands not on his dignity but on his performance. That teacher will best develop responsibility and conscientiousness in his students who is himself responsible and conscientious, who carefully prepares his classes and takes his job seriously, who gives his students teaching rather than preaching. That teacher will best inspire his students to a respect for and love of learning who himself respects and loves learning and regards continuous study as a normal way of life. As a well-intentioned human being, any teacher wants not only to teach his students intellectually but to influence them morally as well, to make them better all-round persons. He will do so by not trying to do it; he will do so by going into the classroom and doing his job to the very best of his ability, thoroughly and with professional competence. In justice, he owes his students nothing less.

QUESTIONS

1. What is the purpose of the school—to teach, to adjust students to society, to counsel, to provide friendly surroundings?
2. Should a Catholic school compel attendance at daily Mass?
3. Should the school attempt to educate the whole man? Should it do what other agencies fail to do?
4. What is the place of the school in such activities as selling milk, collecting money for hot lunches, taking pictures of the students, holding flower shows, running banking programs?
5. Are teachers or parents primarily responsible for instilling Christian principles in the young?
6. How can a teacher encourage use of the library?
7. Should moral objectives be fitted into the teaching of Latin? Of any other subject? Why or why not? If so, how?
8. What are some of the ways in which a day school can

make up for deficiencies in a student's home life? What are some of the ways in which it cannot?

9. Is the aim of education the person who thinks correctly or the person who acts correctly?

10. In taking on religious and moral education, is the school usurping the function of the Church and of the home?

11. How can high schools train their gifted students for leadership?

12. In a conflict between parental authority and school authority, which should take precedence?

13. How democratic or how authoritarian should school administrators be in training inexperienced students for participation in student government?

14. Which are more democratic, public or private schools?

15. How can the school motivate its students to (*a*) study, (*b*) lead morally good lives?

16. Has an accrediting agency a right to require that a school adopt any particular philosophy of education?

17. "The process and the goal of education are identical with one another." Discuss.

18. Is it a sound educational practice which *forces* students to receive a *formal* education?

꙳

chapter five

Two Further Aims

CATHOLIC EDUCATION

If the school exists ultimately because of the classroom, and if the function of the classroom is, directly, an exclusively intellectual one, it would appear at first sight that there is room for dividing schools according to intellectual but not according to any other differences, such as religious ones. Dividing schools into elementary and secondary, for example, is based on differences in the age of the students and in their consequent learning ability; dividing schools into liberal and vocational or professional is based on differences in the interests of students and in their occupational intentions. But schools which are divided on the basis of religious differences among students would seem to be based on something irrelevant to the learning process. Why, if schools are what they have been described here as being, should there be Catholic or Lutheran or Calvinist schools? [1]

Functions of the Church-related School

One reason, of course, is that schools, even as here described, are not exclusively intellectual societies, though they are specifically so. The school is broader than the classroom, and has room in its wider scope of activities for more than intellectual development. True, the school is specifically an agency for the development of intellectual virtues; but it should aim directly, though secondarily, at more than that. There is room in the work of the school, as we saw, for the development of the physical and the social and other abilities of the student. There is also room for the development of his spiritual consciousness and religious practices, by means which have already been mentioned. The Newman Club, for example, does noble work on the secular campus, but it cannot possibly provide an omnipresent Catholic atmosphere which, in every phase of the school's activities, reminds the student silently but powerfully of the place of the supernatural in his life. This is not to say that Catholic students should not attend secular schools or that they will probably suffer spiritual damage if they do so. It is to say that, because the whole man comes to school, a student with religious convictions, say a Catholic, is more likely to deepen his spiritual life at a Catholic school simply because he is offered more opportunities to do so.

The ultimate reason, however, for the existence of Catholic

[1] A detailed explanation of the benefits of Catholic schools is that of Neil G. McCluskey, S.J., *Catholic Viewpoint on Education* (Garden City, N.Y.: Hanover House, Doubleday & Company, Inc., 1959), pp. 89–96. See also John Courtney Murray, S.J., "The Christian Idea of Education," *The Christian Idea of Education* (New Haven, Conn.: Yale University Press, 1957), espec. pp. 155–160.

schools is not a moral but an intellectual one: It makes possible the teaching of sacred doctrine, of knowledge about God and about the created order in relation to God, of divine revelation and its implications.² Because of the religious differences among its students, a secular school cannot teach one particular interpretation of sacred doctrine.³ Yet students who are not instructed in sacred doctrine lose the most important intellectual instruction that they could possibly get. If God exists, then this fact and its implications are the most important knowledge there is, and will have a bearing on one's understanding of all the rest of reality.⁴ In its

² See Leo R. Ward, C.S.C., *Blueprint for a Catholic University* (St. Louis: B. Herder Book Co., 1949), and "Idea of a Catholic University," *A College Goes to School* (Notre Dame, Ind.: St. Mary's College, 1945), pp. 29–44; Edmond Darvil Benard, "Theology as Pivotal: Newman's View," in Roy J. Deferrari (ed.), *Integration in Catholic Colleges and Universities* (Washington, D.C.: The Catholic University of America Press, 1950), pp. 40–65.

³ What the secular college can and should do concerning the teaching of theology is argued in Gustave Weigel, "The College and the Dimensions of Reality," *Liberal Education*, 45, 1 (March, 1959), 44–53. See also John Courtney Murray, S.J., *We Hold These Truths* (New York: Sheed & Ward, Inc., 1960), pp. 134–139. For other views, see E. Earle Stibitz, "A Religious Point of View in Teaching the Liberal Arts," *Liberal Education*, 45, 2 (May, 1959), 249–262. Cf. Horton Smith, "The Interdepartmental Approach to Religious Studies," *Journal of Higher Education*, 31, 2 (February, 1960), 61–68. It may be of interest to note that in 1960 a Canadian Jesuit was a visiting professor of theology at the University of Minnesota, and that in the same year one of his Toronto colleagues began a three-year appointment as associate professor of theology at the State University of Iowa, an institution which grants advanced degrees in religion; see *The Jesuit Bulletin*, Toronto (Ordination Issue, 1960), p. 28.

⁴ "It is not too much to say that the immaturity, or it

upper reaches, in that science and wisdom which is theology, sacred doctrine is the habit of looking at the whole of the reality that one comes to know in its relation to God, the absolutely ultimate cause, and thus of understanding that reality in a way which would be impossible without such knowledge. In its lower reaches, sacred doctrine will be the knowledge of God that immature children are capable of, certainly neither science nor true wisdom, but at least the informational groundwork for them.[5]

It is true that to be a mathematician or a physicist or an electrical engineer, one need not also be a theologian. But to be an educated man one need be, to whatever extent his maturity and ability make possible, a man versed in sacred doctrine. For there is an ultimate cause of reality, and whoever does not know the cause does not fully know the reality. Man, for instance, is not fully intelligible except as the child of God. At best, to know reality thus is to know it only partially, and to be conscious of the fact. At worst, it is to know reality only partially and to be un-

---

might be better to say the incompleteness, of American culture manifests itself at no point so clearly as it does when religious issues are under discussion. There are many reasons why this is so, but the principal one undoubtedly is that theology has been studied so far away from the main stream of university life. Quite without knowing it, we have agreed with Tito and Rákosi in banning religion to the rectory." George N. Shuster in Brand Blanshard (ed.), *Education in the Age of Science* (New York: Basic Books, Inc., Publishers, 1959), p. 40. Reprinted by permission. Cf. Jacques Maritain, "Thomist Views on Education," in Nelson B. Henry (ed.), *Modern Philosophies and Education,* part I, 54th Yearbook of the N.S.S.E. (Chicago: The University of Chicago Press, 1955), pp. 84–87.

[5] See Vincent E. Smith, *The School Examined: Its Aim and Content* (Milwaukee: The Bruce Publishing Company, 1960), pp. 284–285.

conscious of the fact, to suppose that one has the ultimate explanations which the human mind naturally seeks. The name of that mistake is positivism. Men must know things in relation to God if they are to know them as fully as they can. And in a school, an institution devoted specifically to knowledge and the intellectual virtues, simple faith is no longer good enough. Schools exist so that their students may come to know, and to know as fully and as deeply as possible. Catholic schools make possible the teaching of sacred doctrine at whatever level is appropriate to the maturity of the students concerned. It is this function, an intellectual function and hence one proper to a school as such, that primarily justifies the existence of the Catholic school. The earlier reason given —moral and spiritual training and religious atmosphere—is sufficient alone to justify the Catholic school. But it is still secondary, in the school, to the development of intellectual virtue through the teaching of sacred doctrine.

Very briefly, then, the argument runs thus: Schools exist primarily to impart knowledge; the highest knowledge that they can impart is knowledge of God, or sacred doctrine; the religiously affiliated school—for example, the Catholic school—is the best one to impart this knowledge, for theological knowledge begins in faith; therefore the religiously affiliated school is necessary for the fullest development of knowledge in its students. Primarily, Catholic schools exist for the teaching of sacred doctrine and of other disciplines in the light of sacred doctrine.[6]

The Sequel to Rising Costs

There are other possibilities, but in the sense that half a loaf is a possibility. It may be that constantly rising costs of education will make the Catholic burden of supporting two full educa-

[6] Cf. John F. McCormick, S.J., *Saint Thomas and the Life of Learning* (Milwaukee: Marquette University Press, 1937), espec. pp. 17–25. For much the same argument from

tional systems a financially impossible one. In that event some part of the Catholic educational system will be starved out of existence, its students will enter the public school system, and members of religious communities will concentrate on teaching sacred doctrine to these students on a released-time basis or outside regular school hours. Such a solution is better than no religious instruction, but it makes most difficult the coordination of sacred doctrine with other subject matters in the mind of the student. Sacred doctrine is then something apart, something removed from the school and from the life of the intellect, something esoteric and perhaps somewhat meaningless.

Whether the emphasis should be on the grade school or the high school in such a situation is a matter of debate.[7] Father McCluskey favors a concentration of limited resources on the junior and senior high school and the junior college, that is, grades 7 to 14; Monsignor Casey favors withdrawing from the elementary field in favor of secondary and higher education; Monsignor McManus suggests that Catholic students, especially on the secondary level, pursue some of their studies in public and some in Catholic schools.

a Protestant point of view, see Elton Trueblood, *The Idea of a College* (New York: Harper & Row, Publishers, 1959), chap. 2.

[7] See, for example, Z. T. Ralston, C.R., "Parochial Schools in the United States, Grade or High," *The Resurrection Bulletin,* 1, 3 (November, 1959), 11–12, Kitchener, Ontario; Neil G. McCluskey, S.J., "The Dinosaur and the Catholic School," National Catholic Education Association, *Bulletin,* 57, 1 (August, 1960), 232–238; Msgr. George W. Casey, in Driftwood, "The Elementary Grades," *The Pilot,* 132, 32 (Aug. 12, 1961), 4, Boston; *Our Sunday Visitor,* Fort Wayne–South Bend Diocesan Edition, 50, 45 (Mar. 11, 1962), 2, which summarizes the position of Msgr. William E. McManus, superintendent of education for the Archdiocese of Chicago.

Before the final and momentous decision is taken, it is to be hoped that those who make the decision will consult as many as possible of those who are teaching and not only administering in the grades concerned. Indeed, it would be criminal negligence not to do so, for the troops in the firing line know the facts of the situation by a direct experience that the brass cannot have. Their opinions should be carefully solicited and weighed, both because those opinions are informed and consequently indispensable for the making of an intelligent decision, and also because it is the teachers who will have to implement the decision in practice, and the degree to which they put their backs into the job will depend in no small part on the degree to which they have been consulted beforehand. Especially to be solicited are the experiences of those currently trying to teach sacred doctrine—with no school sanctions to back up anything like study assignments or even the requirement of regular attendance—to Catholic students who attend public grade and high schools. Some of these experiences are eye-openers.

It is being taken for granted that the teachers concerned will, in expressing their opinions and their reasons for them, keep primarily in mind the good of the students rather than the advantage or convenience of the religious community to which they may belong. However humanly difficult, this detachment is also indispensable to a sound solution of the problem.

What decision should finally be reached must wait upon such consultation and study, including the effect of diocesan centralization on religious teaching communities. The one decision which would be totally unacceptable would be to keep open only those Catholic schools whose student fees would pay their actual and rising costs of operation. If Catholic education is a good thing, it is a good thing for the poor as well as for the rich. It is a good thing whose costs should fall, not only upon the parents whose children are there at any given time, but upon the community as a whole. But upon what community? Upon the parish? Upon the diocese? Upon the archdiocese? Upon the combined resources of the national Catholic community? Father McCluskey compares the parish basis of organization to the dinosaur, and plumps for the diocese as the unit. Perhaps this organization is also somewhat less than the times require, and it might be possible to consider the national community or at least the archdiocese as a unit for this purpose.

Whatever decision is finally arrived at will involve tremendous upheavals and tremendous investments, and will decide the general shape of American Catholic schooling for generations to come. It should not be reached either hastily or autocratically.

Another solution, proposed for the college level of instruction, is to make sacred doctrine an optional subject in the secular school, taught to those students who elect it. There is as yet no agreement on whether the teacher of this subject should be himself an adherent of the interpretation of revelation that he is to teach. If he is not, it would appear that the course would be largely historical in character; if he is, it would appear that the course would be largely doctrinal in character. The latter would seem preferable, since the aim here is to teach sacred doctrine rather than to teach about sacred doctrine. But difficulties are evident. Would the teacher be a regular member of the faculty? If not, the same question of the coordination of this knowledge with other knowledges would arise, to the probable confusion of the student. If so, something approaching a real solution of the problem of religious instruction on the college level would be at hand. Whether state legislatures would see it that way is another question and, in this context, the crucial one.

A workable answer to the problem, and a time-tested one, exists in the Canadian provinces west of Quebec. As developed in the University of Toronto, this arrangement applies to the undergraduate Faculty of Arts and Science alone. Within this area there are four colleges, one nonsectarian, one United Church (largely Methodist in origin), one Anglican (Episcopalian), and one Catholic. The University alone grants degrees. Each college may teach and examine its students in sacred doctrine (there traditionally called religious knowledge), and the Catholic college may teach and examine its students in philosophy; the University accepts the examination results toward a degree in Arts and Science. Each college may also teach other subjects such as English, foreign languages, and some branches of history, but the University as a whole conducts the final examination, which is the same for students in all four colleges. Other subjects are taught by the University to groups of students who are, for those classes, no longer distinguished by college. Sometimes a college will not teach a subject which it has the right to teach because it does not consider its staff strong enough in that area; sometimes a college will have a specialist in an area, and students from other colleges will attend his classes, especially in one of the honors courses. The arrangements are quite flexible and sometimes pretty complicated. But they do allow a student to get the advantages of both a small college and a large university, of both a religious education and the material aids to education that a tax-supported university can afford. The system works because the people concerned want it to work, because they understand the meaning of pluralism and do not confuse unity with uniformity, and because they believe that people with religious convictions should not therefore be treated as second-class citizens.[8]

[8] For checking the accuracy of the foregoing description, I am indebted to the Rev. John M. Kelly, C.S.B., President, St. Michael's College, University of Toronto. For an analysis of the situation, see Edwin C. Garvey, "Pluralism in the University," *The Commonweal*, 73, 18 (Jan. 27, 1961), 458–

Once more, it has been said above that the function which specifies a school is the development of the intellectual virtues, and that the function which specifies a Catholic school is the development of that intellectual virtue which is sacred doctrine. But it has also been said that, since the school is more than the classroom, it should aim directly, though not primarily, at the development of moral virtue in its students as well—at some degree of character training. Catholic schools can do this in conjunction with and in part by means of the fostering of religious practices such as assistance at Mass and reception of the sacraments. The secular school may and in practice does aim at the development in its students of the natural virtues—at the formation of character. By its very situation, however, it cannot officially deal with or attempt to prepare its students for the reception of the infused, supernatural virtues. The Catholic school cannot actually provide the channels of the supernatural life, for it is not the Church. It can, though, work in close association with the Church by providing opportunities for the reception of supernatural grace and the development of the supernatural virtues that the secular school does not in fact provide. The very atmosphere of a Catholic school is a powerful influence in the direction of religious practice. In view of the absolutely ultimate nature of our supernatural last end, and in view of the moral and spiritual influence, for good or for ill, which a school in all its facets inevitably has on its students, this secondary reason for the existence of Catholic schools is, even taken by itself, quite sufficient to justify their existence. Again, the whole man comes to school, and that fact has educational implications. Indeed, what is at stake in moral and spiritual development is so important that some Catholic schools seem to regard this function as their primary one, to the detriment of their specific work.

---

462. See also Milton Lomask, "Saint Mike's: Best of Two Worlds," *The Sign,* 40, 9 (April, 1961), 41–43, 68–69.

EDUCATION FOR CITIZENSHIP

Another educational aim to which special consideration should perhaps be given is that of education for citizenship, especially in view of the frequency with which it is spoken of as the primary aim of the school.[9] Certainly, a normal human life means a life lived in society, including political society; education for citizenship, then, is not only a worthy educational aim but an absolutely essential one. This does not necessarily mean, however, that it is the primary aim of the school.

Before considering the aims of education, we tried to establish some conclusions concerning the nature of man, since before we can say what a man's education should be we must first know what we are educating. We saw that a man is a human person, a free and rational being capable of knowledge and of love—through

[9] See, for example, Frederick C. Gruber, "Editor's Preface," *Aspects of Value* (Philadelphia: University of Pennsylvania Press, 1959), p. 13: "The American public schools are organized and maintained to promote our democratic way of life. Therefore, they cannot sidestep our most pressing problems, nor can they be indifferent to the inculcation of moral and spiritual values." Reprinted by permission. The present section is one possible commentary on the first statement. One could agree with the second statement while maintaining that children of school age are not as yet in a position to solve these problems or even to do much more than try to grasp the fact of their existence. The last statement is both true and important; it is also true and important, however, that the moral and spiritual values must first be the personal ones that make good men and, as a result and almost incidentally, make good citizens. To reverse the emphasis is to stunt the growth of both man and citizen. For a more detailed statement of Gruber's position, see John L. Childs, "Value Conflicts and the Education of Our Young," *ibid.*, pp. 73–88.

the spiritual principle of his nature transcending the determined natural order, possessing an intrinsic liberty, having a destiny beyond the temporal world—an independent whole and not merely a part of nature, an end and not merely a means.

Precisely because of what he is, man is naturally a social animal. He tends to civil or political society because he is a man and because his nature demands this society for its fulfillment. It is true that society is natural to man because it satisfies his material needs through making possible the division of labor and because it satisfies his intellectual needs through making possible the office of teaching. But society is also natural to man because it allows greater scope for his specifically human powers of knowledge and love; it allows him to communicate his thoughts to his fellows and to express his natural generosity and love to them. Society exists to enable a man to give as well as to take, and thus to reach a fuller degree of human development.

Society, then, is *human* society, erected by the free consent of human persons, and having as its aim the common good of its members, that is, the conditions of the good life through which they can most completely develop their human potentialities. A citizen, then, must first be a man before he can be a citizen, and the better man he is, the better citizen he will make. Jacques Maritain has said it well: [10]

> The essence of education does not consist in adapting a potential citizen to the conditions and interactions of social life, but first in *making a man,* and by this very fact in preparing a citizen. Not only is it nonsense to oppose education for the person and education for the commonwealth, but the latter supposes the former as a prerequisite, and in return the former is impossible without the latter, for one does not make a man

[10] Jacques Maritain, *Education at the Crossroads* (New Haven, Conn.: Yale University Press, 1943), p. 15. Reprinted by permission.

except in the bosom of social ties where there is an awakening of civic understanding and civic virtues.

Those schools which aim only or even first at making a citizen are motivated by a false view of the nature of man and of society; they are putting the cart before the horse.[11] Current events, group projects, and student congresses have a legitimate place in the activities of a school, but they should not be allowed to usurp the place in the curriculum of the traditional intellectual disciplines that develop the specifically human intellectual virtues. For, again, the student is a man first and a citizen afterwards; he is a citizen only because he is a man. An education that aims at making him first a fully developed man by stressing his intellectual and—largely outside the classroom—his moral growth will also make him a good citizen; an education that aims first at making him a citizen by stressing exclusively or even chiefly his social training will only stunt the growth of his human powers. It will risk making him the slave of inhuman forces by regarding and training him as a being whose role is to adapt himself to his environment rather than to form his environment by the free exercise of his human intellect and will.

This leads to another and even more serious criticism of the conception of citizenship as the sole or the primary aim of schooling. This conception implies that man is a means and society his end; it denies, in effect if not in intention, the fundamental liberties of the human person and sees in him only a tool of the state. If education is for citizenship, then the state of which the student is a

[11] Further, "To assume that 'good citizens' can be made to emerge from the schools as hot cross buns do from a bakery is to take a benign view indeed of human nature and the teaching profession." George N. Shuster in Brand Blanshard (ed.), *Education in the Age of Science* (New York: Basic Books, Inc., Publishers, and The American Academy of Arts and Sciences, 1959), p. 32. Reprinted by permission.

citizen will quickly become the power that decides what type of education its citizens shall have. Education for citizenship will come in practice to mean education of the type that a particular state demands, a type subservient to its particular desires and lending itself to its particular aims. Consciously or unconsciously, education for citizenship implies the totalitarian conception of man and of the state, and, if allowed to become the sole aim or even the primary aim of school education, will lead inevitably to the totalitarian state. It is no exaggeration to say that, potentially, education for citizenship, in one of its meanings, is education for tyranny.[12] And this conclusion holds even when the announced aim is education for democratic citizenship.

Brameld: A Philosophy of Education-as-Politics

An example can be found in the reconstructionism of Theodore Brameld. The good intentions lying behind this program are patent. Brameld wants what we all should want: a world in which the ordinary man may at last come into his own and really control his destiny, a world in which he may live at peace with other men, free from the threat of atomic annihilation. No man of good will could quarrel with these ends, or with one who so eloquently pleads for their realization. Yet one who is perfectly in agreement with Brameld about these goals may yet have two reservations about his program. The first concerns the means by which these ends may best be achieved. The second concerns the advisability of turning the schools into agencies whose primary task is the implementation of those very means about which the first question arises.

As Brameld sees it: [13]

The social, political, and economic relations of this period . . . gravitate around two fundamental and related facts. The first

[12] Cf. Maritain, *op. cit.*, pp. 99–101.
[13] Theodore Brameld, *Ends and Means in Education: A*

is the fact of an unstable and precarious economy, with its accompaniment of insecurity, inflation, its cycles of boom-and-bust. The second is the fact of national rivalry and hostility with their potential of atomic war.

His answer to the first problem is the welfare state: [14]

> This is the theory of the positive welfare state of public service as a much more urgent approach to our closely knit industrial culture than the negative state of our *laissez-faire* past. The state, in other words, has a growing number of constructive duties to perform in behalf of popular well-being. . . .

His answer to the second problem is internationalism, involving the surrender of national sovereignty.[15]

> In short, a theory of the state appropriate to the revolutionary conditions thrust upon us by the dubious alliance of economics, militarism, and natural science needs to embrace the coercive power of separate states by a still more coercive power —a supremely enforceable power over all states.

A stable economy and international peace certainly constitute a consummation devoutly to be wished. Yet the battle against *laissez faire* was won long ago, and there are those who, from motives as unimpeachable as Brameld's, consider that further strides into the welfare state will seriously endanger all our liberties. To hold that the good society is identical with the welfare state is to take a defensible position; but it is not at all to enunciate a self-

---

Midcentury Appraisal (New York: Harper & Row, Publishers, 1950), p. 188. Reprinted by permission.

[14] *Ibid.*, p. 65. Reprinted by permission. The same passage appears in Theodore Brameld, *Education for the Emerging Age: Newer Ends and Stronger Means* (New York: Harper & Row, Publishers, 1961), p. 85.

[15] *Ends and Means in Education*, pp. 64–65; *Education for the Emerging Age*, p. 85; cf. *ibid.*, p. 140.

evident proposition. Again, one might agree that the identity of a rational and responsible human nature in all men at all times and places calls for democracy as the humanly ideal form of government and points ultimately to an international community [16] replacing national sovereignties; but even so, one might not consider the time ripe for an effective internationalism. When unilateral disarmament would mean suicide or enslavement, men may not unreasonably prefer a precarious balance of terror, however hard it may be on the nerves. In short, one may legitimately wonder about the relevance of a doctrine of social protest reminiscent of Thorstein Veblen, Father Coughlin, and Wendell Willkie, to the contemporary scene and to the problems that really face democratic society today. If we do not consider these means appropriate to the ends to which they are directed, perhaps we should look for a program other than reconstructionism.

Even if these means were appropriate, a second reservation about reconstructionism concerns the use that the program proposes to make of the schools for its implementation. Among other things, the curriculum will have to undergo radical alteration: [17]

> If the schools are to do their share toward the success that is still possible, and surely desirable, they will have to throw much of the baggage of routine curricula on the junk heap to make room for more imperative tasks.

"What, then, is our proposal? In essence it is that *the hub of every curriculum be the study of the structure and operation of*

[16] How one can draw these conclusions from seeing human nature as "a complex, dynamic fusion of drives" remains obscure. See *Ends and Means in Education,* p. 62; *Education for the Emerging Age,* p. 83.

[17] *Ends and Means in Education,* p. 204. Reprinted by permission.

reconstructed democracy itself." [18]   Or, as it came out later, "In essence my proposal is that *the hub of every curriculum be the problems and prospects of reorganizing democracy itself."* [19]   In short, social studies will save the world, provided they are studies of reconstructionism.[20]

This turning of the schools directly to political ends frightens many who are concerned for the preservation of personal liberties.

[18] *Ibid.,* p. 211. Italics in the original. Reprinted by permission.

[19] *Education for the Emerging Age,* p. 184. Italics in the original. Reprinted by permission. Support for this position is contained in B. O. Smith, W. O. Stanley, and J. H. Shores, *Fundamentals of Curriculum Development,* rev. ed. (New York: Harcourt, Brace & World, Inc., 1957), pp. 574–582, 627–650.

[20] On this and related points, Theodore M. Greene comments: "This need not, and should not, imply an idolatrous veneration for the democratic processes of free association and co-operation under law. For these processes are themselves merely the means—though so far as we can see, *much* the best, and perhaps the *only,* means—for the development of man's highest social potentialities and for steady progress toward the realization of man's proper destiny. The truly liberal goal of education can never be defined merely in terms of a society, actual or ideal; we must resist the temptation to absolutize any form of social organization and to make education *merely* a means to the furtherance of a social goal. In the liberal perspective, education and democracy are *both* institutional means for the achievement of more ultimate human ends. What is here so significant is that they are clearly complementary means, each requiring the lively support of the other." Theodore M. Greene, "A Liberal Christian Idealist Philosophy of Education," *Modern Philosophies and Education,* p. 113. Copyright 1955 by the University of Chicago. Reprinted by permission.

A philosophy of education

It does not frighten Brameld, who can speak calmly of "a philosophy of education-as-politics," [21] and who can hold that "education in its comprehensive sense should become the co-partner of politics." [22] One reason why it does not frighten him is that he cheerfully takes it for granted that a democratic consensus will agree with his position concerning "institutional arrangements, especially of the service state and government." [23] However, in case the majority do not freely arrive at such a consensus, there will be "leaders" to point out to them where their best interests really lie, with teachers receiving the first nomination for the job: [24]

> Leaders are equally articulators and suggesters, that is to say, "pointers" who continually help people to perceive more exactly, more generously, their own best interests. Here is a role so suitable also to the democratic teacher that he himself becomes, in this sense, a democratic leader.

Seen from one angle, reconstructionism is an outdated proposal for the improvement of society; seen from another, it is a plan for the seizure of power. Good intentions and generous impulses and an invocation of democracy are not enough to justify what would in effect, if not in intention, prostitute the schools

[21] *Ends and Means in Education,* p. 67; *Education for the Emerging Age,* p. 87.

[22] *Ends and Means in Education,* p. 59; *Education for the Emerging Age,* p. 80.

[23] *Ends and Means in Education,* p. 66; *Education for the Emerging Age,* p. 86.

[24] *Ends and Means in Education,* p. 67; *Education for the Emerging Age,* p. 87. This position, suggesting something like Big Brother for education, is particularly interesting in view of Brameld's misrepresentation of what he calls "perennialism" as antidemocratic. See his *Philosophies of Education in Cultural Perspective* (New York: The Dryden Press, Inc., 1955), part IV, espec. pp. 365–378; cf. *Education for the Emerging Age,* p. 155.

to the lust for power. However far from its author's mind, this last passage could well describe the commissar of the future serving the unreconstructed rulers of the American version of the "people's democracies." [25]

Should the School Educate for Democracy?

The question is not about the aim, for there must be education for democratic citizenship. The question is about the agencies and about the means. Democracy is not the only possible form of political organization, as history attests. It is not even the only possible form of good government, for not all groups of people are ready to govern themselves. Men have a natural right to good government, to government for the sake of the governed rather than for the sake of the governors, to government *for* the people as well as government *of* the people. But they do not have a natural right to govern themselves, to government *by* the people, to democratic government. For democracy to be practicable there must be, in a preponderant majority of the people who are to run their own political show, a certain development of both moral and intellectual virtues. Principally, there must be a willingness to subordinate one's own individual good to the common good, at least to some reasonable extent; and there must be a considerable degree of the political maturity that comes only with experience. Not all people have enough political prudence to govern themselves successfully; the franchise is a civil rather than a natural right.

Yet there is a real sense in which democracy can be said to be the form of government most in accord with human nature, and

[25] For pertinent remarks on the dangers of a majoritarian tyranny, see John Courtney Murray, S.J., *We Hold These Truths,* pp. 208–209, 324–326, and his "The Church and Totalitarian Democracy," *Theological Studies,* 13 (1952), 525–563. See also Herbert Johnston, "Locke's Leviathan," *The Modern Schoolman,* 26 (1949), 201–210.

therefore a political ideal for all men. For in running their personal lives, people of the most various conditions exhibit an ability to relate means and ends and to direct their actions in view of the relationship that they see. Young people may be apt to consider themselves ready for adult life before they have had enough of the indispensable experience; but it is also possible for them to be tied to maternal apron strings for too long. No one proposes that they be kept under parental authority all their lives; they are recognized as human persons, and the date of their independence is a matter only of time. The same should apply to groups of people, the difference being that the maturity needed is even harder to come by, and the willingness to sacrifice for the common good is needed on an even wider scale. Again, however, the question is one of time only, and the fact that some groups of people are eager to take on the responsibility of guiding their own political destinies before they are likely to make much of a success of it does not at all involve the conclusion that they will therefore never be capable of democratic government. The reasons why they may not be able to do so at any given time are accidental reasons with a historical explanation; they do not spring from the very human nature of the people concerned. Men are capable of governing themselves, and any government which is not *by* the people must, if it is really to be *for* the people, aim ultimately at making itself unnecessary. Imperialism and colonialism are not wrong in themselves; but they involve, for the ruling power, responsibility rather than opportunity.

Education for democracy, then, is required by the facts of the situation, for democracy is that form of government most in accord with human nature as it is observable in men. Where democracy does not yet exist, men must be prepared for it as well and as quickly as possible, though time may here have to be reckoned in generations or even centuries. Where democracy does exist, its preservation must be actively worked for, since it is, in the world's history, a new and still-precarious achievement. There must, then, be education for democracy, even in what is already a democratic society; for even though democracy can be said to be the form of government most in accord with the facts of human nature, it makes demands on its citizens that no other form of government does, and is constantly in danger from fallen human nature itself, from selfishness and ignorance. The question is not whether education for democracy is needed; the question is what the school should and can do about it. Other educational agencies also have a responsibility in this respect, but at the moment we shall confine our attention to the school, for this is the agency generally thought of when the question of education for democracy comes up.

Principally, the school can educate its students for democracy by simply doing its job as well as it can, by helping its students develop the intellectual and the moral virtues needed to govern themselves. Indeed, the school can probably educate for democracy most effectively by not trying to do too much. Inside the class-room each teacher can teach what he is given to teach to the very best of his ability, and can make the utmost intellectual demands that his students are capable of meeting. What he can avoid doing is making his subject matter simply a springboard for organizing his students into busy little committees playing at various projects, the content of which doesn't much matter because the real aim is to get students used to working together. The shallow-minded notion that democracy and committees are synonymous is a grave injustice to the noblest political ideal that the human mind has conceived. Workable democracy requires responsible and thoughtful citizens. One way to develop them is to teach students something with a genuine intellectual content. One way not to develop them is to prepare students for an already committee-ridden society by fostering in them the illusion that they can fruitfully discuss issues before they have learned what the issues

143

are, and that some grasp of Robert's *Rules of Order* is enough to change this extension of the kindergarten into a serious preparation for the future work of deciding grave and complex public issues. The experience of working together is a good experience, a socializing and a civilizing experience. The school can reasonably provide this experience for its students by extraclass activities such as clubs and athletics and social events. As long as they are kept in their place and not allowed to get in the way of the specific task of the school, all is well. They can even be said to be part of an education for citizenship. But they have no place in the classroom, which is an institution for intellectual instruction. When socializing experiences (of which, incidentally, the student already has a great many outside the school) are made the goal of classroom activity, real teaching goes out the window and the student is cheated. So is the nation. The school should certainly see to it that the classroom contributes to education for democracy by the teaching of such subjects as national history and civics, since a knowledge of how our political society came into being and how its various levels of government operate is essential for intelligent participation in self-government. But these are subject matters with an intellectual content, and they should be taught in order to increase knowledge; they should not be made merely means for the organization of childish committees designed chiefly to smooth off rough edges. Rough edges are not, in any case, necessarily undemocratic; perhaps a few more of them might even be salutary in a society which makes so much of togetherness.

It is not only through history and civics, though, that the student is educated for democracy in the classroom; it is through the whole range of a liberal and humanistic education. By imparting to its students a common body of knowledge, the classroom can furnish them with the only ground on which a communication of ideas is possible and the only foundation on which a community can be built. By developing in them the ability to reason and analyze and judge, it can rescue future citizens from the emotional appeal of demagogues to prejudice and passion. In a word, it can develop free minds, and free minds make free men.

Teaching the Christian Conception of Man

At the college level the most important contribution that the classroom can make to educating its students for democracy is to instruct them accurately concerning the nature of man. It is an obvious fact that every organization of society and every system of government applies to men, for men are both rulers and ruled. It is, then, of the utmost importance that we should hold clear and correct ideas regarding the nature of man, for on those ideas will depend ultimately the nature of our society and of our government. If we hold a true view of the nature of man, we can build a society in which men can live a human life. If we hold a false view of the nature of man, we cannot build a society in which men can live a human life. This fact, elementary and even obvious, cannot be insisted on too strongly; for neglect of it leads to the most disastrous consequences. If man is seen as only another biological unit, completely conditioned by heredity and environment to the point at which liberty and responsibility become illusions, if his spiritual nature is denied or even effectively ignored, then he is ripe for the slave state. If man is seen as only another material thing, then he may be treated as any other material thing is treated; he may be regimented, oppressed, coerced. In such a world a man may with perfect logic be made a slave of the machine, of the state, or of other more powerful men; for he is only a thing, and he has no rights which the society has not conferred upon him and which the society may not take away. With such a view of man there can be no moral objection to the actions of Mussolini or Hitler or Stalin or Khrushchev. The only objection can be that they were logical, and that is not a particularly good objection. If students are taught the same materialistic doctrine on the nature of man, it will be only a matter of time until some of them draw the logical conclusions and begin to look around for means of implementing the will to power. Experience says that a man or a family or a business cannot live forever on its inherited material capital; neither can a free society live forever on its inherited spiritual capital.

At the secondary and elementary level there cannot be a great deal of instruction on the evidence for the spiritual nature of man; there can, though, be an introduction to some of the implications of the New Testament, and especially of the Epistle of St. Paul to the Galatians. Even young students can be brought to see the Christian conception of man as a child of God and hence the subject of human dignity and human rights. They can be brought to see that the Fatherhood of God implies the brotherhood of man, and perhaps even the truth that the seeds of democracy lie most fruitfully in divine revelation of the origin, nature, and destiny of man.

At this level, though, perhaps the most effective contribution that the teacher can make to educating his students for democratic citizenship is in the moral order. It is difficult for any of us really to love our neighbor, really to grasp the fact that Christ died for the unlovely and for the almost unlovable as much as He did for us, who are, of course, neither. It is difficult for teachers to love all of the sometimes unsavory specimens put in their charge, though the number of those who obviously do so is a source of constant wonder and awe to those of us who don't quite make it. It is, though, possible for every teacher to do the best he can to love each of his students as his brother or sister in Christ and to treat the student with justice and charity. This does not mean gushing sentimentality or attempts at personal popularity through adopting a buddy-buddy attitude, for it is a fact that the only way in which an adult can become a pal to a child is by becoming childish. It does mean, however, doing one's very best job for each student, trying to see the best in each of them, being willing to give extra time and help to those who need it, making no distinction between the rich and the poor, the black and the white, the Germans and the Irish. If a teacher, while remaining strict and perhaps somewhat impersonal in his attitude, does not abuse his authority but respects the human dignity and the human rights of each one of his students without exception, he will be giving a mighty lesson in the practice of democracy. Moral virtue is developed largely through example, and the teacher who shows his students justice and honesty and consideration and a touch of human kindness is doing what he can to instill the same virtues in his students and to educate them for democratic living. A good many years' observation says that the strength of democracy in this country owes a great deal to the character and example of its teachers.

QUESTIONS

1. What are the most important values of an education?
2. In what ways, if any, should seminary education differ from that of other schools on the high school and on the college level?
3. Should a Catholic school drop, for academic deficiencies, a student who seems to need the moral and religious guidance afforded by the school?
4. "I don't care how much algebra or history they know at the end of the year, but I want them to be good boys." (A high school principal at a faculty meeting.) Discuss.
5. What is the most effective way to integrate religion into the entire curriculum with a lasting effect?
6. What are the aims of a Catholic high school?

7. What may we consider to be the end product of Catholic education?
8. What is the difference between religion and theology?
9. How much training in theology should teachers of religion have?
10. What is the relation between the term democracy and the term education?
11. What does it mean to say that religion is the core of the curriculum?
12. "The chief reason for the Catholic school system is the preservation of the faith." Discuss.
13. "But what those of us who talk as we do are afraid of is something else, the argument that religion is necessary for salvation, that you have got to teach religion, therefore, in such a way as to save students, and that you save them by giving them the truth. At the same time you protect the truth against critical examination. I would be prepared to examine any subject and permit any man who is qualified to teach it, so long as he is committed to the same spirit of inquiry in the study of religion that we follow in all other disciplines. But think what an outcry would arise if somebody made a critical study of Christianity in the classroom, and then announced his conviction that Christ was not only not a divine figure, but was not a historical figure!" [Sidney Hook in Brand Blanshard (ed.), *Education in the Age of Science*, p. 52. Reprinted by permission.] Discuss this position on the teaching of theology.
14. "The ends of education are, in the nature of the case, social ends." Discuss.
15. Would the elimination of the parochial elementary school solve the problem of educating adequately all Catholic students at the secondary level?

chapter six

Liberal and Vocational Education

LIBERAL KNOWLEDGE

In Chapter three [1] a brief reference was made to the liberal arts. Liberal knowledge, however, is not confined to the liberal arts, but includes liberal sciences as well. Liberal knowledge is the same thing as the speculative knowledge described in Chapter one; [2] it is knowledge which, of its very nature, is directed solely to the consideration of truth and not to any operation of doing or making;

[1] See pp. 73–74.
[2] See the section on The Distinction between Speculative and Practical Knowledge.

it is knowledge which exists for its own sake, knowledge which is its own end and reason for being. The phrase "of its very nature" must be kept in mind, for we are concerned here with the end of the knowledge, not with any end personal to the knower and merely accidental to the knowledge itself.

Though the terms "speculative" and "liberal" have Latin rather than Greek roots, the notion which they express originated with Aristotle; and the second term had a more or less fortuitous origin in Aristotle's choice of a figure of speech. In the passage in question he is explaining that, more than any other study, first philosophy (metaphysics) is pursued for the sake of the knowledge itself, and not as a means to any further end: "And understanding and knowledge pursued *for their own sake* are found most in the knowledge of that which is most knowable . . . and the first principles and the causes are most knowable." [3]   And again: "That it is not a science of production is clear even from the history of the earliest philosophers . . . evidently they were pursuing science *in order to know,* and not for any utilitarian end." [4]   Then Aristotle uses a comparison taken from contemporary Greek life in order to make his meaning clearer: ". . . as the man is free, we say, who exists *for his own sake* and not for another's, so we pursue this as the only free science, for it alone exists *for its own sake.*" [5] In its original use, then, the term "free" or "liberal" as applied to knowledge (and, by transference, to education) had nothing to do with the effects of such knowledge or education on those persons

[3] *Metaphysics,* Bk. I, chap. 2, 982 a 30–b 2, in R. Mc-Keon (ed.), *The Basic Works of Aristotle* (New York: Random House, Inc., 1941). Reprinted by permission of Oxford University Press.

[4] *Ibid.,* 982 b 11–21. Reprinted by permission of Oxford University Press.

[5] *Ibid.,* 982 b 25–27. Reprinted by permission of Oxford University Press.

who achieve it. Liberal knowledge or education may indeed, as is frequently said, be the education which makes men and their minds free; [6] but it can do so only by virtue of its original meaning of knowledge pursued for its own sake, and can no longer do so once that original meaning is lost. Liberal knowledge or education may, further, be the education which makes societies free and which makes their members free in the political sense; but, once again, it can do so only by virtue of its original meaning and can no longer do so once that original meaning is lost. Men must see what is before they can see what should be.

Perhaps the best modern expression of the notion of liberal knowledge is that of Cardinal Newman, who has caught and expressed Aristotle's idea exactly in the title of his fourth Discourse: "Liberal Knowledge Its Own End." Within this discourse he puts it in the form of a proposition: ". . . there is a knowledge worth possessing for what it is and not merely for what it does." [7] This, then, is the original, the classical sense of liberal as applied to knowledge or to education—the only meaning that makes any derived ones intelligible. Liberal knowledge, thus understood, is synonymous with speculative knowledge and, in its general sense, with theoretical knowledge. In the rest of this book the terms will be used interchangeably.

[6] A similar conception goes as far back as Adelard of Bath (12th century; *De eodem et diverso*), who sees the liberal arts as liberating the soul from the chains of worldly love. See *The Didascalicon of Hugh of St. Victor: A Medieval Guide to the Arts,* trans. from the Latin with an introduction and notes by Jerome Taylor (New York: Columbia University Press, 1961), p. 18.

[7] John Henry Cardinal Newman, *The Scope and Nature of University Education* (New York: Dutton Everyman Paperbacks, E. P. Dutton & Co., Inc., 1958), p. 94. Reprinted by permission.

It should be but is not unnecessary to point out that Aristotle's comparison does not involve a condoning of slavery, even though Aristotle himself elsewhere argued in favor of it. The comparison is simply taken from an existing fact of Greek social and political life, and, in itself, implies no attitude either for or against that fact. Those who approve of liberal education in its original meaning are not unconsciously and by implication approving of slavery or even of an aristocratic society. Neither does Aristotle's comparison, which includes an example, involve the thing exemplified in the mutability of the example. In order to make an idea intelligible to the people for whom he was immediately writing, Aristotle used a figure of speech taken, naturally enough, from the familiar contemporary society (the Gospel parables come to mind as a parallel). Had he been writing today, he would have used a different one. The fact that the institution of slavery no longer exists openly in contemporary Western society does not at all mean that the original notion of liberal knowledge can have no place in that society. Both of these points are so obvious that one feels apologetic in making them; hard experience, however, indicates that they should be made.[8]

The point that Aristotle was making in the passages quoted above was that metaphysics (and especially, a Christian would add, sacred theology) is supremely liberal because it is sought for its own sake and is not ordained to any further end of doing or even of knowing. Other liberal knowledges may, because of their very nature, be ordained to further knowledge, as the liberal arts are the traditional introductions to the liberal sciences. This fact, however, does not alter their liberal character, though it means that they are liberal in a less complete sense than are those knowledges

[8] Cf. Vincent E. Smith, *The School Examined: Its Aim and Content* (Milwaukee: The Bruce Publishing Company, 1960), pp. 72–73.

that admit of no such ordination. This point has been well made by Father Mullaney: [9]

Theoretical knowledge is knowledge sought for its own sake. But this defining phrase is ambiguous. It might mean either of two things: (a) knowledge sought neither for doing nor for making but solely for the sake of knowing; (b) knowledge which has no character of ordination relatively to higher, purely intellectual disciplines.

Of all men's natural knowledge, metaphysics alone is theoretical in both senses. But physics and the liberal arts are theoretical in the first sense though not in the second. For both physics and the liberal arts, while sought for the sake of knowing, are also related to further disciplines. Hence the liberal arts are theoretical knowledge because they are purely intellectual, are knowledge sought for its own sake. Just as there are degrees of art according to which the servile arts are most fully art and the liberal arts most tenuously so, so there are degrees of theory according to which metaphysics is most fully theory and the liberal arts are most tenuously so.

LIBERAL ARTS AND SCIENCES
IN THE CURRICULUM

In the traditional medieval schema the liberal arts were divided into the trivium, comprising logic, grammar, and rhetoric or composition, and the quadrivium, comprising arithmetic, geometry, astronomy, and music; in brief, these were, respectively, the logical arts and the mathematical arts. These are the arts, it has been said,[10] which guide the making of things by the mind, for the mind, and in the mind. The completed product of the liberal

---

[9] James V. Mullaney, "The Liberal Arts in the Aristotelian–Thomistic Scheme of Knowledge," *The Thomist,* 19, 4 (October, 1956), 493–494. Reprinted by permission.

[10] See above, pp. 73–74.

arts is something known, something remaining within the mind of the artist or the knower. Hence, alone among the arts, the liberal arts are virtues of the speculative intellect and are also speculative or liberal sciences.[11]

The Place of Liberal and Fine Arts

What is the place of these arts in the curriculum? On the primary, the secondary, and the undergraduate levels, it would seem that logic, grammar, and composition could best be taught as liberal arts. At these levels the student needs to know and can learn *how to make* an argument or a sentence or a paragraph; at the graduate level he can more properly be introduced to the intricacies of philology and of the nature of the various logics. There seems to be fairly general agreement on this point, both in theory and in practice. The aim of the teaching of grammar appears to be much the same from the elementary through the college years, though the amount of attention given it and the manner of its teaching will vary with the convictions of each teacher or superintendent. Much the same can be said of the teaching of composition, though with a qualification which will be made in a later paragraph. Logic is seldom taught formally and under that title below the college level. Yet a great deal of logic, taken as a liberal art, is necessarily taught in connection with grammar and composition, especially when the subject concerns the construction of some form of argument.

Of what was once the quadrivium, some phases of plane geometry are still taught as a liberal art, involving the construction of figures as a means of exploring their properties. Music, however, is now thought of and taught as a fine art, and arithmetic and

[11] Cf. Bernard I. Mullahy, C.S.C., "The Nature of the Liberal Arts," *The New Scholasticism*, 23, 4 (October, 1949), pp. 361–373.

astronomy as sciences. As a division of the liberal arts, then, the quadrivium is now pretty well a dead issue.[12]

Concerning the teaching of composition as a liberal art, a qualification was mentioned above. In that art which is composition, the liberal arts and the fine arts overlap. The liberal arts, according to the classification that we have been using, guide the making of things by the mind, for the mind, and in the mind, whereas the fine arts guide the making of things by the mind and for the mind, but not in the mind. So far as composition involves a mental construction, a relating of the parts of a literary composition to each other and to the whole, it remains a liberal art and is so taught. So far as composition involves outward expression in the medium of language, it becomes a fine art and is so taught. Indeed, it would appear that, on the basis of the definitions given above, all of the fine arts are to some degree liberal, since they involve a preliminary mental construction before any expression in a given medium. Perhaps the difference would lie in the emphasis given, in the fine arts, to the medium of expression and its demands. Whether composition in its various forms up to what is called creative writing is taught primarily as a liberal art or as a fine art will probably depend on the teacher's convictions about the extent, if any, to which composition is a form of rational discourse.[13] This writer's present view, though one open to correction, is that composition of an expository or argumentative nature is closest to what

[12] For an interesting examination of the liberal arts, including the suggestion of calling the humanities the quadrivium and organizing them around history, see Mullaney, *op. cit.*, 481–505. For another position on the liberal arts in the curriculum, see Smith, *op. cit.*, pp. 97–104. See also William F. Cunningham, C.S.C., *General Education and the Liberal College* (St. Louis: B. Herder Book Co., 1953).

[13] For the basis of this debate, see Aristotle, *Poetics,* 1451 a 1–12. Cf. St. Thomas, *Summa Theologiae,* I, 1, 9, ad 1; Smith, *op. cit.*, pp. 64–68.

Aristotle meant by rhetoric, and is that which most involves mental construction and rational discourse and which therefore lends itself best to being taught as a liberal art. On the other hand, such a form of composition as lyric poetry would involve highly personal insights and modes of expression rather than rational discourse, and, if teachable at all, would have to be dealt with much more as a fine art than as a liberal art. Between these extremes would fall many types of composition, each with its own teaching problem.

The fine arts, in turn, can rightly claim a place at all levels in a liberal education,[14] with their more theoretical aspects commanding a larger share of instruction at more advanced levels. It is true that they are not the same as the liberal arts, since they must be expressed in a medium outside the mind. They are like the liberal arts, however, and unlike the useful arts, in that they involve a making *for* the mind, an operation whose products are to be enjoyed for themselves rather than to serve as means to any further end. If liberal knowledge is that knowledge which is its own end, such fine arts as music, painting, sculpture, and dancing have a place in an education called liberal. Such an art as architecture seems to be in part a fine art and in part a useful art, and, in practice, is usually taught in a separate professional school rather than in a school of fine arts.

A different teaching task is involved when the aim is to enable the student to appreciate rather than to practice the fine arts, to read or to listen with intelligence and sensitivity rather than to write or to compose music or to play an instrument. As an example let us take composition in the medium of words. When such composition is considered as a fine art rather than as a liberal art, its product is called letters or literature. In the teach-

[14] For a description of a course emphasizing music and painting, see Brother Leo B. Wren, F.S.C., "Aesthetics in the High School," *The Catholic Educational Review*, 59, 8 (November, 1961), 544–549.

ing of literature, whether in the English or in a foreign language, the student is to be led to grasp an imaginable and intelligible object by a sort of intuitive perception that is certainly not the result of any rational process through which a teacher can lead him. What the teacher can do is to make this operation somewhat easier by removing biographical, historical, and other obstacles to understanding. Ultimately, though, he must rely on the luminosity, on the beauty and truth of the literary work itself and its appeal to the student's natural intelligence and sensitivity; exhaustive grammatical or rhetorical analysis and dissection simply kill any possibility of appreciation.

These remarks would hold for any instruction below the graduate level, and even for graduate work designed primarily to develop a teacher rather than a research scholar; for the latter, a deeper analysis in such fields as philology, psychology, and history would be appropriate. With the requisite changes, what has been said concerning the teaching of literature would apply to the other fine arts as well.

Before turning to the liberal sciences, it might be worth remarking that a person can become liberally educated without necessarily becoming proficient in each one of the liberal arts and sciences, especially the latter. A general education is a good thing, but it is not synonymous with a liberal education. Indeed, as long as specialization does not occur too early, it is quite possible to get a better liberal education by the investigation of some discipline or area of knowledge in depth than by a more superficial introduction to a greater number of disciplines. A person who has a gap in his knowledge occasioned by a comparatively deep exploration of another field will at least recognize it as a gap, and will also know from the experience of thorough study in a particular area something of the indefinite reaches possible to the human mind. A person who emphasizes breadth of knowledge at the inevitable expense of depth runs the risk, not only of knowing

157

nothing really thoroughly, but of not even realizing his predicament.

Preparing for the Development of Science

In Chapter three [15] the notion of science was briefly discussed and was applied to sacred theology (which is also wisdom) and to the philosophical, the mathematical, the natural, and the social sciences. In current practice the last three are taught at all levels of instruction, and the first two in undergraduate and graduate work in colleges and universities. Under the wider heading of sacred doctrine, some knowledge of divine revelation and its implications is also imparted, though probably not scientifically, in primary and secondary church-related schools. Whether sacred theology can be successfully taught as the science and the wisdom that it is to undergraduates is a matter of debate; my own conviction is that it can and should be taught in this way even though not all students will grasp it scientifically, and, indeed, that such intellectual instruction is the principal reason for the existence of Catholic colleges.[16]

[15] See the section on Intellectual Virtues.

[16] See above, pp. 69–70, 124–127. From an immense literature on the subject, see, for example: *The Curriculum of a Catholic Liberal College* (Notre Dame, Ind.: Notre Dame College of Arts and Letters, 1953), chap. 4; Smith, *op. cit.*, pp. 260–267, 276–282; Cyril Vollert, S.J., "Theology and University Education," *The Modern Schoolman*, 21 (November, 1943), 12–25; Eugene M. Burke, C.S.P., "The Content and Methodology of the College Religion Program," in Roy J. Deferrari (ed.), *The Philosophy of Catholic Higher Education* (Washington, D.C.: The Catholic University of America Press, 1948), pp. 161–171; John Courtney Murray, S.J., "Towards a Theology for the Layman," *Theological Studies*, 5 (1944), 43–75, 340–376; W. H. Russell, "Principles for a College Religion Course," *Journal of Religious Instruction*, 8 (1937–38), 697–710; W. H. Russell, "Why Not Religion

The same question is posed concerning the teaching of the other sciences. Should the effort be made to teach these disciplines scientifically to young people below the instructional level of the graduate school? Jacques Maritain has answered the question negatively. He contends that the aim of liberal education at the high school and college levels is essentially to develop the natural intelligence on an infrascientific level—"what Plato would have called 'right opinion' " [17]—and thus to *prepare* for the development of intellectual virtues such as science. Basic liberal education has as its objective the grasping of the *meaning* of science, or

---

for the Sisters and the Laity?" *Journal of Religious Instruction*, 16 (1945–46), 220–225, 325–332, 397–412; John M. Cooper, "Religion in the College Curriculum," in Roy J. Deferrari (ed.), *College Organization and Administration* (Washington, D.C.: The Catholic University of America Press, 1946), pp. 148–174; Joseph C. Fenton, "Theology and Religion," *The American Ecclesiastical Review*, 112 (January–June, 1945), 447–463; Thomas C. Donlan, O.P., *Theology and Education* (Dubuque: Wm. C. Brown Co., 1952), chaps. 7–9; Johannes Hofinger, *The Art of Teaching Christian Doctrine* (Notre Dame, Ind.: University of Notre Dame Press, 1957); Reginald Masterson, O.P. (ed.), *Theology in the Catholic College* (Dubuque: The Priory Press, 1961); Roy J. Deferrari (ed.), *Theology, Philosophy, and History as Integrating Disciplines in the Catholic College of Liberal Arts* (Washington, D.C.: The Catholic University of America Press, 1953), pp. 45–190.

[17] "Thomist Views on Education," in Nelson B. Henry (ed.), *Modern Philosophies and Education*, part I, 54th Yearbook of the N.S.S.E. (Chicago: The University of Chicago Press, 1955), p. 61. Reprinted by permission. Cf. Herbert Johnston, "College Education—For What Habits?" *The Catholic Educational Review*, 53, 8 (November, 1955), 505–513. Much of the following discussion is taken from this article; reprinted by permission.

art, or wisdom, the understanding of its nature and scope, rather than the acquisition of that intellectual habit itself.[18] The reason is that: [19]

At each stage the knowledge must be of a sort fitted to the learners and conceived as reaching its perfection within their universe of thought during a distinct period of their development, instead of laying the foundations of a single sphere of knowledge which would grow in a continuous and uniform way until it became the science of the adult, where alone it would attain perfection.

It would appear, then, in such a view, that at various stages of human development the knowledge of which a person is capable differs in kind and not only in degree, and that basic liberal education below the graduate level should not attempt the impossible task of developing in students the intellectual virtue of science. To do so would inevitably result in cramming students with a set of memorized conclusions which they would be unable to relate to the principles involved in such a way as to see *why* the conclusions are and must be true. Until the end of the college years, then, studies should aim merely at right opinion; they should be *about* a science rather than *in* a science. One need hardly emphasize the difference that acceptance or rejection of this position will make to what is taught and how it is taught.

[18] Maritain, *op. cit.,* 79–80.
[19] Maritain, *Education at the Crossroads* (New Haven, Conn.: Yale University Press, 1943), p. 60. Reprinted by permission. Cf. *ibid.,* p. 63. In an unpublished address delivered at the University of Notre Dame in 1953, entitled "The Liberal Arts and Education," Professor Maritain developed the same theme; here he called the attempt to develop true intellectual virtues before the end of college "encyclopedic inculcation" and "indoctrination of adult science in the young person," a process resulting in the production of "a learned intellectual dwarf."

With this question in mind, let us run rapidly through the list of those disciplines which we agreed to call sciences, whether in the fullest or in an attenuated sense. In the field of the social sciences and of history, experience indicates that it is possible at least to some extent for students at all levels to see conclusions in their principles, to see results in their causes, sometimes with some degree of necessity and sometimes only probably. Much of the work of these, as of other, disciplines will consist in the student's mastering factual material. This operation involves a twofold benefit. First, it supplies indispensable raw material without which further development in the field is impossible. Second, it develops habits in the interior sensitive powers of the imagination and the memory,[20] and these powers play a large part in further intellectual development.

The student's maturity and the point to which his intelligence has developed will certainly make a crucial difference concerning what is presented to him and the way in which it is presented to him. But where the subject matter itself allows of it, the teacher should always aim at leading the student to see results in their causes, at getting an answer to the question *why* on the level appropriate to the student's maturity and abilities. In history, for example, a study of the causes of World War I on the most elementary level might be restricted to the statement of the assassination of an Austrian archduke. The same study with more advanced students—perhaps those in a secondary school—might involve the distinction between an occasion and a cause, and some notion of the background of Balkan politics. For undergraduates this consideration could be broadened and deepened to include cultural, economic, and other factors. The graduate school might appropriately go into some of the more abstruse elements of Serbian nationalism. All these are different *levels* of knowledge, but they

[20] St. Thomas, *Summa Theologiae*, I–II, 50, 3, ad 3.

are not different *kinds* of knowledge. If history is in any sense a science, then that science was being developed to some degree from the first and most elementary answer to the question *why*.[21] Examples drawn from such a social science as economics might support this conclusion even more firmly.

In the natural sciences the same sort of effort can and should be made to lead the student to see some intelligible necessity in the relation between conclusion and principle. There are many levels at which the connection between heat and the expansion of metal may be investigated, some of which are appropriate to high school students, others to students in a liberal college, and others to students in a graduate or professional school. To the extent that inductive sciences are truly sciences, the student at any of those levels is actually developing and not merely preparing for the habit of science. This is the manner of developing the natural intelligence of the student which is proper to this subject matter; the differences will be in degree only.

The same is true, and perhaps more obviously so, of mathematics. Once the preliminaries have been mastered, to teach mathematics as anything less than an exact science is to do violence to its object. The grade school or high school student, and probably the ordinary undergraduate, need not necessarily become familiar with the intricacies of number theory or the infinitesimal calculus. But if he learns only the first book of Euclid he must

[21] See *ibid.*, 51, 3, c, in which St. Thomas explains why the habit of science can be caused by one act but not opinion or habits of the internal cognitive sense powers. A habit of science formed by only one demonstration is less perfect than the same habit formed by several demonstrations, since it extends to only one conclusion (*ibid.*, 54, 4, ad 3). A habit of science can be increased by addition when someone learns, for example, more conclusions of geometry; it is increased intensively when one becomes able to reach conclusions more quickly and more clearly (*ibid.*, 52, 2, c).

learn it demonstratively, that is, scientifically, or he cannot be said to have learned it at all.

In philosophy and theology, too, there are various possible depths of penetration. It is a commonplace that the aim of an undergraduate course in a liberal college is not to develop the professional theologian or metaphysician. Yet here, again, the choice is among different degrees of the development of that habit which is the intellectual virtue of science or even of wisdom; it is not between science on the one hand and opinion or faith on the other, even right opinion and true faith.

When a teacher proposes for the student's consideration truths which either cannot be or are not on that occasion reduced to self-evident principles, he is not inducing science in the student but either opinion or faith. By opinion the student holds a conclusion as probable; by faith he holds it as certain. But in neither case does he *see* its necessity. To argue that at any level below the graduate school students are intellectually incapable of grasping such relationships seems to be to fly in the face of daily teaching experience. To say that, even if they can, they should not be taught to do so, suggests an interpretation of the word science that would restrict its application to the more or less (it is always a matter of degree) fully developed, articulate, and self-conscious knowledge of the professional economist or chemist or theologian. There is no question of developing such competence below the level of the graduate school, and sometimes not even there. Such an attempt would indeed be doomed to failure, and might well lead to the hopeless substitute of indoctrination, of presenting the student with a neat package of conclusions which he is to memorize and repeat rather than understand. This is simply bad teaching, and everyone is against it. But opinion, even right opinion, is not the only alternative. Another possibility is that, in the consideration of those disciplines which can be called sciences, the student should be led to relate conclusions and principles, effects

163

and causes, in whatever depth his intellectual development allows. The question *why* is one of the first and most persistent that a child asks; it can be answered in ways that involve many levels of penetration, but it can be answered and answered truly at any one of them. This effort to lead the student to achieve something more than opinion need not deliver him to an arid intellectualism that stunts the natural development of his intelligence in close concert with his imagination, that closes to him the wonder and the beauty of the reality that he is coming so eagerly to explore. This, once more, is simply bad teaching, and has nothing to do with science.

It would appear, then, that the liberal sciences as well as the liberal arts are part of a basic liberal education and should be taught as what they are at whatever level and in whatever way the student can grasp them. Where science at some level is possible, opinion is not enough. Indeed, there is a sense in which opinion, even right opinion, is no preparation at all for the future development of science and may well get in the way of its future development. In a text which is central for this problem, St. Thomas explains that what he calls a disposition can be distinguished from a habit in two ways. In the first way, a disposition differs from a habit as the imperfect differs from the perfect in the same species; this same quality is called a disposition when it exists in us in such a way that it can be easily lost, and is called a habit when it exists in us in such a manner that it cannot be easily lost. A disposition of this kind can become a habit as a boy becomes a man. In the second way, a disposition differs from a habit specifically; that quality which is called a disposition in this sense, such as sickness and health (and opinion), is called such because from its very nature it has *changeable causes,* whereas that quality which is called habit, such as science and moral virtue, is called such because from its very nature it has *unchangeable causes.* A disposi-

164

tion of this kind cannot become a habit, because the two are different specifically.[22]

A disposition in the first sense is science imperfectly possessed and easily lost; but it is truly science because its causes are unchangeable. A disposition in the second sense is opinion; however long it may remain, it can never develop into science because its causes are changeable. If the teacher begins with a problem which the student understands and is interested in, and then leads him by discussion to reach a conclusion which is related to a principle on however elementary a level, a beginning of science has been accomplished, that beginning perhaps appropriate to the secondary or undergraduate level, but allowing of further development in later life and not requiring graduate instruction (something which very few students receive) for such development. If, on the other hand, the teacher begins with a problem and then either leaves it unresolved or leaves the student in doubt or confusion about the reasons why a certain conclusion should be held, no beginning of science has been accomplished that would make possible any further development. The use of a discussion method that becomes its own end instead of a useful method of attacking certain kinds of problem; the use of rhetoric that aims merely at persuading when demonstration is possible; the resolving of conclusions into principles whose nature (for example, philosophical or theological) is undifferentiated and confused in the student's mind—all these are sure ways to prevent the development of the virtue of science, to vitiate the work which is liberal education, and to guarantee that the student will get little more, intellectually, from his years in school than some sound advice from his elders. And he need not come to school to get that.

[22] *Ibid.,* I–II, 49, 2, ad 3; see also I–II, 55, 4, c, in which it is explained why opinion cannot be called an intellectual virtue.

To stop at opinion, even right opinion, is to make impossible any further development by way of understanding that deepens with study and experience, for there is no understanding to begin with. On whatever level is proper to the student in those disciplines allowing of it, some degree of the development of science, some habit of resolving conclusions into principles, is the only goal of teaching which can justify the existence of that institution which is the school. And at the college level it is the only possible preparation for the further habit of resolving conclusions into absolutely first principles, that habit of Christian wisdom which is the crown and the ideal of the Catholic liberal college.

VOCATIONAL EDUCATION

"Vocation" is a Latin word that means calling. Every man has the same ultimate vocation—eternal union with God—and education in the first and partially in the second of the meanings we saw above [23] is relevant to the attainment of this final goal to which all mankind is called. In ordinary usage, however, the term vocational education is restricted to education in the third and the fourth of its meanings, to formal education in the school and particularly in the classroom or its equivalent. In what follows we shall largely confine ourselves to this meaning of the term. In ordinary usage, too, vocational education is restricted to education for that occupation to which a person is called as the means by which he makes his living.

This very meaning of the term suggests a connection with the first and ultimate meaning of vocation. In the Puritan notion of the calling and in the Catholic notion of the duties of one's station in life, there is made explicit the relation between that calling which is one's daily work and that calling which is eternal life. That relation is the relation of end and means, for a person's work

[23] See Chapter four, Education as a Potential Whole.

166

is not only the means of his making his own and his family's living; it is also and even primarily the means of his doing his share of the world's work, of living a life useful to others through his co-operation with divine providence, of reaching that goal which is his final vocation. This fact means that the school which provides vocational education in its usual meaning has, as a vital part of its task, to make clear this relation between the various senses of vocation so that the student can see his future occupation as a means of giving as well as of taking. Even on the purely natural level something of this sort can be done by way, perhaps, of the example of those occupations which are called professions, and their tradition of service before profit. Such teaching is realistic in the basic sense of being in line with reality, with the facts of life, however imperfectly it may be applied in general practice. And it is not inconsistent with informing students about the harsh realities of the economic arena and the necessity for hard battling within that arena.

There is another meaning of vocation that has relevance here, a meaning narrower than that of the final end of life and broader than that of a particular occupation. On the natural level every human person is called to be as fully human as possible, as well as and before he is called to be clerk, teacher, business executive, journalist. This is the basic meaning of education on the natural plane, and it involves the development of human powers, and especially of the powers peculiar to human beings, to their fullest possible extent. For the school, and especially for the classroom within the school, this means the development of the intellectual virtues and of the desire for their further increase. It means the development, so far as is possible for each student, of the liberal arts and sciences, for the sake of what they enable the student to be rather than for what they enable him to do. It means, in brief, a liberal education for all, to the extent that their own abilities and interests and circumstances allow of it.

A philosophy of education

The Position of Dewey

Reference was made above [24] to possible misinterpretations of the notion of liberal education arising from the confusion of Aristotle's example with what he was exemplifying. One influential instance of such misinterpretation is that of John Dewey, in a chapter entitled "Labor and Leisure." Dewey's own summary of the chapter follows: [25]

Of the segregations of educational values discussed in the last chapter, that between culture and utility is probably the most fundamental. While the distinction is often thought to be intrinsic and absolute, it is really historical and social. It originated, so far as conscious formulation is concerned, in Greece, and was based upon the fact that the truly human life was lived only by a few who subsisted upon the results of the labor of others. This fact affected the psychological doctrine of the relation of intelligence and desire, theory and practice. It was embodied in a political theory of a permanent division of human beings into those capable of a life of reason and hence having their own ends, and those capable only of desire and work, and needing to have their ends provided by others. The two distinctions, psychological and political, translated into educational terms, effected a division between a liberal education, having to do with the self-sufficing life of leisure devoted to knowing for its own sake, and a useful, practical training for mechanical occupations, devoid of intellectual and aesthetic content. While the present situation is radically diverse in theory and much changed in fact, the factors of the older historic situation still persist

[24] See in this chapter the section on Liberal Knowledge.
[25] John Dewey, *Democracy and Education* (New York: The Macmillan Company, 1916), p. 305. For contemporary discussions of these and many related problems, see A. H. Halsey, Jean Floud, and C. Arnold Anderson (eds.), *Education, Economy, and Society: A Reader in the Sociology of Education* (New York: The Free Press of Glencoe, 1961).

168

sufficiently to maintain the educational distinction, along with compromises which often reduce the efficacy of the educational measures. The problem of education in a democratic society is to do away with the dualism and to construct a course of studies which makes thought a guide of free practice for all and which makes leisure a reward of accepting responsibility for service, rather than a state of exemption from it.

Dewey is wrong in seeing the distinction between a liberal and a vocational education, between the speculative and the practical orders, as the product of and as logically dependent on a particular social theory and practice. The notion of a liberal education does not depend for its existence on the slave-owning society of Aristotle or even on the aristocratic society of Newman. It is true and it is deplorable that in each of these societies, though in much different degree, a liberal education was in fact restricted to a fortunate few who, by reason of birth, were to rule the society; the education open to the many, who were to be ruled, was often haphazard and generally utilitarian in character. At least two things, both of which Dewey saw and fought against, are wrong with this situation. The first is the idea that only the group actually exercising power in any society should, for whatever reason, receive an education designed to develop them as persons. The second is the idea that there is a complete separation between the two kinds of education, so that a vocational in the sense of a utilitarian education should make no attempt to develop the specifically human powers of the person concerned. Aristotle was indeed mistaken in dividing men into free and slave. Yet this fact should not entail the abandonment of the liberal education that he rightly considered proper to those whom he saw as fully men. It should rather entail our seeing all men as Aristotle saw free men—as fully human, as capable, though in varying degrees, of the development of those powers which make them human, as calling for a liberal education as the condition of their growth. Perhaps it was par-

169

ticularly difficult for Dewey to do this because he considered even the explanation that Aristotle gave of human powers and habits to be the product of his social environment,[26] and because, ultimately, his biologically oriented picture of the world and of men within it ruled out the possibility of the existence of the speculative order and of liberal knowledge as these have here been described.[27]

Dewey is right, however, in condemning as undemocratic—and, indeed, inhuman—the effort to perpetuate the division between rulers and ruled by denying to the latter the educational advantages of the former. The passion for social justice that drove Dewey all his life led to his fierce and unrelenting demand for equality of educational opportunity for all, regardless of the accidental circumstances of their birth. Those who believe in God and who see all men, regardless of circumstances, as equally the children of God, can reasonably be no less fierce and no less unrelenting in their demand for that aspect of social democracy which is genuine equality of educational opportunity. There may be room here for some examination of conscience.

Dewey is also right in his denial of an "intrinsic and absolute" distinction between liberal and vocational education and in his insistence on the possible cultural value of the latter. In our earlier discussion of the virtues of art and of prudence[28] we saw that one classification of the first virtue was into the liberal, the fine, and the useful arts. We saw, too, that the virtue of art—the virtue of making things well—perfects the thing made rather than the

[26] *Ibid.*, pp. 294–298.
[27] *Ibid.*, pp. 216–221. Cf. John Dewey, *Reconstruction in Philosophy* (New York: Mentor Books, New American Library of World Literature, Inc., 1950), *passim*.
[28] See in Chapter three the section on Intellectual Virtues and in this chapter the section on Liberal Arts and Sciences in the Curriculum.

maker, whereas the virtue of prudence—the virtue of doing things well—perfects the agent himself.

It was also argued, however, that this classification of the arts is not absolute, that the fine arts overlap both the liberal and the useful arts, and even that all of the fine arts are to some degree liberal, since they involve a preliminary mental construction before their expression in a given medium.[29] For the same reason—and it is this point which is of interest in a consideration of vocational education—even the useful arts can be said to be liberal, though in a lesser degree than the fine arts, for these too require that the thing be made in the mind of the artist before it can be made in a material medium. This is more evidently true of those arts which are usually classed as handicrafts, such as weaving and pottery, in which the same person is usually both designer and maker, than it is in those arts in which the maker does no more than operate a machine that produces, say, textiles or pottery designed by another person and actually fashioned by a machine designed by yet someone else. The more directly a human person is involved in the making of something—in head, heart, and hand—the more of his personality is stamped on the thing made, and the more, conversely, the act of making has in turn influenced his own personality.

For just as there is not an absolute separation between the liberal and the fine and the useful arts, so neither is there an absolute separation between art and prudence, between making things well and doing things well, for the reason that every making is also a doing, and every artist is also and always a man. This fact has one consequence in the perennial problem of art and prudence, which in turn manifests itself in such areas as those of censorship, academic freedom, and technology. It also, though, has another consequence beyond such questions as whether it would be pru-

[29] See p. 155.

dent to make this particular weapon or movie or laborsaving device; it has the consequence that every conscious act of making makes not only the product but also the maker. It is true that the perfection of the virtue of art, as such, is in the thing made rather than in the maker, that it is possible to be a good artist and a bad man or a bad artist and a good man. But the good artist is a bad man, if he is, in spite of and not because of his artistic ability. For in the natural order we are what we do, in the sense that it is through repeated actions, including those of making, that we develop those habits that in sum form what we call our character. Making, like all the other things that we do, has an effect on us as well as on the medium in which we work, an effect on our intellectual and volitional and emotional and even physical life. This is why do-it-yourself projects are so often prescribed as a form of therapy, and why adult education classes in handicrafts are swamped with applicants even though the things made could be more easily and cheaply bought as the product of a machine. For there is a deeply human joy in making, a joy that springs from the use and the consequent development of human powers; to make a thing well is, supposing it to be a thing worth making, something that is proper to men and something that makes them, to that extent, better men.

It is this truth that John Dewey has in mind when he insists that vocational training in schools should be not only—and even not primarily—to enable the student to get a job as a result of such training. It should rather be carried on for its immediate benefits to the student, for what it enables the student to be rather than to do. Vocational education, as Dewey sees it, is a part of what has been described above as liberal education, though he would not use that terminology because of his misconception of the notion of liberal education. Another result of this broad and human conception of vocational education that Dewey has would be to rescue the student from a narrow specialization that would effectively condemn him to one type of occupation for the rest of his life, to the atrophy of personal powers, and to permanent economic and social subservience.[30]

Manual Work in a Liberal Education

A more recent consideration of the same subject, and one which refers to Dewey's earlier work, is that of John W. Donahue, S.J. He points out that "the official cultural tradition, especially in its academic form, has been dominantly intellectualistic in a rather constricted sense. . . . But if culture is defined exclusively in these terms, the workman is left to sink with his labor below the level of the fully human." [31]   Manual work, he insists, can be part of a liberal education: "For if the demands of craftsmanship challenge any workman to reflect, plan, choose, and endure, then they too are liberalizing, for they nurture the uniquely human powers of thought and free choice." [32]

The school, Father Donahue continues, cannot give the primary place to vocational education, but it can do a number of things. First, it can acquaint its students with the existence of various careers, including those in science and technology; it can develop "a philosophical and theological understanding of work itself," including a consideration of social questions involving labor. At the high school and college level this theoretical approach could be made in courses in "history, sociology, ethics, and theology." Second, the school can "find place for education *through* work," through shop work and hobby clubs that make no attempt to reproduce the exact conditions of contemporary industry, for "The detailed division of labor, so fruitful for mass output,

[30] Dewey, *Democracy and Education,* pp. 358-374.
[31] *Work and Education* (Chicago: Loyola University Press, 1959), p. 17. Reprinted by permission.
[32] *Ibid.,* p. 204. Reprinted by permission.

is pointless when the workman's own development is the aim." At the elementary and especially at the secondary level this formation could be aimed at through such activities as home economics, wood and machine work, and pottery making.[33]

Granting that vocational education is susceptible of a broader meaning than is generally given it and that what are usually called vocational subjects can and should be liberally taught, there remain some further and related questions. Should vocational education in the sense of direct preparation for a particular occupation be the concern of the school? If so, of what kind of school, at what level, in what occupational areas? Is such occupational training compatible with a liberal education? [34]

On the elementary level there is or should be no problem. To these years belong the formation of the basic skills and the acquisition of the basic information that make possible progress in any field of knowledge. It is true that the reading and writing and reckoning learned in the elementary school are practically indispensable in the earning of a living; but this fact is accidental to the knowledge, which remains speculative considered in itself.

On the secondary level, as we saw above, Dewey opposed job training for two reasons. The first was that specialization too early in life, before the student had a real chance to discover his aptitudes and interests, would result in the forced growth of one set of powers and the neglect of other and as yet unsuspected ones, with the consequent impoverishment of the student's intellectual and aesthetic life. The second reason was that another result of such early specialization would be to condemn the student, for

[33] *Ibid.*, pp. 205–210.
[34] See Edward M. Bridge, M.D., "The Relationship between Liberal and Professional Education," *Educational Record,* 37 (October, 1956), 267–276; Harlow H. Curtice, "Industry and Education in a Free Society," *The Journal of Higher Education,* 26 (October, 1955), 357–360, 399–400.

lack of the required schooling, to an occupation that would tie him to a low social and economic status for the rest of his life, thus hardening the existing division of social classes and effectively preventing what afterwards came to be called vertical mobility.

Both of these objections have force, though the first one is perhaps somewhat less valid today than it once was because of the expansion of methods of testing and guidance. What remains true, however, is that each person has a right to the opportunity to develop his capacities to the extent of his ability and interest so that his future life, as a human being and as a member of the city of God and the city of man, may be as rich and as rewarding as possible. When the limit of that capacity or interest or both has apparently been reached, it might be better to accommodate the students concerned in special classes until they have reached the legal school-leaving age rather than use shop or home economics or secretarial courses as dumping grounds, to the detriment of those students who would otherwise receive a better vocational education. Those who lack the money or the desire to go to college, and who want some technical preparation to help them get started in a highly competitive economic order, may reasonably look to the secondary school to provide that preparation along with as much liberal education as the circumstances permit. They may also reasonably expect that these vocational classes will be conducted on a high level, for on the proficiency of their instruction will depend in large measure the future course of their lives. The precise organization of the schools in which this instruction would be given is a matter that would depend largely on local circumstances. What seems clear is that a considerable number of students in high school have a genuine need, for one reason or another, of vocational training at a level of competence that will enable them to get and hold a respectable position in business or industry. It is true that in a society dedicated to social as well as to political democracy no able and willing student should miss the opportunity for a college education because he cannot afford its costs. But it is also true that even in this society the ideals of social democracy are not as yet fully realized. Dewey's (and others') objections to job training in the high school are sound as far as they go, but they overlook the needs of some real people in the real world. Job training for those capable of a more humanistic education does indeed mean that some of their capacities will be less fully developed than they could and should be; it also means that most of the higher positions in the economic order will be permanently closed to them because they lack that union card which is the college degree. It was, however, long ago pointed out that men must first live before they can begin to live well, and they are not as likely either to continue intellectual pursuits or to rise in the world economically if the high school denies them any job training and then turns them into a world in which the first thing they need is a job, and as good a one as possible.[35] Vocational education in the sense of job training has a place in the secondary school.

Further, for most girls of high school age, the occupation called homemaking is either an immediate or a remote prospect. Many of them learn such arts as cooking and sewing at home, but many of them do not. In any event, a professional teacher may well add much to the earlier home apprenticeship. Whether the glossy, automated equipment often available for home economics instruction is the best preparation for working with what a young couple's budget can afford is another question. But that such in-

[35] The problem of employment is especially acute for these young people. Unemployment among those under the age of twenty-five is double the average for all workers; see *U.S. News and World Report* (Dec. 4, 1961), 91. Cf. Naomi Barko, "Dropouts to Nowhere," *The Reporter,* 26, 7 (Mar. 29, 1962), 34–36; James Bryant Conant, *Slums and Suburbs* (New York: McGraw-Hill Book Company, Inc., 1961), pp. 33–53.

struction should be made available to those students who need and want it seems a reasonable proposition, especially if family life is as important as we say it is.[36]

Vocational Problems of the Liberal Arts Graduate

On the college and university level, schools of medicine, law, architecture, engineering, and many others have long prepared students for the technical requirements of specific occupations. Vocational education on this level differs from that on the secondary level largely by the intellectual content of the sciences, chiefly mathematical and natural, that underlie instruction in these professional fields. Society needs scientists and professional men, and it needs them trained at the highest possible level, that is, at the university level. Society also needs liberally educated men, and, again, it needs them educated at the highest possible level. The members of the first group have few worries concerning employment after graduation, for their professional education is also vocational education in the sense of training for a specific occupation. The members of the second group have considerably more worries, for their education has usually not trained them for any specific occupation.[37] It is widely known that liberal arts graduates have a harder time finding employment than their technically trained counterparts. It is almost as widely acknowledged that the cultivation of the liberal arts and sciences is the very condition of the life of Western civilization. Yet industry continues to hire specialists, with an eye only to the present, and liberal colleges con-

[36] For an uncompromising contradiction of this position, see Mortimer J. Adler, "Labor, Leisure, and Liberal Education," *Journal of General Education,* 6 (October, 1951).

[37] The remainder of this chapter is adapted from Herbert Johnston, "Can Liberal Arts Students Get Jobs?" *Columbia,* 34, 1 (August, 1954), 6, 17–18. Reprinted by permission.

tinue to train nonspecialists, with an eye only to the past. Both the colleges and industry can do something about this situation; so far, though, neither has done much but talk.

A recent news release from a university placement bureau listed, for the information of aspiring students, the firms whose representatives would shortly visit the campus to interview prospective employees. Reading that release must have been a pretty discouraging experience for the liberal arts students, though possibly not a novel one. Physicists, chemists, and engineers of every variety were in eager demand; but the market was a bit slow for historians, for philosophers, for linguists. Those who had devoted four truly precious years to some beginnings of the development of wisdom may have wondered whether their devotion to the speculative virtues, to the humanizing disciplines, had been such a good idea after all.

For the hard fact remains that even the pursuer of wisdom must eat, and, if he has given hostages to fortune, so must his family. Without the necessities and some degree of the comforts of life, the ordinary man finds truly human living so very difficult as to be practically impossible. Worrying about the fuel bill while he lives the glory that is Shakespeare is apt, in time, to dim even that glory, to kill even that life, in the harsh demands of immediate existence.

Certainly, wealth is not the end of human life, though too many people live as though it were. But it remains one of the means to that end and, ordinarily, an indispensable one. Material goods are important to men because they supply their material wants and thus allow them that sufficiency and independence of the demands of the body that are prerequisite for the pursuit of a really human life. It is true that men are not beasts, and when their bodily needs and comforts have been looked after, they have secured the opportunity to live as men but have not yet begun to do so. Neither, however, are men angels, disembodied spirits;

178

and without enough wealth they cannot develop their intellectual and moral capacities and achieve a properly human perfection.

One sometimes wonders if this last fact is sufficiently realized by those who, from the comparative safety of established positions within an academic organization, eulogize the benefits of an exclusively liberal education. It is true that the end is more important than the means, and that the means exist only for the sake of the end. But it is also true that the means must be there before the end can be reached. It is true that living is more important than making a living, and is the only reason for making a living. But it is also true that for most men it is necessary to make a living before giving much attention to the good life. It is true that, other things being equal, the liberally educated man will be the better because the more humanly developed man; that he will be the better because the more critical and mature citizen. But it is also possible that, disappointed and embittered by years spent on an economic treadmill, he may simply give up the effort for the good personal life, the good family life, the good civic life as beyond his tired powers. It is questionable whether that man could afford a liberal education and could profit from its very real advantages.

Happily, business is increasing its help to education. Further, and still more happily, industry's interest in the higher learning extends beyond the more technical fields into that of the liberal arts and sciences. There are many and increasing examples of industries granting full scholarships for liberal as well as for technical education. There is, however, a further question. When the fortunate young men and women who received these scholarships are ready to graduate, will the companies that educated them be willing to hire them? In spite of what it bears upon, the question is not academic. For notwithstanding the good words of business executives, backed up to some extent by the good deeds of their scholarships and research grants, the lot of the liberally educated man in today's labor market is not a happy one.

The university employment bureau, numerous follow-up studies, and almost anyone's casual observation tell the same story. Technically trained male college graduates—engineers, chemists, physicists, and mathematicians—are hired in the greatest numbers and at the highest salaries because in the North America of the latter twentieth century there is greatest demand for their services. From colleges of business administration, students trained in accounting have the best employment opportunities, with those taking finance, marketing, and business organization trailing. Bringing up the rear, badly handicapped in the economic race, come the graduates of the liberal college. There are jobs for these men and women, sometimes at quite attractive starting salaries, but they must seek the job rather than having it seek them. And they must sell themselves on the basis of personality, part-time experience, and extraclass activities, not on the basis of their college training.

It makes no difference what they majored in, except that some fields will do them less harm than others. Philosophy majors may disguise the inauspicious truth by emphasizing their study of psychology, and hope for some form of personnel work. English majors, discreetly concealing Chaucer, may talk fluently about the arts of communication, and hope for an opening on the company house organ. Most of them, though, just hope. Whatever type of employment they finally stumble into, liberally educated graduates can, at least on the basis of their formal education, expect to start at less money than their vocationally educated brothers, and receive fewer and slower promotions.

For twentieth-century America is not nineteenth-century Europe. It took one kind of education to prepare the sons of the landed or mercantile aristocracy for positions of civic responsibility in local or colonial administration while they lived off inherited wealth. It takes a somewhat different kind of education to prepare the sons of the ordinary American family for competition in an economic order in which they must earn their own and their family's living. And it is simply dishonest to pretend that nothing has changed since Newman wrote, and that the average student entering a liberal college is not immediately taking on himself a heavy financial sacrifice, perhaps a heavier one than he can afford.

Yet it is still true, and will always be true, that man does not live by bread alone. The exclusive concern with things material does not make a good human being, a good husband and father, a good citizen. It is still true that liberal knowledge is good in itself because it is an end and not just a means, worth having for what it enables a man to *be* and not just to do. And the only point of doing, in the long run, is to *be* somewhat better than one was before. A technological civilization that loses all contact with its spiritual roots is headed for that horror described by Aldous Huxley and George Orwell.

Liberal colleges exist to preserve, develop, and transmit certain ideas and values which are the very breath of life to a free society. But these ideas and values do not exist in a vacuum. They do not even live in great books. They come alive only in human beings, in men and women who treasure them and extend them and lovingly hand them on. In men and women who build and maintain free societies with them. In men and women who must also eat before they do much else, and who find that in today's labor market a liberal education is a real handicap.

One way to pretend to solve a problem is to ignore it, and this is the easy road that has been taken by many of those professionally engaged in the liberal education of the young. Knowing the nature of man, of the human person to be educated, these teachers rightly argue that a liberal education is the one most fitted to his nature, the one which will best develop his truly human capacities, that will incidentally make him a better businessman and a better citizen because it first makes him a better man.

What they overlook are some of the implications of the fact

that human nature is always realized in particular men who live in particular circumstances of time and place and must work out their human lives and aim at their final end within those circumstances. And much as liberal educators may deplore the fact, and in many respects rightly deplore it, the stubborn fact remains that in the America of the latter twentieth century the liberally educated man, the man who cannot lay claim to some technical specialty at graduation, is under a handicap in relation to economic opportunities that very few can fully overcome in a lifetime of striving. And since economic opportunities are important not only to individual physical comfort, but to the possibility of developing fully as a human person, liberal educators may be contributing to the defeat of their own purpose.

It works both ways. Let us say that a businessman works very hard in order to make enough money for his family to enjoy the material basis on which to build a really good family life. Somewhere there comes a point, the point of diminishing returns, at which his continued absence from home on business, his continued inability to share personally in family life, will do his family more harm than the opportunities for good afforded by the money earned by that extra work. There comes a point at which too much of a good thing defeats its own purpose. In the same way a liberal education, designed to make a better man and hence a better citizen, may take so much of the student's time in equipping him for the good life that it leaves him no time to equip himself to make a living. And unless he can make a living, his chances of tasting the good life are slim. Again, too much of a good thing defeats its own purpose.

Another way to pretend to solve a problem is to surrender to its difficulties and give up the fight. There are many people who for many reasons are ready and even eager to throw overboard the task of cultivating the intellect, of fostering a consciousness of the spiritual roots of our civilization, of keeping alive a vision of man as something more than a maker and a minder of machines.

One reason is the anti-intellectualism that has always been a part of the American outlook, stemming both from a vigorous conviction of the benefits of material productivity and from a confusion concerning some of the implications of democratic equality.

Another reason is the subtler anti-intellectualism of the professional educators themselves. Many of these, confusing liberal education with the pseudointellectualism of such a period as the Enlightenment, despair of the unaided human reason in the face of the terrifying problems facing man today. They fail to remember that the human reason need not remain unaided, but that the very faith to which they would turn, whether in divine or in human things, becomes itself a blind fideism when divorced from human intelligence, fatal alike to human reason and to true faith.

Still another reason is simply the general weariness of men engaged in what is certainly a long battle and what looks like a losing one, at least for the present. Men may be convinced of the value of a liberal education in the abstract, but understandably reluctant to pay the personal price, and to ask their wives and children to pay it, to keep in existence the spiritual and intellectual capital that other men squander recklessly to their individual material advantage. The temptation to sell out is almost overwhelming.

Yet there need be no sellout, no abandoning of liberal education, just as there need be no blinking of the unpleasant contemporary facts. Both the liberal college itself and the business community can contribute to alleviating the situation.

How the College Can Help

So far as the college is concerned, there seem to be two possible lines of action. One is to keep the liberal arts college in a large university, but to emphasize its function of providing liberal instruction for the students in the professional schools of the university. These professionally trained men and women form the group from which, at least for the immediate future, the leaders of our technologically oriented society will largely be drawn, and it is imperative that they receive as much truly liberal education as possible along with their necessary technical training. And it is also imperative that, for this purpose, a strong liberal college exist in the university, within which its faculty may be at home in an intellectual atmosphere conducive to study and thought in the liberal tradition, and from which they can carry the results of such scholarly work to instruction in the professional schools as well as in their own college.

Another possible line of action, and one more suited to the small liberal college which is not part of a larger university, is to compromise the traditional liberal training to the extent of including some frankly vocational instruction aimed at enabling the graduate to compete on somewhat more even terms in the labor market. This last expression falls under the heading of offensive language to some of the more delicate-minded teachers in liberal colleges and to the fledgling aesthetes who look up to them and ape their attitudes. Yet even these students must find employment when their years of schooling are over, and some modicum of vocational education might prove helpful in the process. Incidentally, if they could observe their revered instructors jockeying for place and power and pay within the academic marketplace, they might be more likely to admit the possible compatibility of a liberal education and consciousness of the economic facts of life, of a liberal college and the existence of vocational courses within that college. It is true that these vocational courses have no place in a liberal college as such; but without them the small liberal college may come to have no place in our contemporary society. And without the values that the liberal college represents, our society will not long remain. The first line of action seems preferable, in that it keeps intact the liberal character of the college within the university; but the second course seems to be the only one possible for the smaller college.

It is essential, however, that the compromise be recognized and acknowledged for what it is, and that courses directed to an immediately practical end not be called liberal—something they are not. Teachers and administrators of a liberal college will do themselves and their students no good by invidiously contrasting liberal and vocational studies, or by a superior attitude toward bread-and-butter subjects. Neither, on the other hand, will they do any good by confusing the two areas, by pretending to themselves, to their students, and to the public that training aimed at getting the graduate a decent start in the work of earning his living is the same thing as a liberal education.

It is not necessarily a question of superiority and inferiority; it is a question of difference, of seeing that one thing is not another. Vocational training dressed up under any other name is still vocational training. In itself it is good, and for most young Americans in the latter half of the twentieth century it is probably necessary. But it is not liberal education, and confusing the two will only lead to the gradual loss of the notion of what a liberal education is, to the drying up of the spiritual springs from which its values rise, and finally to the conversion of America into a mechanized Sparta, with Sparta's inevitable fate.

What the liberal college can do, then, will depend on its situation. The college which is part of a large university might concentrate more of its work on the students in the professional schools. The college which is not so situated might include in its curriculum a certain number of vocational courses. Perhaps neither policy is ideal; but at least each is designed to face contemporary facts realistically and to grapple with a real problem.

185

Only Business Can Do the Hiring

Business, however, as well as the college, must face these facts and must grapple with this problem, for the whole community and not just the school is affected. The gradual decline of the liberal college, its losing battle against the spirit and the circumstances of modern America, should be a source of profound concern to all who think beyond today's dividend and tomorrow's vacation.

In the light of this stubborn problem, what becomes of industry's acknowledgment that it needs liberally educated men, and of its increasing willingness to underwrite their education? It has been frequently remarked that, whereas the top brass and elder statesmen among business executives are busily deploring the emphasis on specialization in education and calling for more broadly educated men in business,[38] their personnel recruiters are just as busily hiring specialists and neglecting the nonspecialists. The elder statesmen can afford to sit back and take the long view; their harried personnel men do not have time to read the articles in which that view is expressed.

There is a certain irony in the situation. Our society is based, in the economic order, on the principle of capitalism, on the idea that it is necessary to use part of the harvest for seed, part of the profit for investment, else there will be no further harvest and no further profit. We are smart enough not to kill the goose that lays the golden egg, and are somewhat arrogantly conscious of the fact. At the same time, by putting real economic and social burdens upon the graduates of our liberal colleges, by effectively discouraging the more able members of our society from entering these colleges, we are recklessly spending our spiritual and intellectual capital with no thought of renewal. It is the same mentality

[38] See, for example, Clarence B. Randall, "The Myth of the Specialist," *Dun's Review*, 76, 5 (November, 1960), 34-36.

that, until recently, neglected conservation of natural resources, with the disastrous results that have long worried thoughtful men. It is time for the neglect of our intellectual resources to be brought to a halt before there is nothing left to conserve.

Conservation, unfortunately, involves sacrifice. The potatoes that we plant this spring we did not eat last winter, and we may occasionally have been hungry. The young trees that we spare for future growth are not available for present building needs, and we may now have a smaller house. The young men and women that we educate liberally are not, immediately upon graduation, equipped to keep our books or build our highways. Yet the capitalistic principle works in one instance as it does in the others. And a society that applies the principle in its material life should, to be consistent, apply it also in its intellectual life—if it cares about having any intellectual life, and about remaining human rather than merely efficient technologically.

Who is going to pay that price? Who is going to make that investment? At present our society is asking its young liberal arts graduates to pay the price, while society as a whole, in its economic and its political institutions among others, reaps the advantages. But he who would reap should also sow. For years the personnel representatives have been hiring the technically trained college graduates, cheerfully assuming, if they thought about it at all, that the liberally educated graduates would find some sort of job somewhere, and would continue indefinitely to keep alive those abilities and those values without which there would be no properly human community, no freedom of enterprise, and no business world. But the supply is running out, and understandably so, for the liberal college graduate can recognize the discrepancy between the words of commencement day and the deeds of the day after.

Only business can solve this problem, because only business can do the hiring. Even if the government subsidized students

187

undertaking liberal studies, the problem of their making a living after graduation would remain. Even if business more heavily endowed private liberal colleges—and a case can be made for both these projects—the same problem would remain. National associations to help corporations choose recipients for their donations and councils for financial aid to education are promising ventures, but they are only half the battle. Top executives must see to it that their representatives are directed to hire, pay, and promote men who cannot, immediately after graduation, perform efficiently a certain technical function. An expansion of the existing industry training programs should help here.

Perhaps the key lies in what one business executive called "talents which can be developed." Corporations can hardly be expected to pay young men just to sit around being liberal. But they can reasonably be expected to pay good salaries to young men who are serving as business apprentices, who can bring the admitted values of a liberal training to the world of business, who form a promising and a precious pool of future executive talent. That is, if they honestly mean what they say about liberal education. If they want to protect their growing investment in that education. If they really believe in the capitalistic principle.

For the individual person, liberal education is often a luxury. For the nation and for its economy, it is a necessity.

QUESTIONS

1. What knowledge is of value for its own sake? Is science a part of it?
2. How can one convince pragmatic-minded students of the value of theoretical subjects?
3. Should the secondary school emphasize preparation for

college or preparation for life? Are these necessarily different?

4. Should all students follow a college preparatory curriculum as far as their abilities allow?

5. What are the broad purposes of education in our modern society? What difference, if any, does the word "modern" make?

6. In a democracy is it possible to give a really liberal education to everyone?

7. What should be the curriculum of a secondary school in which the greater number of students will not go to college?

8. Is there any difference between a general education and a liberal education?

9. What should one teach junior and senior high school students who cannot grasp such things as bookkeeping and shorthand?

10. What is the specific end of teaching (*a*) the liberal arts, (*b*) the fine arts, (*c*) the useful arts? What would be the ideal balance among these in the curriculum of the average high school?

11. Are students justified in attending college for the social and economic advantages that such attendance brings?

12. Does the teaching of logic have any place in the secondary school? In the elementary school?

13. Should a student with a very high IQ be permitted to take a vocational course?

14. Are vocational subjects being crowded out of the secondary school curriculum by an undue emphasis on "intellectual" subjects?

chapter seven

The Learning and the
Teaching Process

One of the most frequently repeated themes of this book has been
that the term "education" is susceptible of at least four interpretations, all of them proper and all of them distinct.[1] Though the
professional teacher, to whom these observations are particularly
directed, must keep all these meanings in mind, his special concern
will be with the fourth of those meanings, education in the sense
of classroom teaching. Another repeated theme has been that the
terms "art" and "science" and "teaching" are likewise susceptible

[1] See, for example, in Chapter four the section on Education as a Potential Whole.

of several proper but distinct interpretations.[2] Again, though, because of the immediate professional function of the classroom teacher, the meaning of teaching that will most concern him will be that of intellectual instruction. It is true that there is more to education than classroom instruction and that there is more to teaching, at least taken in a broad sense, than helping students develop the arts and sciences. Yet the task of the classroom teacher is specifically—though, once more, not exclusively—this last task, and if he fails in this he fails as a teacher, however admirable he may be in other respects. There should, then, be some point to our examining as closely as we can what goes on in the reciprocal activities of learning and teaching as these apply to the student and the teacher in the classroom.

THE DE MAGISTRO *OF ST. THOMAS AQUINAS*

A useful instrument for such an examination is provided by the small work, *De Magistro* (Concerning the Teacher), which forms one question of a larger work entitled *De Veritate* (Concerning Truth).[3] St. Thomas is here concerned directly with the intellectual rather than the moral, with the true rather than the good, with teaching and learning in the sense of the acquisition of

[2] See above, p. 67.
[3] *Quaestiones Disputatae,* vol. I (*De Veritate*), Spiazzi ed. (Turin: Marietti, 1949), qu. 11. A convenient edition and English translation of the *De Magistro,* including an introduction by James Collins, is *The Teacher* (Chicago: Gateway Editions, Henry Regnery Company, 1953 and 1954). A later Gateway Edition, *The Teacher—The Mind,* includes a second question from *De Veritate* and has a new introduction. It will be taken for granted here that the divisions called questions and articles are familiar to the reader. If they are not, he might usefully consult Collins's introduction mentioned above.

knowledge and the development of intellectual virtues. Indeed, his examples throughout the four articles of the question suggest that he was thinking of learning and teaching in terms of the development of that virtue which is science. It would, though, be a mistake to consider that the example which St. Thomas consistently uses is anything more than an example, to consider that in his doctrine the only knowledge really teachable is scientific knowledge.

The history of the problem to which the first article of *De Magistro* is addressed is too complex to be considered here. In general, it concerns the efficacy of secondary causes, the question whether a merely created cause is truly a cause or whether the only real causality in the universe is exercised by God. In particular, it concerns the question whether that creature who is a human being can really teach another human being, or whether God alone can properly teach and should alone be called teacher or master. Consistently with his Aristotelian rather than Platonic view of reality, St. Thomas takes the position that secondary causes are really efficacious, that they can properly be said to bring results into being, and that one man can truly teach another in the sense of causing him to know the truth.

There are, however, causes and causes. St. Thomas sees God, of course, as the primary cause of human knowledge because He is the primary cause, the creator, of man's intellectual nature; without God there would be no one who could know and nothing which could be known. In creating man, however, God has made a being who, though only in a secondary manner, can do his own learning and his own knowing. Hence a man who learns can be called a secondary principal cause of his own learning—secondary because he depends on God for the possession of his intellectual power, but principal because that power does allow *him* truly to learn and to know. Finally, a teacher is a secondary instrumental cause of someone else's learning—secondary because he too is a creature and receives his ability to be any kind of cause from God, and instrumental not because he is himself an instrument but because he can furnish instruments or aids which will make it easier for the student to learn. God, then, is the primary and principal teacher and the primary cause of knowledge in the student; the student is the secondary but principal cause of his learning, for, unless he performs the necessary intellectual operations, nothing happens; the human teacher is a secondary and merely instrumental cause of learning, though he is also, in many situations, an indispensable one. This, briefly, is the position on teaching and learning that St. Thomas is going to explain and defend in this brief question on the teacher. The rest of this section will be devoted to a sort of running commentary on selected parts of that question in an effort to make as intelligible as possible the soundest examination of this problem that I know.[4]

Acquisition of Knowledge

After explaining, in the body of the first article, what his position is on the efficacy of secondary causes, St. Thomas proceeds to apply his doctrine to that particular example which is the acquisition of intellectual knowledge. The beginning of human knowl-

---

[4] Another commentary on the same work is that of Francis C. Wade, S.J., "Saint Thomas Aquinas and Teaching," in Donald A. Gallagher (ed.), *Some Philosophers on Education* (Milwaukee: Marquette University Press, 1956), pp. 67–85. Cf. Vincent E. Smith, *The School Examined: Its Aim and Content* (Milwaukee: The Bruce Publishing Company, 1960), pp. 1–33. For an illuminating consideration of the subject from the point of view of an experienced and perceptive teacher, see Gilbert Highet, *The Art of Teaching* (New York: Alfred A. Knopf, Inc., 1950); for the same kind of consideration from the point of view of a psychologist, see Jerome S. Bruner, *The Process of Education* (Cambridge, Mass.: Harvard University Press, 1960).

edge, he reminds us, lies in the possession by men of that virtue called understanding,[5] through which we are enabled to grasp immediately the concepts and propositions which, themselves self-evident, form the principles from which we proceed to further knowledge which is not self-evident. In a certain way, then, it can be said that all further knowledge is contained in these general principles, as the developed organism is contained in the seed. The seed, however, is the organism only potentially, not actually; the process of development is still necessary before that potentiality can be actualized. More particular knowledge of reality is contained only potentially in such self-evident principles as the notions of being or of unity or in such propositions as that a whole is greater than any of its parts; a process of development is necessary before that potentiality can be actualized. This process, carried on by one who learns, is the acquisition of further knowledge.

Observe the order of the stages in St. Thomas's argument. First, though briefly and taking for granted on the reader's part some familiarity with his reasons for such a position, he establishes the efficacy of secondary causes and the possibility of creatures as well as the Creator bringing into being effects of their own. Then he narrows his concern to that particular effect which is acquired knowledge, establishing the position that there is such a thing as natural knowledge and the natural acquisition of truth, that men can really be said to learn for and by themselves. Finally, in considering this acquisition of knowledge, he reaches first the possibility of learning and only afterwards the possibility of teaching. For there can, as St. Thomas sees it, be learning without teaching, but there cannot be teaching without learning. In the process of learning, once more, both student and teacher are real though only secondary causes; but the student is a principal secondary cause whereas the teacher is only an instrumental secondary cause.

[5] See in Chapter three the section on Intellectual Virtues.

195

To return to the notion of the actualizing of more particular knowledge from the general principles in which it is contained only potentially, St. Thomas points out that there are two ways in which one thing may be said to exist in another potentially. One is what he calls active potency, in which situation the potentiality can be actualized without the intervention of any outside agency. In this way a man who is ill, and in whom health exists only potentially, can become well, can have that potentiality actualized, simply by the natural forces inherent in his body. The other kind of potentiality is what St. Thomas calls passive potency, in which situation the potentiality in question cannot be actualized unless by the intervention of an outside cause. Thus, air does not ignite spontaneously, but requires the application of some form of heat for the actualization of this potentiality which it has.

In the first instance, no outside agency is required for the bringing into actual being of what previously existed only potentially. But the help of an outside agency is not necessarily ruled out. The human body tends naturally toward health and has its own forces for fighting disease. There is still, though, a place for the physician. What he can do is to assist nature, to provide aids by which the natural forces of the body may more readily operate in overcoming disease and bringing into actual existence the physical health which existed only potentially as long as the man was ill. It is still, though, the body itself which is the principal cause of the alteration; the physician is only an instrumental cause in the actualizing of what is already an active potency. In the second instance, in which an outside agency is always required, that agency itself is the principal cause of the actualizing of what is only a passive potency. Thus, in the example, heat is the principal cause of the igniting of air, which is not spontaneously combustible.

In which of these kinds of potentiality should we place the new knowledge which men are capable of acquiring but have not yet acquired? St. Thomas maintains that this knowledge exists in people in active potency, and as evidence points to the fact that the process of discovery exists, that men do learn by their own efforts and without the aid of others. The relatively ignorant person, then, is like the relatively ill person; his natural powers enable him to become well. But just as the natural process of healing can be aided by the work of a physician, so can the natural process of learning be aided by the work of a teacher.

When art is called upon to aid nature, it does so by imitating nature. The human body tends by nature to correct a chemical imbalance within it, and the physician prescribes by his art medicine to assist this correction and to make it more certain. The human mind tends by nature to acquire new knowledge by the process of discovery, and the task of the teacher is to use teaching methods to bring the student to acquire new knowledge in the same way in which he discovers it for himself. The teacher is an instrumental cause of knowledge as the physician is an instrumental cause of health; the student is a principal cause of knowledge as the patient is a principal cause of health.

The Teacher as an Instrumental Cause

In the example of teaching which St. Thomas gives, he is evidently thinking of that knowledge which is demonstrated, scientific, and even deductive in nature; yet there seems to be no reason to suppose that he is using this as anything more than an example, the clearest but not the only one, of learning and teaching. In the process of discovery, he continues, the one who learns for himself starts from general and self-evident principles, and then reasons to particular conclusions which were implicitly contained in the principles. Using these conclusions, in turn, as the principles of further reasoning processes, he arrives at yet further conclusions. What a teacher does is to use signs of some sort—oral, written, pictorial, etc.—to show the student how to go through those reasoning processes. These signs are instruments which the student uses to enable him to carry on the reasoning process that would be called discovery if he did it without such instrumental aids. In furnishing these instruments, the teacher can be called an instrumental cause of the student's new knowledge and of his developing ability to acquire further new knowledge for himself. It is the student's own reason which arrives at the conclusion, for no one can know for him; yet the teacher really teaches by supplying the instruments which the student uses. It is the patient's own physical and psychic forces that bring about his cure, for no one can be well for him; yet the physician really heals by supplying the instruments that the patient uses in becoming well. The job of both the physician and the teacher is to make himself superfluous. As the physician really causes health in his patient, so the teacher really causes knowledge in his student, even though the knowing itself—an active rather than a passive process—must be done by the student.

Still thinking of the virtue of science as his example, St. Thomas goes on to say that even when the result of teaching and learning is not scientific knowledge, but rather opinion or faith, this result too is in some way related to the first principles of knowledge. And since these principles of all further knowledge are evident to us through the power of that reason which God gave us at our creation, God can be called our primary and interior teacher, for He gave us the natural powers through which alone we can come to know anything. Yet a human teacher is still a teacher; to teach is an analogical term.

This is the position that St. Thomas develops in the body of the first article, his formal statement of the reason why a human teacher can properly be called a teacher. Further light may be shed on this position and on some of its implications by a consideration of some of the objections raised against it and by the answers that St. Thomas gives to those objections.

The third objection concerns the signs that the teacher is said to use as the instruments by which the student acquires new knowledge. The difficulty is that when a teacher proposes signs to a student, the student either knows or does not know what the signs represent. If he already knows what they represent, he is not learning anything new and is not being taught. If, on the other hand, he does not know what the signs represent, he cannot understand them and thus cannot learn anything new from them. In either instance he does not learn and is not taught. If, then, the work proper to a teacher is the presenting of such signs, no man can teach another.

The answer given is that in different ways we both know and do not know what the signs in question represent. We may, for example, know very little of the nature of man, that is, very little of the reality designated by the term man, which is a verbal sign of the reality. Yet we have had enough experience to know roughly that there are beings so designated, that they are living things, and probably more. From this beginning we can go on to learn more of the nature of man by whatever further signs the teacher may use. Again, if we are led to see that a certain conclusion is true and why, we at least understood previously the meaning of the terms which constitute its subject and predicate, though we still had to be brought to grasp the relationship between them. All teaching of new knowledge builds on the existence of previous experience, and ultimately on discovery which the student has made for himself. Teaching does not and could not begin from something absolutely blank; if there could be no discovery from previous personal experience there could be no subsequent teaching. But all students have some knowledge of their own as they come to their teachers, and it is this fact that the objector has overlooked.

The Student as the Principal Cause

The sixth objection argues that knowledge is an accident which, as an accident, does not change the subject, the knower, in which it inheres. But teaching, as described above, consists in the transferring of knowledge from teacher to student, a process that does involve a change by way of addition on the part of the student. If this is teaching, then, one man cannot teach another.

This, however, is not teaching as St. Thomas understands and has explained it. The teacher does not take something that he has and implant this thing in a student; he does not pour something into a passive receptacle. Rather, by teaching, he brings the student to go through the same kind of process that the teacher went through when he learned whatever is in question. Thus the student's knowledge is like the teacher's, for both know the same thing and probably learned it in much the same way. Yet the student has still and necessarily done the learning; he is still the principal cause of that learning. What he formerly knew only potentially he now knows actually, and his teacher has been the instrumental cause of the change. For the student is changed accidentally, though not substantially; he is still the same person, but now he knows more than he did and can better gain still further knowledge. The objector's misconception of teaching makes the teacher the principal cause of the student's learning. This is an error that progressive educators have fought with pretty substantial success, and it is to their credit that they have done so. Every great theorist of education, however, has known that the student is the principal cause of the learning process, and it is unfortunate that a general weakness in history has often led this modern rediscovery to be mistaken for an original vision.

The Teacher As an Essential Cause

A similar difficulty, similarly handled, is raised in the eleventh objection. Knowledge, the argument goes, involves a representation of things in the soul of the knower. But if one man could impress these representations on the soul of another man, he would be doing what only God has the power to do. Only God, then, can really be said to teach.

St. Thomas's reply is much the same as the one he gave to the previous objection. The representations in question, he says, are caused in the soul of the learner directly by his own intellect and only mediately by the teacher. Things existing in the external world can properly be said to cause knowledge, though the intellectual power of the knower is the principal cause. In the same way the words or other signs that the teacher uses can properly be said to cause knowledge, though the intellectual power of the knower is, again, the principal cause. Once more, the various contributions to the teaching-learning process are compared and contrasted, with emphasis on the principal role of the learner.

The answer to the following objection, on the other hand, places the emphasis on the contribution of the teacher. The objector has cited Boethius to the effect that all that teaching really amounts to is the stimulation of someone's mind. But when you stimulate someone to know, the objector continues, you don't cause him to know, any more than you cause someone to see when you point something out to him. One man, then, does not really cause another to know, and does not teach him in the meaning of the term that St. Thomas has been maintaining.

In his reply to the twelfth objection, St. Thomas argues that the comparison of intellectual "seeing" to bodily seeing is inexact. When a man sees physically, his ability to see one thing does not depend on his having previously seen something else. Indeed, he can see any material thing as soon as it comes within his range of vision. It is true, of course, that intellectual knowledge which is habitually held functions in this same way. For example, a person who has already acquired to some extent that intellectual habit or virtue called biology can recall to mind any biological conclusion that he has previously learned simply by focusing his attention on it. He can "see" these conclusions as readily and as immediately as he can see things physically. In both situations the only assistance that anyone else could offer would be to direct attention to the thing to be seen, by pointing it out or by way of a reminder.

When it is a question, however, of learning something for the first time, the comparison is invalid; for, though everything is equally visible physically, not everything is equally intelligible, or visible intellectually. Self-evident principles are intelligible immediately as physical objects are visible immediately; but the more particular conclusions can be reached from these principles only discursively, step by step, with each step depending on the previous one and leading to the next one. And for a man to learn to reason thus, to advance from potential knowledge to actual knowledge in this way, a teacher is essential, though in what sense remains as yet to be seen. The mind is in essential potency to such conclusions, whereas it is in only accidental potency to conclusions which it knows habitually but is not at the moment actually considering, just as anyone is in accidental potency to seeing things which are visible but at which he is not at the moment looking. When it is a matter of reaching new conclusions from principles, therefore, a teacher really causes knowledge in his student and really teaches him.

There are certain difficulties in this position. One is a seeming contradiction with this article's insistence on the learner as the principal cause of the acquisition of knowledge. In the body of the article St. Thomas distinguished between active potency and passive potency, the former of which did not require anything more than an intrinsic principle to come to actualization, and the latter of which did require more. The example of the former was becoming healthy and the example of the latter was the igniting of air. Learning was linked with the first rather than with the second example, and the evidence offered was the observed fact of learning by discovery. The cooperation of a teacher was not ruled out, but the point was made that a teacher is not necessarily required, in the very nature of the case, whereas heat is necessarily required for the igniting of air. What was there called active potency seems to be equated with what is here called accidental potency, at least to the extent that in both instances that outside agent called a teacher is not essential or necessary or indispensable to the actualizing of knowledge. Again, what was there called passive potency seems to be equated with what is here called essential potency, for in both instances an extrinsic agent is required or necessary or indispensable for the actualizing of potential knowledge. Then just as fire is the principal cause of the igniting of air, so should the teacher be called the principal cause of the learner's acquiring new knowledge. The process of discovery seems to be ruled out.

A possible explanation of this apparent discrepancy is that in the body of the article St. Thomas was speaking theoretically and absolutely: There is such a process as discovery, and this fact indicates that the human mind is capable of acquiring new knowledge by its own power. In the reply to the twelfth objection he may have been speaking practically, referring to what occurs for the most part, to what the usual situation is. Euclid did achieve his conclusions by original thinking, by discovery; but the rest of us are not Euclids, and if we are to learn Euclidian geometry we need a teacher.

Another possible explanation, however, is that there is no discrepancy, not even an apparent one, and that the reply to the twelfth objection should be read strictly in the light of that objection, with no immediate reference to the body of the article. According to this interpretation, "essential" should not be equated with "indispensable," as is done in the translation referred to.[6] On the contrary, when St. Thomas speaks of the teacher as *motor*

[6] See above, p. 192, note 3.

essentialis, he means, not "an indispensable mover," but simply "an essential mover" in the sense that the teacher indicates the steps in the reasoning process that the learner is to follow. This is really and essentially to move the intelligence of the student, though only instrumentally. Merely to point out, however, as one does to bodily sight, is not to move the sense power of the student except accidentally, for the power of sight does not operate through a process of comparison, but simply and immediately sees. The intellective power, however, does not simply see (except when principles or habitual knowledge are in question); it does not have immediate intuition, but goes step by step to new knowledge. And this fact does not at all rule out the process of discovery, whereby one makes such progress himself. There is still a mover here, and an essential mover; the soul can here be said to move itself as in one respect active and in another respect passive.[7] There is, however, no movement, except accidentally, in the instance of either bodily sight or intellectual knowledge held habitually, for there is no comparison involved. Hence, there is no room for teaching.

This second explanation seems more likely, given the fact that St. Thomas is addressing himself to a particular objection. The objector's whole position is based upon the identification of teaching with simply pointing out or calling to mind. St. Thomas's reply is based upon the falsity of this identification, upon this confusion of causality *per se* and causality *per accidens,* or essential causality and accidental causality. There is always the possibility of discovery, of learning through one's own efforts exclusively; a teacher is, at least sometimes, not indispensable even when the acquisition of new knowledge is in question. When, however, a teacher does teach, he does something more than point

[7] Cf. St. Thomas, *In V Metaph.,* lect. 14 (Turin: Marietti, 1950), Spiazzi ed., No. 955, 956; *In IX Metaph.,* lect. 1, No. 1776, 1777, 1782.

out or call to mind. When the object to be known is not immediately evident, as it would be to bodily sight or in habitual knowledge; and when, further, the learner does not go through the necessary discursive process by himself, as he does in discovery; then the teacher acts as a *per se* cause and as an essential mover in contrast to a *per accidens* cause and an accidental mover.

The dividing line could, then, be drawn from the point of view of the one who causes knowledge, whether essentially or accidentally; and only the first of these can be called a teacher and be said to teach. It could also be drawn from the point of view of the one in whom knowledge is caused—again, whether essentially or accidentally. When knowledge is caused essentially, a power subject to habituation is in question, a power that is either the intellect or another power subject to it in some way.[8] These powers are, before any habituation occurs, able to be used well or badly and are indefinite and unpredictable in relation to their attaining or not attaining their objects. After some degree of habituation occurs, these powers are at least somewhat inclined to act one way or another in relation to their objects, to be more definite and more predictable. Thus a man who has learned some arithmetic is more likely to grasp an arithmetical conclusion, and a man who is habitually honest is more likely to tell the truth. Powers which are not susceptible of habituation either cannot receive any impression or cannot retain whatever impression they receive from being put to use. Unless the powers come to some degree and in some way under intellectual control so that they can both receive and retain effects of their use under that control, there can be no habituation and no development of the powers in question. Neither can there be any teaching, for teaching is precisely the bringing of another's powers under the control and direction of his reason in such a way that a habit is developed. To direct these

[8] See in Chapter three the section on Habits in General.

powers in this way is to be an essential mover, a *per se* cause of knowledge and of the ability to acquire more. To direct powers which are incapable of such habituation—for example, to point something out to bodily sight—is to be merely an accidental mover, a *per accidens* cause of knowledge. The first activity is to teach; the second is not to teach. The question, then, is not whether a teacher is essential in the sense of indispensable, for discovery remains an open possibility. The question is whether a teacher is an essential mover of a power that is in some sense under the control of the intellect and able to receive that quality which is a habit or virtue, that is, whether a teacher is an essential mover in the meaning of a *per se* cause of knowledge. St. Thomas maintains that a teacher is precisely such a cause. The practical importance of this discussion to the question of what is teachable and what can reasonably be included in a curriculum in any of its meanings is quite evident.

The Role of Principles

Turning now to the thirteenth objection, we find that once more it is science that is in question. Scientific knowledge, the objector argues, involves certainty; and without certainty one has only opinion or faith, not science. But the sensible signs by which one man is said to teach another cannot produce certainty, for the sensible is the area of the contingent and the changeable, which is not directly intelligible and cannot itself produce certainty. Therefore it follows that one man does not really teach another.

The certainty of scientific knowledge, St. Thomas answers, does not arise from the sensible signs used by the teacher but from the self-evident principles of human knowledge. What the teacher does is to show us how conclusions are reduced to or contained implicitly in principles. What causes us, directly, to hold new conclusions with certainty is the fact that, through the power of intelligence that God gave us at our creation, we can see the truth of these principles, and, consequently, the certain truth of con-clusions that we see as reducible to those principles. Our certainty, then, does not directly come from and depend on the contingent, sensible signs that the teacher uses; rather it comes from our previous certainty of the truth of self-evident principles—or of other con-clusions previously established and now usable as principles in further reasoning.

The eighteenth and last objection resembles the third to some extent. Students do not really learn, the objection runs, from those called teachers; for, if you questioned the student before he received instruction, he would show some knowledge of the subject.

Still apparently thinking of science as his example, St. Thomas answers that the knowledge the student displays about a given subject is the knowledge of principles, which are self-evident and need no teaching. He has still, though, to learn conclusions that can be drawn from these principles, and it is to a knowledge of these that a teacher can lead him.

Can a Man Teach Himself?

Having established the conclusion that one man can properly be said to teach another, St. Thomas asks in the following article whether a man can accurately be said to teach himself. He im-mediately grants that through his own intellectual power and without a teacher a person can come to the knowledge of many things. But this does not, he argues, allow us to say that this person actually teaches himself.

In the reason given for this position we meet language which, like the constant example of science in the first article, could lead to misunderstanding if narrowly interpreted. One cannot be said to teach himself, St. Thomas maintains, because one who teaches must have the knowledge which he teaches explicitly and perfectly. This is not the situation of one who learns by discovery; he has the principles of knowledge, but this is not the same as to have, explicitly and perfectly, the further knowledge which is to be derived from those principles. No one, then, can be said properly to teach himself. The difficulty, to be considered below, concerns the meaning of "explicitly and perfectly."

The first objection to this position harks back to the doctrine outlined in the body of the first article, the doctrine that the teacher is only an instrumental cause of knowledge, furnishing instruments by means of which the learner, as principal cause, brings new knowledge into existence. If, then, the instrumental cause is called a teacher, much more should the principal cause be called a teacher, and we should be able to say that a man teaches himself every time he learns something.

In his answer St. Thomas returns to the argument of the body of the second article. It is true, he grants, that the learner's intellectual power is the principal agent in the learning process and that the teacher is only an instrumental agent. Nevertheless, the knowledge to be acquired pre-exists completely in the teacher, but not in the learner. And it is because of this condition that the former can properly be called a teacher and the latter cannot.

The fourth objection is based on the argument that it exhibits greater perfection to learn something on your own than to do so through someone else. So, if a man is called a teacher because of his part in a less perfect manner of coming to know, one who learns by himself and hence in a more perfect manner should with even better reason be called a teacher.

From one point of view, St. Thomas answers, learning by yourself may indeed be a more perfect way, for it shows great intellectual ability. The results, though, are apt to be less perfect, since one can learn much more readily and surely from one who already has the knowledge explicitly than he can through his own gropings on the basis of general principles and experience.

In the second article of *De Magistro,* then, St. Thomas maintains that, properly speaking, a man cannot be said to teach himself or to be his own teacher. Just as the first article involved the possibility of confusion through the consistent use of deductive science as the example of teaching and learning, so the second article involves the same possibility through its emphasis on the completeness of the knowledge that the teacher must possess before he can be called a teacher. This position should not be interpreted to mean that before one becomes a teacher he must know all the conclusions, materially speaking, that have thus far been reached in a particular area of knowledge. If this were so, which of us could hope to qualify? The position taken in this second article should rather be understood as this, that to be a teacher one must hold, explicitly and in full consciousness, whatever knowledge he is going to try to bring someone else to grasp. He need not know every latest development in chemistry to teach chemistry, though it is well to know as much as possible; he need not know every latest technique in one of the fine arts to teach it to others, though, again, he should know as many as possible. What he must know, clearly and competently, is what conclusion, what technique, he is trying to impart, and must accordingly know quite clearly what teaching methods he adopts and why he adopts them. He may not be nearly as intelligent as the genius who gropes in brilliant originality on the far frontiers of his discipline, and may never contribute an original idea to that discipline. But he is teaching, whereas the pioneer is not. It is not, once more, a question of better or worse, of more important or less important; it is a question of difference: To discover is not to teach.

Knowledge of the Truth

In the third article of this question St. Thomas maintains that not only God and other men but even angels can properly be said to teach men. Since this is more obviously a theological than a philosophical question, we shall give attention only to the sixth objection. The objector defines teaching as the process of leading someone to the truth and thus being the cause of truth in his soul. But truth comes into existence all at once, through a process of creation, rather than gradually. And this is an operation which can be attributed only to God, and not to an angel.

St. Thomas replies that a teacher does not really cause truth in the soul of the learner, but rather the knowledge of the truth. What the student learns was true before he learned it; and its truth depends on the way in which reality is, not on the student's knowledge of reality. What is of interest to us here is not whether an angel can teach, but where truth originally lies. Is truth something that we create by our knowledge, or something that was created by divine knowledge and that we discover by observation and reasoning? Do we make the truth or find it? Does reality conform to our knowledge or vice versa? Is there only practical truth or is there also speculative truth? Though this is not the place to go into the matter, a definite position on these basic epistemological questions must be established as one of the preliminaries to a consistent philosophy of education. The educational process is going to be very different depending on one's view of the nature of man, of the nature of reality, and of the relation between man and the reality external to him.

Teach Child or Subject?

The fourth article of *De Magistro* asks whether teaching belongs primarily to the active or to the contemplative life, and considers contemplation on both the supernatural and the natural levels. These different ways of life are distinguished first of all by the end to which each is directed. The contemplative life, St. Thomas explains, looks to the contemplation of truth, and ultimately of that truth Who is God, whether imperfectly in the present life or perfectly in the Beatific Vision. The active life, on the other hand, looks to those human acts, performed here and now, which are designed to be of help to our neighbor.

How is this distinction to be applied to teaching? Here St. Thomas addresses himself to a question that has reappeared in contemporary education literature, the question whether one teaches the child or the subject matter. If we put the emphasis on the child, we are looking chiefly to the active life of classroom work; if we put the emphasis on the subject matter, we are looking chiefly to the contemplative life of study. As might be expected, St. Thomas points out that one teaches both child and subject matter, the sign of which fact is the double object of the verb "to teach." If, again, we put the emphasis on the subject matter, then teaching is a sort of offshoot of the contemplative life of study and thought, whereas if we put the emphasis on the learner, then teaching is a matter of the active life of pedagogy. If we have to make a choice, it must be said that teaching belongs more properly to the active than to the contemplative life, for its ultimate purpose is achieved only in aiding another human being, in bringing that human being to learn something that he had not previously known. Teaching is an activity; specifically, it is that sort of activity which is an art. And what this art aims at making is a man, in the sense that it is directed to leading a human being to bring about a change in himself through the development of some ability, some quality, that he did not previously possess, at least to the same degree.

In order to illustrate this point, let us use the example of the intellectual virtue of science. One of the meanings of this term, and probably the one that we commonly have in mind when we use it, is that of a body of conclusions, a subject matter considered more or less quantitatively. When we say that a certain man is a chemist, we ordinarily mean that he has learned, whether by teaching or discovery, some considerable part of what is known in the field of chemistry, or, more accurately, in one of its branches. We mean, too, that he has a certain command of this knowledge—that he understands why the conclusions concerned are true, and probably that he can explain them to others.

Ultimately, knowledge of this kind (and science is only one example, though perhaps the clearest) is the whole reason for *learning*, at least in the speculative order. One is a better and a fuller man when he knows than when he does not know. But knowledge of this kind is not the whole reason for *teaching*. Indeed, if teaching is that art which aims first at making a man, such knowledge is not even the primary reason for teaching. For the teacher it is, or should be, a means by which the learner can be brought to develop the ability to gain this knowledge for himself, and thus to become independent of a teacher and capable of indefinite progress on his own initiative.

The primary meaning of science, to continue the example, is not the one explained above—that of a body of conclusions—but rather that of an intellectual virtue, a habit, a quality, perfecting the intellectual power and thus the person in whom it comes to exist.[9] The chemist, then, is primarily a man who has developed the virtue or good habit of chemistry, the ability to reason successfully from principles to conclusions in this area. For him, the point of this development is precisely the conclusions, the body of knowledge, which he thus becomes able to grasp through someone's teaching (for example, in professional journals), or which he thus becomes able to discover for himself through laboratory experimentation and his own thought. For the classroom teacher, however, the emphasis is reversed. His job is not primarily to see that the student masters a body of knowledge and the reasons why it is true. His job is rather to use some small part of this body of knowledge as examples of how one reasons from principles to conclusions in this area, in such a way that the student will develop

[9] See in Chapter three the section on Intellectual Virtues.

the ability to do the same thing for himself. What the classroom teacher is primarily after is not the student's knowledge but the student's ability to get knowledge. He is after science in the meaning of an intellectual virtue; and for this purpose he uses science in the meaning of a body of conclusions chiefly as a means. Ultimately, a learner learns and wants to know a subject matter, a body of knowledge, a set of conclusions; he wants to know what is, or how to do or make something. But in school a learner wants chiefly to learn how to learn, precisely so that in the future he may achieve the mastery of subject matter. And in school the teacher should, so far as possible, try to use subject matter principally as a means by which to teach the learner how to learn. As Stephen Leacock once reminded us, one should never let his schooling interfere with his education.

It is for this reason that in the question about whether we teach a child or a subject matter, St. Thomas comes down finally on the side of the child. Teaching, he is saying, is not the same as contemplation or research or invention; it is rather bringing someone to be in a way in which he was not before one did that work which is teaching; it involves doing something to and for a person before it involves doing anything to or for a subject matter. This position would still leave wide open the question of what proportion of the operations of such an institution as a university should go to research and what proportion to teaching, and whether the same operations should go on in the same institution. It would insist, though, that one is not the other, and that teaching involves the work of bringing someone else to see what one already sees himself, either because he has discovered it, or, more likely, because someone else has taught him. Teaching involves more than knowing reality and more than bringing someone else to know reality, whether speculatively or practically; it involves bringing someone to know how to know reality.

And yet, as St. Thomas has also pointed out, the verb "to

teach" does take two objects. Just as you cannot teach something unless you teach it to someone, neither can you teach someone without teaching him something. You cannot run a successful course in just anything in general or nothing in particular. It is this point that is brought out in the fourth objection, which argues that teaching should be said to belong rather to the contemplative than to the active life. For it is the same perfection, the objector holds, that enables one to become perfect himself and also to communicate this perfection to others; in this context it is meditation on truth that allows one both to possess that truth himself and also to communicate it to others by teaching. In brief, it is one's own learning that makes his subsequent teaching possible.

St. Thomas replies that the conclusion from these premises should be that teaching has its *source* in the contemplative life, but not that it is itself a part of that life.[10] Even this conclusion has important consequences for those who are teachers. Teaching is, indeed, an active life; but it is an active life that cannot possibly succeed unless it has its source in the contemplative life. This truth points up one of the thorniest difficulties in contemporary education. You cannot, once more, teach a student without teaching him something. But what you are to teach him you have to have time to learn, and to learn not in the sense of keeping a couple of chapters ahead but in the sense of becoming as proficient in the subject matter in question as is humanly possible. Personally, I have always been somewhat suspicious of the teacher of whom it was said that he didn't know much but he could teach well what he did know. If what is being taught has no intellectual content, it does not belong in classroom work. If it has intellectual content, the teacher cannot really impart it as the science or art that it is unless he has had the opportunity to study it at some

[10] For a further consideration of most of the points touched on in *De Magistro*, see St. Thomas, *Summa Theologiae*, I, 117, 1.

length, to do more than read a textbook or two in the field, to think about it and actually come to grips with the problems involved. It isn't going to do the students much good to be introduced to a set of conclusions if they don't even understand what the problems are. For preparation of this sort, obviously, teachers need more time to study and to think than most of them now have. It may be that the shortage of teachers in relation to the numbers of students now in school makes such preparation impossible. If so, the quality of teaching is bound to suffer, and we face again the old dilemma of quality or quantity. It might be possible to try to teach fewer subjects and to teach them on the basis of a more adequate preparation on the teacher's part, since a smattering of many subjects, as Newman pointed out, is not the same thing as proficiency in any of them. It might also be possible to relax laws concerning school-leaving age so that the relation between numbers of teachers and numbers of students would be improved, though the effect of this course of action on the labor market would have to be considered. It might also be possible to attract even more teachers into the field, though the cost would have to be taken into account. What does not seem to be possible, at least if we want quality in schools, is the continued proliferation of subject matter put on the course of studies with little or no regard to the question of whether it can be taught, along with all the other subjects on the curriculum, at an intellectually significant level.

WHAT IS TEACHING AND WHAT IS TEACHABLE?

Let us return to the problem raised in the twelfth objection of the first article of *De Magistro,* the complex and difficult question of what it means to teach. If the interpretation suggested above [11] is correct, St. Thomas holds that only one who is a *per se* cause, an essential mover, can properly be called a teacher and be said to teach. This distinction is certainly a real one, for to cause only accidentally is not to cause essentially. Further, the identification of teaching with the second of these ways of causing knowledge but not with the first seems also to be based on our experience of reality and to constitute a valid position. Yet the notion should not be interpreted too narrowly or applied too rigidly, for the term teach is another of those whose various applications are not easily made and which involve some degree of arbitrariness in decisions concerning those applications.

The Speculative Order

First let us consider learning and teaching in the speculative order—the order of what is, the order that we discover and study as it is. We can say that there certainly seems to be no teaching in the process of discovery, for here the learner does everything by and for himself without the aid of any extrinsic cause, even an accidental one. In everyday life we are constantly learning in this way by observing, remembering, imagining, and drawing conclusions from what we observe. On a higher level, this is what happens when scientists do research, when mathematicians and philosophers speculate, when artists grasp a facet of reality and create a form in which to express it. This knowledge is discovered rather than taught. Yet some, at least, of the discovery would never have been made without previous teaching. Scientists and artists go to school to other scientists and artists before setting up shop for themselves, and all of us have received lessons in the interpretation of experience from our elders. Indirectly, then, even discovery depends on prior teaching, at least to a great extent. Indeed, it was maintained above, the primary function of a teacher

[11] See pp. 201–206.

is to make himself superfluous, in the sense that his job is less to impart knowledge than to impart the means of gaining knowledge for and by oneself, that is, to help the student develop the intellectual virtues whereby he will be able to learn for himself. Discovery does not directly involve teaching, but there is some relationship.

Teaching seems to be a little more directly related to discovery when controlled discovery is used as a means of guiding learning. Thus a chemistry teacher sets up an experiment in his laboratory so that his students may learn a chemical law. There is no discovery here on the teacher's part, and no real experiment, for he made the discovery under similar circumstances when he was a student of chemistry, and the original discovery was probably made many years before that. What he does is to control the environment in such a way that the students will find out for themselves that a certain chemical event occurs under certain circumstances. Is this teaching? Taken alone, it is probably discovery, which does not involve teaching, for the students see the results of their controlled experiment themselves. But this is not all that happens. When the teacher leads the students, by a process of induction, from this single example to the general chemical law that has been thus exemplified, he certainly teaches and leads the students to new knowledge as a *per se* cause, an essential mover. Taken as part of the whole learning process, then, the laboratory experiment can be looked on as one of the instruments through which the teacher functions as an instrumental cause of new knowledge. Thus something which in itself involves only discovery becomes an integral part of a total process that can certainly be called teaching. This time, there is an even closer connection between discovery and teaching.

A similar relationship exists between teaching and simply pointing things out or calling them to mind. St. Thomas has explained that he would not call this sort of activity teaching because it involves only accidental and not essential causality. Taken alone, this operation, like that of discovery, should probably not be called teaching. But in actual fact, at least in the classroom, it seldom occurs alone. As part of a more inclusive teaching process, a teacher must constantly be reminding his students of knowledge which they have already acquired, and must constantly be pointing out this or that object or event as one part of the basis of an explanation. It would be possible to call such pointing out or reminding a preliminary to teaching. In view of the fact, however, that this accidental causality is inextricably mingled with essential causality, it would seem more accurate to look on the whole procedure as a unit and to call it, as a whole, teaching.

Much the same can be said of faith, which involves a person's willing to make an act of intellectual assent to the truth of a proposition which he accepts on someone's authority. Faith is a less perfect substitute for knowing, for seeing intellectually for oneself; and, whenever possible, one should try to see why a proposition is true rather than merely accept it on faith. Very often, though, we have to be content with faith, and it is quite reasonable that we should be so content. In the Beatific Vision, faith in divine revelation will be superseded by direct knowing; but in this life faith is the best that we can do, and faith is quite reasonable, considering the nature of the authority involved. Faith in human authority is also reasonable, and in fact our reliance on it is immense. A man who has never seen the continent of Africa is yet certain, on the basis of a very reasonable faith, that Africa exists. Anything else would require the existence of a huge and quite incredible conspiracy. A professional historian who has worked with the original documents can probably be said to know that Napoleon existed and did what he is credited with doing. His students, however, only believe that he existed, though to believe anything else would be patent folly.

When one person asks another to believe something on authority, no matter how good the authority and how reasonable the faith, there has not been teaching, for the one doing the believing has not been brought to know anything but only to believe it through an act of assent generated by his own will. Given the willingness to believe and the acceptance of the divine or human authority, the person who points out things to be believed is moving or influencing another accidentally, just as one who points out things to the bodily sight or recalls things already learned is causing knowledge accidentally. Properly speaking, this is not teaching. Once more, however, in ordinary classroom procedure this pointing out is contained in a larger process that does involve teaching, and can be said to be absorbed into that total process. A geography teacher, for example, does ask his students to learn geographic facts and to accept them on faith as true. This, however, is only the first step. He then uses this factual information as the basis on which he explains intellectually to his students relations of cause and effect. And since the imparting of the facts through authority becomes an integral part of a larger teaching and learning process, it can, when considered as part of that whole, be called teaching. The same holds true of historical facts. Taken alone, they are merely chronology; but history is more than chronology, and involves relationships that must be intellectually explained, that must be taught and learned. And so with many other disciplines. To require that we believe nothing, that we start at the beginning as though nothing had been achieved, is to condemn ourselves to perpetual barbarism. In many fields of knowledge, factual information accepted on faith is a prerequisite to any understanding and certainly to any further discovery. In itself, this imparting of information to be believed can hardly be called teaching; but as part of a broader, more complex, and yet single and continuing process, it can be called teaching.

When we consider opinion we find a somewhat different situation. Unlike faith, opinion involves a person's seeing reasons why a certain proposition is probably true. Unlike science, on the other hand, opinion generates only probability and not certainty, leaving in one's mind the fear of error. Sometimes scientific certainty is not possible; there simply is no necessary connection between the conclusion in question and a self-evident principle. An example would be the prediction of future historical events. Sometimes scientific certainty is possible but is not achieved, because the learner does not succeed in grasping the necessary connection. If he was not engaged in direct, personal discovery, the learner has in either instance been brought by a teacher to see why the conclusion in question is probably true. Such teaching is true teaching, even though its result is only opinion. For it involves the teacher in a process through which he directs the intellectual activities of the learner as an essential mover. He does much more than simply point out or recall something; he directly leads the student to see the relation between a conclusion and a principle, even though the student does not see the relation as a necessary one but only as probable. This is teaching, and a form of teaching that necessarily occupies a prominent place in the work of the classroom.

The area of science, and especially of deductive science, is that in which teaching most evidently occurs, and this is no doubt the reason why St. Thomas consistently uses it as his example of teaching in *De Magistro*. Here the teacher is a *per se* cause of the learner's acquisition of knowledge, leading him to use his reasoning power to grasp the necessary connection between a conclusion and an established or a self-evident principle. In this way the student is brought to know a number of conclusions in the science in question, and to see why they are and must be true; he is also brought, by repeatedly doing such reasoning, to develop, as a quality perfecting his intellect, that virtue which is the science in question. To bring a student to do these things is to teach in the fullest and most evident sense of the word, though not, once more, in the only proper sense of the word.

Thus far this section has been concerned with finding out in what way and to what extent a process which can properly be called teaching goes on in the speculative order, in the knowledge that we can have of reality as we find it. It began with discovery, which does not by itself involve teaching, and ended with science, which involves teaching in the fullest sense. Let us now look at the practical order, the order of the reality that we make and of the actions that we do, and try to find out, first of all, whether teaching is involved in the knowledge that we can be brought to have of this order.

The Practical Order

First of all there is that intellectual virtue which is a practical science, an example of which would be ethics or moral philosophy. If the position taken in the first chapter is correct, it is this virtue that you are now trying to develop in the course which you are now taking. Ethics, whether individual or social, is practical knowledge in that its conclusions are in terms of what is to be done rather than in terms of what is. Yet it remains a virtue of the speculative intellect in that it is scientific knowledge which is only remotely practical; its conclusions are in universal rather than in particular terms. Practical science involves a process of demonstration as does speculative science, though the demonstration is, because of the difference in the subject matter, not as incontrovertibly clear. A demonstration in ethics is not ordinarily as clear and indisputable as it is in algebra or even in biology. Yet it remains a demonstration, leading the student to see intellectually the necessary connection between a conclusion and a principle. As such, it involves teaching, in the same way and to the same degree that any other science does.

Turning now to the arts, to that knowledge through which one is enabled to make things well, we find virtues which are perfections of the practical intellect. The liberal arts which are grammar, composition, and logic could be said to form a bridge back to the sciences, for they are and can be taught as sciences as well as arts. Below the graduate level, however, they are seldom so taught, and our present question is whether bringing someone to acquire these arts as arts, as virtues of the practical intellect, properly involves teaching. There would seem to be little room for doubt here, for bringing someone to see how he should go about developing an idea in a paragraph, for example, involves much more than simply pointing something out. One shows him what he should do to develop the idea intelligibly, how he should go about each step in the development, and *why* he should develop it in this way. Intellectual explanations are required here; the learner must grasp relations of cause and effect, of end and means; and he cannot grasp them by simply looking, by having them pointed to. It is true that natural aptitude plays a great part here, as it does in the other arts, and that flashes of intuition which could probably be called discovery play a large part in the formation of even the liberal arts. There is something to any art that cannot be taught. But there is also something that can be taught, some intelligible relationship involving a *why*. There is, for example, a natural logic through which, without any formal instruction, one can reason validly. But there is also something to be taught in logic, something involving theory, and something which ordinarily makes logical operations that much surer. When these relationships are in question, much more than just pointing out is required. Here there is need of a teacher, of an essential mover, of a *per se* cause of knowledge.

The same can be said of the fine arts and even of the useful arts. The student of painting and the student of carpentry—the latter sometimes called an apprentice—are ordinarily instructed in what to do, how to do it, and why they should do it thus and not so. The development of these and other arts as virtues perfecting the practical intellect of the one who learns them requires much more than learning by rote a number of physical actions to be performed in sequence. For the artist is one who *knows* how to make something, who *understands* what is to be done to bring into being a certain kind of object. It is true, and perhaps even more than with the liberal arts, that there is much here that depends on sheer native ability, on personal power of insight. Yet even genius can learn something from others, and what the others can do for the aspiring artist amounts, once more, to teaching, to acting as an essential mover.

Perhaps this is the point at which one should mention, more or less parenthetically, the question of teaching the appreciation of the fine arts. Here we are concerned, not with practical knowledge, but with the speculative knowledge of an operable object, of something made. For the one who sees or hears this work, it is part of the order that he finds and that someone else has made. Can the efforts that another person makes to help him appreciate its beauty properly be called teaching? Can the teacher do any more than hold up the sonnet or the portrait or the fugue, and say, "Look"? Should he really be called a teacher?

In the earlier discussion of this point,[12] it was said that ultimately he must rely on the luminosity, on the beauty and truth of the literary work itself and its appeal to the student's natural intelligence and sensitivity. Teaching in the sense of essential and not merely accidental moving thus seems to be ruled out. Yet even here there may be room for teaching in a tenuous and delicate sense. There is certainly no room for the deadening reduction of a fine imaginative flight to a poor imitation of a syllogism, something it was never meant to be. It is, though, possible for all concerned

[12] See in Chapter six the section on Liberal Arts and Sciences in the Curriculum.

223

to rise somewhat above "ooh" and "ah." It is also possible to rise above "I don't know anything about art but I know what I like," to the point where one knows not only what he likes but why he likes it, and has achieved some understanding of the work of art. Here the classroom teacher functions largely as art critic. A good instructor, while avoiding what could be called dissection, might be able to show how the artist obtained certain effects and why the means he used led to the beautiful expression of his vision. Such a line is a fine one and is difficult to draw in practice; when it is drawn, however, it would appear that the result could fairly be called teaching, in a reduced but still proper meaning.

It might be argued that certain manual techniques are of the essence of most fine and useful arts, and that these cannot, properly speaking, be taught, precisely because they are no more than manual. There are, however, two objections to this position, the first of which is that such physical techniques as manipulating a brush or a saw are not of the essence of the arts of painting or carpentry. The goal aimed at in these techniques is the development of the appropriate muscles and the required nervous responses so that their possessor may handle these tools smoothly and without having to stop and think of each successive step. The goal aimed at in teaching an art is the development of a good habit of the practical intellect so that its possessor may successfully plan the production of something. The point of an art is not to eliminate thought, but to strengthen the practical intellect so that thought about how to make something may be more accurate and more surely successful. An art is more intellectual than physiological, whereas a technique or skill is more physiological than intellectual. The technique is important for the expression of the idea, but it is not of the essence of the art itself.

The second objection to the position mentioned above is that even skills can properly be said to be taught. It is true that such skills, for example, as swimming and skating and typewriting are learned pretty largely by doing, by practice and repetition until the necessary neuromuscular patterns are developed and the feel of the thing is acquired. It is possible to pick these things up entirely through one's own efforts, by a process paralleling that of discovery. The results, however, are apt to be better if one has a teacher; and it will be maintained here that the function of instructing in these areas, if competently carried out, is properly teaching.

On the most elementary level the one whom we shall provisionally call a teacher may simply indicate *what* should be done. He tells the learner to perform this step first, that step second, and so on, and to practice each step for a certain length of time in a certain series of combinations. If this is all that he does, he seems to be acting on the theory that one develops these skills entirely by doing, and that there is nothing to be explained intellectually. This person certainly understands what he is about; he provides the pattern through which the student does just the right things in just the right order to build up the needed neuromuscular combinations. But he does not communicate to the student the reason for what he asks him to do. It is true that such a reason exists, and the learner is guided through these steps by someone who knows precisely what he is doing and who plans the steps in a definite order so as to obtain a definite and foreseen result. Yet as long as the student is not led to see why he does what he does, to see for himself the relation of cause and effect, there does not seem to be any essential moving, any teaching.

On the next level the teacher may show the student *how* to do each step in the process through doing it himself by way of example. He actually gets into the water, on the ice, at the typewriter; he backs up the signs that his words are by the more vivid signs that his actions are, and thus makes learning easier and more certain. Again, though, if he stops short of explaining why the student should do these things, there may be an operation that can be called training, but hardly one that can properly be called teaching.

Finally, the teacher may explain *why* such a way of doing the thing is better in the sense of being more effective than another way of doing it. This person does not consider that these skills are exclusively a matter of doing, but that they involve some sort of intelligible process, some sort of understandable relation of end and means, which the student can grasp at whatever level his maturity allows and which he can use in further developing the skill in question.

The first level of instruction in skills or techniques seems to involve chiefly the memory, the second the imagination, and the third the intellect. Taken alone, the first and even the second should not be called teaching. Like controlled discovery, however, these are probably seldom found alone, or should not be. The best teaching practice, and probably the usual one, would seem to be a combination of all three levels. It is true that these are skills or techniques rather than knowledges, and that they are done most efficiently when the swimmer or skater or typist can perform the needed actions without stopping to think of each one. But it is also true that they are human skills, and in learning them, if not in doing them, the most human and ordinarily the most effective way will involve learning not only what to do and how to do it, but also why to do it. It will, in short, involve teaching.

Can Moral Virtue Be Taught?

If the analysis in this section is valid up to this point, then a process that can properly be called teaching is in some way, though by no means always in the same way, involved in the development of the intellectual virtues and even, in the best practice, of skills and techniques. There is, however, one intellectual virtue which is also a moral virtue, and whose consideration will thus carry us over to the subject of moral virtue.[13] As an intellectual virtue perfecting the practical intellect, it would appear that prudence can be learned but not taught. We can be said to learn from experience, in the sense that we examine new situations in the light of our knowledge of past similar situations and the remembered outcomes of certain courses of action. But *we* must see the relationship of similarity; otherwise it is not *we* who have learned from the experience. If someone else points out the similarity to us and advises us to choose a particular course of action on this basis, it is his prudence rather than our own that we are going on. If he points out the similarity to us, perhaps provides further examples, and draws a general conclusion that in this kind of situation a certain sort of action is called for, he is, on however rudimentary a level, teaching moral science. The particular application, again, must be our own; and the virtue of prudence by which we make the application successfully must also be our own.

As a moral virtue involving the rectitude of the will, prudence, or rather the question about the possibility of teaching prudence, becomes one example of the general problem of the possibility of teaching moral virtue. It is impossible to teach the natural moral virtues themselves because these are directly developed by each person's actions rather than by his knowledge. God can infuse supernatural moral virtues in men, but men must develop their own natural moral virtues by performing good acts. And the performance of good acts, as we all know from hard personal experience, requires more than our knowing what we should do; it requires, among other things, a definite act of the will, an act which is radically free and which each of us must perform himself.

[13] For an excellent explanation of prudence and the question whether it can be taught, see Charles J. O'Neil, "Prudence, the Incommunicable Wisdom," in Robert E. Brennan, O.P. (ed.), *Essays in Thomism* (New York: Sheed and Ward, Inc., 1942), pp. 187–204.

The only act which can lead to the growth of moral virtue is a free, human act; the only *per se* cause of such an act, the only essential mover to such an act, can be the agent himself. Because of the nature of its cause, moral virtue is not teachable.

The fact remains that we all speak, however loosely and improperly, as though moral virtue were teachable. Parents and schoolteachers, among others, say that they are trying to teach the children under their care to be honest and kind and loyal. Strictly speaking, the word teach is here being used improperly. All that can be taught is knowledge of some sort, and knowledge alone does not produce the actions from which moral virtue grows. Yet it is largely on the basis of our knowledge, however arrived at, that we decide what actions to perform. It is a matter of universal experience that the ideas of moral right and wrong to which people are exposed, especially by way of precept and example, have a tremendous influence on their decisions about what they will do. And it is these decisions and the acts that follow them that cause the development of moral virtue or moral vice. One cannot, properly speaking, teach anyone moral virtue. But this fact does not mean that one cannot effectively help others to develop moral virtue. Especially, it does not mean that one should abandon the young to the inner clamor of their own emotions and the outward pressure of whatever environment they find themselves living in. People, and especially young people, can and must be helped to develop moral virtue, to become men and women of character. They cannot, accurately speaking, be taught moral virtue. But they can be taught something that will go a long way toward helping them act in such a way that they will develop moral virtue. Perhaps it would be worth our while to look at some of the possibilities, even though these cannot be said to involve the teaching of moral virtue in any proper sense.

Moral science, that is, moral theology or moral philosophy, is one way of bringing to others knowledge that may be of help to them in their moral growth. As sciences these are virtues of the speculative intellect; as practical sciences they are directed, though remotely, to action. They arrive at conclusions that certain species or kinds of act are right and are to be done, and, given the good will of the agent, these sciences can help him come to a more accurate decision about what he should do in given concrete circumstances. Moral science does not develop moral virtue; it is not even an indispensable condition for the development of moral virtue; but for those who are willing to use it, it can be quite helpful in their efforts to decide what they should do. We all act, among other things, on the basis of certain general moral convictions; it is better to have these convictions scientifically established in our own minds than not to have them so established. It is better, for example, for an employer and an employee to understand the nature of the employment contract that they have entered into and their mutual rights and obligations under it; such understanding does not guarantee that either party will act justly toward the other; but it does mean that, given the will to be just, they will the better understand what justice requires of them and will thus be more likely to act in an objectively just manner. And it is by such acts that the virtue of justice is developed.

The teaching of moral science, however, is a complicated business, usually confined in practice to college students who are following a certain course of studies. For most people, including the relatively young (and perhaps for many college students as well), scientific knowledge in this area is impossible, and faith is the best that can be done. It is important that a small child should learn that telling the truth is right and lying is wrong; it is impossible to demonstrate this to him as a scientific conclusion because he is too immature to grasp the demonstration; something else must take its place. One of the things that can take its place is faith, a statement that telling the truth is right and that lying is wrong, given on divine or on human authority, and appealing to the child's faith in the authority. The child then believes rather than knows that lying is wrong, and does not know why. This is less than scientific knowledge and is a substitute for it; but it is the best that can be done in the circumstances. Morally, it may be equally effective as long as it produces a subjective certainty in the believer, for the point of either knowledge or belief of this sort is to help the agent decide on courses of action that will gradually develop his moral virtue. Intellectually, knowledge is always preferable to faith, for it is more human to see than not to see. When knowledge is impossible, however, faith is a quite reasonable substitute, and its indirect effect on the development of moral virtue is probably much the same.

Influencing Individual Actions

When we leave the area of statements about right and wrong species or kinds of moral act and come to that of the individual act, a different kind of knowledge is involved. Persuasion and advice culminating in opinion have a place here. One person is convinced that another should, in the given circumstances, do this as opposed to that, both because it is objectively right and because it will help the person doing it develop a moral virtue rather than a moral vice. For this purpose he offers advice to the other person, putting his own experience and prudent judgment at the latter's disposal, and perhaps even tries to persuade him to do the action that the adviser considers right. This is not to teach the moral virtues, but it is to provide a form of knowledge, below the scientific level, which makes it more likely that one action rather than another will be done and thus that a good moral habit rather than a bad one will be acquired.

Another way of helping a person make what one regards as the right decision is to tell him what to do in the form of precept. In generalized form this is expressed as law, and in particularized form as a simple command. The influence of precept, and especially of the sanctions standing behind law or command, was briefly examined [14] in connection with the question of the transfer of moral training. All the evidence seems to indicate that the existence of rules of conduct backed by sanctions can, if carefully administered, lead to the sort of action that directly develops moral virtue. We all need the constant rule of law. But perhaps young people are especially in need of the kind of guidance, both in general and in particular terms, that precept provides. Since knowledge is always better, because it is more human, than lack of it, those who lay down the law or who issue particular commands would do well to explain not only *what* action they are requiring but also *why* they are requiring it. Ultimately, however, they are requiring the action, and it is this action that, if wisely ordered, will develop moral virtue in those who perform it. Precept is not, properly speaking, the teaching of moral virtue; but it is a strong influence for the performing of those actions that will ordinarily lead to moral virtue. The peculiar strength of its influence probably comes from the fact that it not only points out what is to be done—though this is its primary function—but adds an appeal to the will through the threat of sanctions if the precept is disobeyed.

Another strong influence on conduct is example. Like precept, this is primarily a form of instruction leading directly to a knowledge of what should be done (presuming that the example is good). When parents, for example, consciously and carefully set a consistent standard of honesty for their children to observe, they are using actions rather than words as signs of their meaning, but the result in the children is the same—knowledge of what their parents consider right. The further difference between example and precept is that example appeals to admiration and love

[14] See in Chapter two the section on Transfer of Training.

231

rather than to fear. It does not threaten punishment for disobedience, but offers something positive to be admired and emulated. Both precept and example have their place, and experience indicates that both are needed. When a choice exists, though, example would seem preferable. Casual observation would indicate that it is also probably more effective practically; what we do speaks more loudly than what we say. It is for this reason that parents and others responsible for young people rightly pay a great deal of attention to the example that they themselves offer and to the environment to which those under their care are exposed. To offer example is not, properly, to teach moral virtue or vice; but it is to have a tremendous influence on the performing of those acts which lead to moral virtue or vice.

Throughout this chapter we have been concerned with trying to find out what it means to teach and what kinds of teaching there can be. To teach, we found, is to be an essential rather than a merely accidental cause of another's knowledge. In classroom practice, these kinds of causality are often mixed; the effort, however, should always be to come as close to what is clearly teaching as the situation allows, to aim at intellectual explanation, at the student's understanding of the reason *why*. It is such explanation, in the final analysis, that is the reason for the existence of that society which is the classroom, the heart of the school. On the other hand, we should avoid the mistake of seeing teaching as a univocal term, in such a way that we would admit only science and the liberal arts taught as sciences to be properly teachable and properly included in the curriculum of the classroom. The following chapter will attempt to distinguish the notion of curriculum as applied to the classroom and the laboratory from the notion of curriculum as applied to the whole school, and to arrive at some general conclusions about what should be included in each. The material of the present chapter should serve as a foundation for that effort.

QUESTIONS

1. Do television and tape recordings as teaching methods lessen the personal influence of the teacher?
2. What is the difference between indoctrination and teaching?
3. Is "spoon feeding" of students ever justified? If so, in what areas of study, at what levels, and for what reasons?
4. What difference would a teacher's philosophy of education make in his teaching when he has to follow a given curriculum and syllabus?
5. "Each man discovers for himself what is already well-known." [15] What are some of the possible interpretations of this sentence that come to your mind? Pick out one of the interpretations that has some relation to the educational process, and, in its light, evaluate the statement.
6. Does a "teaching machine" really teach? Is it more than a device for reviewing and drilling?
7. Can a foundation for original, independent thinking be given on the secondary level? If so, should it be? If so, how?
8. Do drill and memorization have any place in the contemporary classroom?
9. "Teaching is a waste of time unless it results in changes in behavior." Discuss.
10. "Education is the process whereby a pupil who requires teaching is transformed into a student who teaches himself." Discuss.

[15] From *The Making of a Modern Educator* by William Van Til, copyright 1961 by The Bobbs-Merrill Company, Inc., Indianapolis; used by special permission of the publishers; p. 51.

chapter eight

Curriculum Planning

THE RELATION OF CURRICULUM TO PHILOSOPHY OF EDUCATION

Four possible meanings of the term education have already been distinguished; [1] they all concern the growth of human powers, but growth of different powers and growth induced in different ways. In the first meaning education is taken as the growth induced by the total experience of a lifetime; in the second it is taken as that induced by educational agencies other than the school; in the third it is taken as that induced by the school as a whole; and in the fourth it is taken as that induced by the work of the class-

[1] See in Chapter four the section on Education as a Potential Whole.

room, the laboratory, and the library. The rest of Chapter four was devoted to trying to discover the functions proper to the various educational agencies on the basis of the different meanings of education. The rest of this chapter will be devoted to trying to discover, on the same basis, the different meanings of the term "curriculum" and the kind of curriculum best suited to each educational agency.

The basic meaning of curriculum is that of a course of study, something that one travels (literally, "runs") over or through. To call something a course—for example, a race course or a golf course—implies that it has been laid out according to a plan, and that travel on it is not haphazard. With this in mind one could hardly speak with much meaning of curriculum as corresponding to the first meaning of education, involving the experience of a whole life. For only another person can properly be called a teacher, and only another person can consciously and deliberately lay out a curriculum or course of studies for a student to follow. One does learn from experience of life, and this is truly education; but such learning largely occurs by discovery rather than results from teaching. It is true that others control to some extent, especially when we are young, the environment in which we spend most of our time and thus, to a limited degree, the experiences that we undergo. Most of this control, however, will be found to involve the activities of such persons as parents and school authorities, and to be exercised through some definite educational agency such as the home or the school. For life as a whole there is no curriculum; even sound advice from others leaves most future experiences uncertain.

Corresponding to the second meaning of education, involving the efforts of agencies other than the school, there would seem to be a real though somewhat informal meaning to the term curriculum. Parents consciously set out to teach their children how to say their prayers, how to clean their teeth, how to tell time. However informally, they decide to some extent what means they are going to use and in what order they are going to use them in order to bring the child to know these things; that is, they lay out a curriculum. The same could be said of the teaching work of the church, a work which proceeds, in however flexible a manner, according to some plan that the particular teacher has in mind. And so, though perhaps less evidently, with other educational societies. Important as these notions of curriculum may be, however, they are not those with which we are professionally concerned as schoolteachers or administrators.

The third meaning of education concerns that more formal agency of education which is the school. In this context the term curriculum would cover all the activities sponsored by the school which consciously look to the development of the students in any way. Thus, social events and athletics, the school play and the salute to the flag, would be considered part of the curriculum of the school. Some of these activities aim ultimately at a moral rather than at an intellectual result. Like the action of setting an example, however, they aim immediately at conveying some kind of knowledge; or at least at the process which we have called controlled discovery, through which the student discovers knowledge for himself, but discovers it in circumstances designed by someone else to bring about a desired learning result. All of these efforts, involving the laying out of some definite experiences directed to an equally definite learning result, may properly be called curriculum. It is important, however, that its nature as a school curriculum be kept in mind.

The fourth meaning of education that was distinguished above has to do with the specifically intellectual work of the teacher in the classroom or the laboratory. Paralleling this narrower meaning of education is a narrower meaning of curriculum, that of a

237

course of studies or the total of such courses offered as a means of instructing students in some phase of intellectual knowledge and developing one or other intellectual virtue.

A Necessary Distinction

It should be evident what confusion in practice could result from the failure to distinguish clearly between the school curriculum and the classroom curriculum. If no such distinction is made, then there is no theoretical basis for distinguishing algebra as more properly the work of the classroom than calisthenics, or history than stamp collecting.

As professional educators, again, we are directly concerned with education in the third and fourth of the meanings outlined above, and hence with the corresponding meanings of currriculum, that is, the school curriculum and the classroom curriculum. We have already seen something of the confusion concerning the various agencies of education and the aims proper to each that can and does result from the mistake of considering education as a strictly univocal notion. Another expression of the same mistake, and one resulting in the same confusion, is that of considering curriculum as a strictly univocal notion, of failing to see that it can be used in different but still proper ways. An example can be found in the work of Krug, which may perhaps be taken, from a host of possibilities, as fairly representative of contemporary writing on the subject. He is arguing for a notion of what we have been calling the school curriculum as preferable to the narrower conception involved in the classroom curriculum: "A narrow definition of the curriculum restricts the scope and range of curriculum planning, while a broad one provides more readily for orderly and reflective guiding of educational change in all aspects of the life and work of the school." [2]

[2] Edward A. Krug, *Curriculum Planning*, rev. ed. (New York: Harper & Row, Publishers, 1957), p. 4. Reprinted

This is an example of what might be called the fallacy of the false dichotomy. It is not, as Krug supposes, a question of either-or, as though curriculum could have only one meaning; it is a question of both. We are back again to the notion of a

---

by permission. Other writers in the field express similar notions of curriculum. For Alberty, the school curriculum —and he mentions no other—is made up of all the activities that it provides for the students; Harold Alberty, *Reorganizing the High School Curriculum,* rev. ed. (New York: The Macmillan Company, 1953), p. 125. The same idea is expressed in Marshall C. Jameson and William Vernon Hicks, *Elementary School Curriculum: From Theory to Practice* (New York: The American Book Company, 1960), p. 39; and in Nolan C. Kearney and Walter W. Cook, "Curriculum," *Encyclopedia of Educational Research,* 3d ed. (New York: The Macmillan Company, 1960), pp. 358–365. The same notion, with added emphasis on the social purposes of students' experiences, is found in W. Ray Rucker, *Curriculum Development in the Elementary School* (New York: Harper & Row, Publisher, 1960), p. 3; and in Vernon E. Anderson, *Principles and Procedures of Curriculum Improvement* (New York: The Ronald Press Company, 1956), pp. 9–12. In this last work, the author first gives the usual broad definition of curriculum as the experiences that pupils have under the guidance of the school, and then, inconsistently, attempts to illustrate this notion by an even broader definition of curriculum as the total environment of the students' waking lives. Similar confusion is found in George A. Beauchamp, *Planning the Elementary School Curriculum* (Englewood Cliffs, N.J.: Allyn and Bacon, Inc., 1956), pp. 34–35; and in M. D. Alcorn, R. A. Houseman, and J. R. Schunert, *Better Teaching in Secondary Schools* (New York: Henry Holt and Company, Inc., 1954), p. 167. A useful summary of many definitions of curriculum may be found in James A. Fitzgerald and Patricia G. Fitzgerald, *Methods and Curricula in Elementary Education* (Milwaukee: The Bruce Publishing Company, 1955), pp. 100–103; the authors do not clearly

potential whole, examples of which are education, and, as a corollary, curriculum. There is more than one kind of education, and there is more than one educational agency; because of this fact there is more than one kind of curriculum, and the curriculum proper to one educational agency will not be the curriculum proper to another one.[3] The school is a much broader educational agency

---

indicate their own preference, but seem to approve one that would include all school activities. An early example of this broad conception of curriculum as identical with what we have been calling the school curriculum occurs in a letter written by William B. Brown and printed under the title, "New Approaches to Curriculum Building in the Los Angeles City Schools," *School and Society*, 42, 1080 (Sept. 7, 1935), 332; reprinted in Hollis L. Caswell and Doak S. Campbell, *Readings in Curriculum Development* (New York: American Book Company, 1937), p. 173. An earlier passage suggesting this expanded meaning is provided by Florence Stratemeyer, *The Effective Use of Curriculum Materials* (New York: Bureau of Publications, Teachers College, Columbia University, 1931), p. 3; reprinted in Caswell and Campbell, p. 160. See also Franklin Bobbitt, *The Curriculum* (Boston: Houghton Mifflin Company, 1918), p. 42; reprinted in Caswell and Campbell, pp. 66–67.

[3] A few authors distinguish clearly between what we have been calling the school curriculum and the classroom curriculum, though reserving the term curriculum for the former. Saylor and Alexander see the curriculum as the school's total program for its learners, including situations both within and without the school; for what we are calling the classroom curriculum they use the term program of studies; J. Galen Saylor and William M. Alexander, *Curriculum Planning for Better Teaching and Learning* (New York: Rinehart & Company, Inc., 1954), p. 4. The point is that, whatever the terminology, the distinction between school curriculum and classroom curriculum is made, and the confusion noted in note 2 is avoided. Gwynn makes the same distinctions, em-

than the classroom, and hence its curriculum will be broader than that of the classroom. The school is much more than the class-room and aims at developing a much wider range of the student's capacities. And since, again, the whole man cannot be educated as a whole, the classroom and the laboratory will have to con-centrate on one phase of that development—the intellectual one— as their specific purpose; otherwise, this purpose will not be achieved. If chemistry is worth learning, then the chemistry teacher had better concentrate on teaching chemistry rather than, say, democratic living, for certainly no one else will teach the former. For this reason the idea of curriculum as applied to the school as a whole will simply have to be distinguished, under pain of scholastic confusion and ineffectiveness, from the idea of cur-riculum as applied to the classroom.

The first step, then, in deciding what a curriculum should contain is to decide what curriculum you are talking about, just as the first step in deciding what the aims of education are is to decide what education you are talking about. Let us first consider the classroom curriculum. If the specific work of the classroom and the laboratory is the development in the student of intellectual virtues—of the arts and sciences—then the classroom curriculum will have to be geared to help accomplish that end.

It is true, of course, that the ability of the teacher is of far

---

ploying curriculum for all the activities of the school and course of study for the classroom curriculum; J. Minor Gwynn, *Curriculum Principles and Social Trends,* 3d ed. (New York: The Macmillan Company, 1960), pp. 240– 241. For an early example of this same distinction, see R. L. West, Charles E. Greene, and W. A. Brownell, "The Arith-metic Curriculum," in Guy Montrose Whipple (ed.), *Report of the Society's Committee on Arithmetic,* part I, The 29th Yearbook of the N.S.S.E. (Bloomington, Ill.: Public School Publishing Company, 1930), p. 65.

more immediate importance than the construction of any curriculum. Good teaching involves the personal communication of teacher and students, a spiritual process that lies beyond and defies any attempt at mechanical direction. A curriculum is, in a sense, mere machinery, and working on a curriculum sometimes looks like nothing more than tinkering with machinery. Yet a curriculum is machinery which, if properly organized, can immensely facilitate the personal and spiritual communication which is teaching, and which, if improperly organized, can make that communication greatly and needlessly more difficult. For one does not only teach students; he teaches them something; and what he teaches them, as well as how he teaches it, obviously has a great influence on the ultimate outcome.

THE CLASSROOM CURRICULUM

It will be impossible in this section to go into detail about exactly what should be taught in any given academic situation, both because the situations are too numerous and diverse and because such detail lies beyond the scope of this book and beyond the competence of its author. It should, however, be both proper and possible to examine some of the philosophical conceptions that inevitably lie behind convictions about what should or should not be included in any given course of studies. The most pertinent of these conceptions is that of the purpose of classroom instruction and the place that the work of the classroom holds in the total educational process.

Returning to Krug as our example, we find descriptions of four bases on which curricula are commonly organized. These he calls subjects, broad fields, problems of living, and experience.[4] Let us look at each in turn.

[4] *Op. cit.,* pp. 103–108. Other writers on curriculum use varied, though generally similar, descriptive expressions.

Subject and Broad-fields Curricula

The first category pretty well explains itself. Over the ages men have developed the arts and the sciences as so many ways of achieving some understanding of various facets of reality. Obviously, not all arts and all sciences can be taught to all students;

Stratemeyer, Forkner, McKim, and Passow also find four major types of curriculum organization, which they call separate subjects, subject fields (groups of related subjects), broad areas (which cut across subject fields), and problems or needs of the group; F. B. Stratemeyer, H. L. Forkner, M. G. Mc-Kim, and A. H. Passow, *Developing a Curriculum for Modern Living* (New York: Bureau of Publications, Teachers College, Columbia University, 1957), pp. 86–105. The authors favor the last of these divisions, a child-centered program based on "persistent life situations." Smith, Stanley, and Shores speak of the subject curriculum, the correlated curriculum, the broad-fields curriculum, and the activity curriculum; B. Othanel Smith, William O. Stanley, and J. Harlan Shores, *Fundamentals of Curriculum Development*, rev. ed. (New York: Harcourt, Brace & World, Inc., 1957), pp. 230–275. These authors add to their four divisions the notion of core curriculum. The first meaning of the term as they explain it can be largely reduced to their broad-fields curriculum, and the second to a particular plan for education for citizenship, though the authors themselves see their meanings of core curriculum as constituting distinct forms; *ibid.*, pp. 311–387. Faunce and Bossing see the core curriculum as part of the experience curriculum; Roland C. Faunce and Nelson L. Bossing, *Developing the Core Curriculum* (Englewood Cliffs, N.J.: Prentice-Hall, Inc., 1958). Alberty uses the two broad divisions of subject-centered and experience-centered curriculum, and recommends combining the values that come from direct experience with those that come from systematic organization; *op. cit.*, pp. 125–155. Using further distinctions, Alberty sees six kinds of what he calls core

but some more or less judicious selection from among these has constituted the traditional classroom curriculum. It has also constituted the proper classroom curriculum, since the work of the classroom is precisely the development of its students' intellectual capacities, including, of course, aesthetic sensitivity and some skills.

One difficulty with this approach is that the arts and especially the sciences are ramifying so rapidly as to make judicious selection among them increasingly difficult. The problems inherent in the intense and increasing specialization of knowledge are particularly acute in universities and research institutes, where communication among men who are supposed to be colleagues is becoming

---

curriculum, ranging from one based on separate subjects to one consisting of activities planned by teacher and students; *ibid.*, pp. 169–193. Beauchamp follows much the same method. He describes the subject-centered and the experience curricula as the extremes, and, as intermediate conceptions, the correlated, fused, broad-fields, core, and integrated curricula; *op. cit.*, pp. 18–36. Leonard speaks of reorganizing the subject curriculum into what he calls topical, cultural, and problem types; J. Paul Leonard, *Developing the Secondary School Curriculum*, rev. ed. (New York: Rinehart & Company, Inc., 1953), pp. 270–305. He also devotes some space to core courses; *ibid.*, pp. 396–435. Saylor and Alexander provide a thorough description and a balanced evaluation of approaches to curriculum construction which they term subject-centered, broad-field, major social functions of living, and interests, needs, and problems of learners; *op. cit.*, pp. 250–304. They give a similar treatment to the notion of core curriculum; *ibid.*, pp. 306–345. Jameson and Hicks describe briefly four types of curriculum as separate-subjects, correlated, broad-areas, and needs-development, and prefer the last type; *op. cit.*, p. 40. Beck, Cook, and Kearney use the terms separate-subjects, correlated (including core), broad-fields, and developmental-activity to describe kinds of cur-

increasingly rare. Secondary and even elementary schools, however, are also affected by this situation, and are under constant pressure to add more and more subjects to an already crowded curriculum. Yet if we do not graduate our students, at whatever academic level, with some connected and intelligent grasp of reality as a whole, if we confine them to isolated fragments of that reality with unbridged and unimagined chasms gaping between the fragments, we can hardly claim to be doing much of a teaching job.

The attempt to overcome some of these difficulties involved in the specialization of knowledge has led to the second category, which Krug calls broad fields, or integration. The aim here is to help the student relate various aspects of reality in his own mind by explicitly relating their study in the classroom. Within this category Krug distinguishes correlation, which "implies the establishment of relationships among two or more subjects without necessarily destroying the identities of these subjects as such" from what he calls fusion, "under which two subjects are brought together in such a way that they lose their separate identities and form a new pattern." An example of correlation would be cross

---

riculum; they, too, prefer the last type; Robert H. Beck, Walter W. Cook, and Nolan C. Kearney, *Curriculum in the Modern Elementary School* (Englewood Cliffs, N.J.: Prentice-Hall, Inc., 1953), pp. 237–241. Anderson keeps to the two broad classifications of subject-centered and experience-centered approaches to curriculum development, and favors the latter; *op. cit.,* pp. 67–81. Fitzgerald and Fitzgerald describe curricular organizations as subject, broad-fields, core, and activity, and provide a critical comparison and contrast between conventional and newer curricula; *op. cit.,* pp. 129–149. Gwynn speaks of a correlated, fused, core, and experience curriculum, with some minor variations such as interrelation; *op. cit.,* pp. 241–245, 410–412, 453–455. A high point of Gwynn's contribution is a definition of curriculum that includes "extracurricular" activities; *ibid.,* p. 245.

references between a history and an English class, in both of which the same chronological period was under study. An example of fusion would be a single course in social studies or in problems of democracy.

Correlation should help the student see relationships among his various glimpses of a complex reality, thus allowing him to build up gradually an intellectual framework or context within which new knowledge can be intelligibly situated. Fusion aims at the same end, and, in addition, at helping reduce the proliferation of subjects within the classroom curriculum. Yet, because of the very nature of reality and of the human mind, there are limits to what can be done in this direction. Knowledge may be a singular noun for the infinite mind of God, but it is to a large extent a plural noun for the finite minds of men. We have knowledges rather than knowledge, and our chief intellectual endeavor is to reduce that plurality as much as we can to singularity, to comprehend the many under the one, to coordinate our knowledges. But coordinated knowledge, properly understood, does not mean confused knowledge. There are several ways in which the one and the many are related; there are different kinds of whole, each with its own type of unity. Coordinated knowledge is a unity of order among several kinds of knowledge, each of which, in order to come into relationship with the others, must be and remain itself. You cannot, for example, coordinate historical and geographic and economic knowledge unless you first have these knowledges as they are in themselves, each specified by its own object, and unless, in approaching a problem involving all of them, you carefully keep each kind of knowledge distinct from, though related to, the others. Coordinated knowledge is a unity of order. To speak of the unity of knowledge in any other sense, to aim at a unity which ignores the ultimately irreducible differences among types of knowledge—this is to achieve, not coordination, but chaos.

In the first place, then, if the student is going to coordinate

246

his knowledges, he must first have those knowledges. So before worrying about coordination, we must first teach him and teach him well. In the second place, he must continue to see the distinction as well as the relation between the various disciplines that we teach him. If he cannot tell the difference between historical and geographic and economic knowledge, he is not likely to have a very clear grasp of the complexities of problems that involve all those knowledges and more. One does not, for example, resolve a social problem by blurring and confusing its complexities; one simply guarantees that he will never resolve it because he does not even understand it. The broad-fields approach to the classroom curriculum has much to be said for it as an effort in the direction of an important educational goal. It does, though, have limitations.

Organization by Problems

As Krug points out, the subject and the broad-fields approaches to the construction of the classroom curriculum differ in their conception of what constitutes a single, teachable subject, but are in agreement that the basic aim of any classroom curriculum is to help the student develop knowledges and skills. He continues: [5]

> It is possible, on the other hand, to depart from the traditional categories of human knowledge and skill as the bases for organizing the classroom studies. One possibility is that of human problems or needs, such as selecting and preparing for an occupation, developing one's personal effectiveness, establishing and maintaining good family relationships, and assuming responsibilities.

In what the author is here describing we have an example of confusion about the meanings of curriculum that has its origin in confusion about the meanings of education and the functions of the various agencies of education. The problem comes finally to

[5] *Ibid.*, p. 105.

what kind of whole one considers education to be. If education is, as this book maintains, a potential whole, and if education is an analogical rather than a univocal term, then different agencies of education will have specifically different functions, even though these inevitably overlap to some extent. The classroom, this book has also maintained, is specifically directed to the intellectual; if it aims directly at any other goal it is attempting something for which other educational agencies are better equipped, and it is also leaving undone something for which no other agency is as well equipped. Selecting an occupation is an important procedure, but it seems to involve some sort of guidance program in which many agencies of education cooperate, rather than anything that can or should be organized as a classroom course of studies. Preparing for an occupation may indeed, as the section on vocational education pointed out, be the basis of a classroom program, but as a means of handling a special rather than a general situation. The aim of developing one's personal effectiveness seems so vague and general as to lose all meaning, at least as the basis of a classroom course of studies. Effectiveness for what? And how do you teach it? It is this sort of thing that brings schools into disrepute and supports sometimes well-founded charges of devotion to trivialities. Establishing and maintaining good family relationships is certainly a worthy aim, but surely the family itself is the educational agency that could best achieve this end. Something can be taught in the classroom about the nature of the domestic society and the relationships involved in it; and it is important that students gain such knowledge. Yet actually maintaining good domestic relationships seems to require moral virtues like patience and kindness rather than knowledge, however important it is, of sociological or anthropological or theological conclusions about the family. And moral virtue cannot be taught in the classroom. Finally, coming to assume responsibilities is also an essential part of the education of young people. Again, however, this is a moral matter more than an intellectual one. Parents and others can try to control the environment in such a way that situations will arise in which young people will be required to assume responsibility; but they cannot do more than this.

While classroom teachers were making whatever ineffectual gestures such a curriculum would call for, the proper work of the classroom would go undone because there is no other agency to do it. This is not to say that a classroom curriculum should be so unrealistic as to divorce itself from "human problems or needs." It is to say that few human problems can be resolved without bringing knowledge and clear thought to bear on them; it is also to say that one of the prime human needs is precisely the development of intellectual virtues, of human knowledge and the desire and ability to increase it. The classroom, chiefly through its teacher and its curriculum, is the central agency for the achievement of such an end. If it tries to be all things to all men, it succeeds in being nothing of value to any of them. The problems-of-living or life-adjustment curriculum cheats the students out of what they have a right to expect from their classroom teaching, and puts nothing effective in its place.

It may be worth pointing out that the addition to this type of curriculum of the adjective "Catholic" or "Christian" does not materially alter the situation; it merely changes the emphasis from temporal life to eternal life. No one is objecting to adjustment either to this life or to the next; the objection is to taking up precious classroom time in the process. The work of the classroom is still specifically intellectual rather than religious or social or moral or anything else. If there is such a thing as the natural order, and if knowledge of this natural order is good in itself, as an end and not just a means to a higher end, then the classroom had better devote its strictly limited time to helping its students acquire this knowledge and the ability to get more. Confusion is still confusion, even when sprinkled with holy water.

It was pointed out above [6] that in his encyclical Pope Pius XI used the term education in a much wider meaning than that of

[6] Chapter four, p. 86, note 5.

schooling. Failure to distinguish the various meanings of the word has sometimes led to misinterpretations of the encyclical and to unfortunate conceptions of what Catholic schools are supposed to be doing. For example: [7]

> The place for Catholic children to receive their education is in the Catholic school. There the Christian philosophy of education, based on the Christian philosophy of life, receives its implementation. In his encyclical on the *Christian Education of Youth,* Pius XI tells us that the aim of Christian education is "to co-operate with divine grace in forming Christ in those regenerated in Baptism." Paraphrasing this definition and applying it to our own circumstances here in the United States, we might say that the aim of Christian education is to provide those experiences which, with the assistance of divine grace, are best calculated to develop in the young the ideas, the attitudes, and the habits that are demanded for Christlike living in our American democratic society.

Here, again, the work of the school is seen as that of education for citizenship; the only difference is that now the city of God has been added to the city of man. And the ideal means of achieving this end is the activity or experience curriculum: [8]

> The successful school organizes its curriculum into a series of things to be done and offers a plenitude of opportunity for first-hand experience. The successful school is a place where children live and do, not merely sit and listen. . . . They live, they act, they do; and through living, acting, and doing their characters are formed. Basically, character is something that is resident in the will.

[7] Right Reverend George Johnson, "Education for Life," in Sister Mary Joan, O.P., and Sister Mary Nona, O.P., *Guiding Growth in Christian Social Living* (Washington, D.C.: The Catholic University of America Press, 1946), vol. III, p. 5. Reprinted by permission. Cf. *ibid.,* p. 13.
[8] *Ibid.,* p. 7. Reprinted by permission.

The formation of character, then, is the primary function of the school. It is true that intellectual development is also important, but intellectual development for the exclusively practical end of solving problems concerning courses of action.[9] As with other life-adjustment and experience curriculum programs, there is here a complete lack of any notion of knowledge as speculative, as liberal, as its own end. What really matters is doing and living and acting, for by these means, rather than by sterile speculation, will we and our charges storm the gates of heaven. What has Jerusalem to do with Athens? [10]

The Experience Approach

The fourth category that Krug describes is one that bases the classroom curriculum on the experience, not of the teacher, but of the students. "The organization of the experience curriculum," he says, "is therefore in a continuous process of development in

[9] *Ibid.*
[10] See also The Rev. Gerard S. Sloyan, *The Recognition of Certain Christian Concepts in the Social Studies in Catholic Elementary Education* (Washington, D.C.: The Catholic University of America Press, 1948). The author makes no distinction between education in the sense of a total life process and education in the sense of classroom instruction, with the result that the latter, like the former, is to aim directly at salvation. The question then arises in one's mind whether social studies will be taught at all. See also Sister Mary Janet, S.C., *Catholic Secondary Education: A National Survey* (Washington, D.C.: Department of Education, National Catholic Welfare Conference, 1949). The author sees the proper aim of the school as that of producing Christians rather than scholars (p. 138), and calls for less emphasis on the intellectual and more on the moral virtues (pp. 92 ff., 134). Indeed, it is there argued, Catholic colleges should accept students on the basis of their Christianity rather than their scholarship (pp. 139–140).

251

which the learner participates."[11]   After considerable experience in formal education most students become sufficiently conscious of their intellectual interests and sufficiently definite in their vocational plans to select, say, a college major in mathematics rather than in modern languages or a college of arts and science rather than a college of medicine.   Even these relatively mature students, however, do not set the classroom curriculum of the courses of instruction that they follow; even at the college level a distinction is made between the student body and the faculty.   At lower levels, the necessity for such a distinction is even more apparent. It is, of course, simply a matter of good teaching to begin with what the student now knows and, so far as possible, what he is now interested in.   But the whole point of the teaching process is to guide the student in directions that the teacher, on the basis of his maturity, experience, and professional training, considers he should go.   The experience curriculum, if it means what its proponents say it does, would seem to amount to something like the problems-of-living approach plus a built-in guarantee of perpetual juvenility.   Apart from the physical order, most children are not in a position to know in what direction or by what means they most need to grow; to build a classroom curriculum on their limited experience would be something like extending the kindergarten throughout the school.[12]   This is not democracy; it is chaos.   Even Rousseau, who confused teaching with indoctrination and insisted that Emile learn geometry and physics by what we have been calling controlled discovery,[13] did, after all, himself control the situa-

[11] Krug, *op. cit.*, p. 106.
[12] One basis of the permissive curriculum is the uncritical application to classroom procedures of certain theories of growth; see Ralph W. Lewis, "Growth, in Biology and in Education," in Helmut Schoeck and James E. Wiggins (eds.), *Scientism and Values* (Princeton, N.J.: D. Van Nostrand Company, Inc., 1960), pp. 181–201.
[13] See Jean Jacques Rousseau, *Émile: or Education*, Bar-

tion so that Emile would learn something of these disciplines. And that he should so learn resulted from a decision made by Jean Jacques Rousseau and based on his experience, not from a decision made by Emile and based on his lack of experience. It is Rousseau who gave us the dictum that "The art of teaching consists in making the pupil wish to learn," [14] and who insisted that appealing to children's present interests is the best motivating force.[15] Yet even Rousseau, with all his permissiveness of attitude, did not go as far as the experience curriculum, probably because he wanted Emile to learn something.

THE SCHOOL CURRICULUM

In Chapter four [16] there was some discussion of the role of the school as one educational agency. The position there taken was that the school is a more inclusive agency than the classroom, and hence should take direct means to educate its students on more than the intellectual level. It was also maintained, however, that the school exists, as an institution, for the work of the classroom, and hence that it should not let its other educational efforts interfere with classroom work and with the intellectual development of its students.

Even in the classroom and the laboratory, of course, much more than intellectual education constantly goes on. The impact

---

bara Foxley, trans. (New York: Everyman's Library, E. P. Dutton & Co., Inc., 1911), pp. 110–111, 138–139. Cf. in Chapter seven above, the section on What Is Teaching and What Is Teachable?

[14] Jean Jacques Rousseau, *Emile: or Education,* B. Foxley, trans. (New York: E. P. Dutton & Co., Inc., 1911) (Everyman's Library), p. 250. Reprinted by permission.

[15] *Ibid.,* pp. 81, 140–144.

[16] See the section on The School.

of one personality on another, the way in which the teacher goes about his work and treats the students, and a thousand other experiences of the daily classroom round inevitably have a strong influence on the moral, the social, the emotional, and other related facets of the student's personal development. These results are of such importance that one should be able to take it for granted that the classroom influences in these respects will be beneficial rather than harmful. The teacher, for example, who ridicules students or plays favorites should be taken to task and even, in extreme cases, discharged, no matter how successful a history teacher he may be; the student who has a bad moral effect on other students should also be taken to task or even expelled, no matter how successful a student of physics he may be. Yet, directly and immediately, the job of all concerned with classroom teaching and learning is intellectual, is concerned with arts and sciences and skills. Growth of other kinds occurs in the classroom, but it occurs incidentally and indirectly.

The Place of Extraclass Activities

The school as a whole, on the other hand, aims directly at more than intellectual growth, and hence may employ means of fostering that growth that would be out of place in the classroom and would perhaps interfere with its work. Extraclass activities have, by definition, no place in the classroom; but they have a definite place in the school. The fact remains, however, that the school came into being for intellectual reasons and that it exists ultimately for what goes on in its classrooms; without the school young people can still grow morally and socially and in other ways because of other educational agencies, but without the school they cannot grow very much intellectually. If, then, extraclass activities come to the point of interfering seriously with intellectual pursuits, they must yield the ground, however beneficial they may be in themselves. With these general notions in mind, let us look briefly at some of the activities which may fittingly find a place within the school curriculum.

Krug's summary is that "Extra-class activities include inter-scholastic and intramural athletics, school publications, music programs, plays, student body organization and management, debates and other speech projects, plus a great variety of student clubs." [17] To these should be added, for a Catholic school, various religious practices, such as assistance at Mass and an annual retreat.

The value of these activities to students is surely so widely acknowledged as not to require the support of argument; the record speaks for itself. Through a judicious handling of these means, the school can make a direct and immensely valuable contribution to the student's development in moral, social, physical, and other ways. Each school administration will no doubt have to make its own decisions in the light of its own circumstances about what extraclass activities will find a place in its curriculum and what amount of emphasis will be given them. A few general points, however, can probably be made.

One is that there should be restrictions on the amount of time any student may give to these activities; the social virtues are important, but schools do not exist to turn out a generation of professional joiners. Another general point is that everyone should be given the opportunity to take part in at least some extraclass activity, no matter how poorly he is doing in his classroom studies. For the school is, after all, directly interested in more than the intellectual virtues, and should make at least some part of its wider educational functions available to all its members. In any event, no student is going to spend all his time in study, and he could be doing a lot worse than engaging in some school-sponsored ac-

[17] *Op. cit.*, p. 114. A much more detailed list is that of Harold C. Hand, *Principles of Public Secondary Education* (New York: Harcourt, Brace & World, Inc., 1958), pp. 163–167.

tivity. A third point is that, so far as possible, students should take a part, and often the chief part, in planning the details of the program involved; it is here, rather than in the classroom, that the experience curriculum has a reasonable place. As a corollary, students should also be held responsible for the results of their planning, including the financial results. A fourth point is that the cost of any of these activities to the student should be small enough that no one is excluded for lack of money.[18] Any other arrangement encourages snobbishness and pride in those who have the necessary money, attributes that extraclass activities are definitely not supposed to be promoting. It could also foster a sense of injustice and do serious psychological harm to those who do not have the wherewithal. And in both groups it encourages a false set of values.

In summary, the school curriculum can hope to achieve much more in the development of the whole man than can the narrower classroom curriculum. If it is itself prudently handled, it can do much for the student's acquisition of prudence as well as of other virtues.

QUESTIONS

1. Should method or content, professional preparation or academic education, be stressed in teacher training?
2. Should the curriculum emphasize the past or the problems of the present?
3. Should the same secondary school try to educate all types of student?
4. What extraclass activities should be included in and ex-

[18] For a good discussion of this important point, see Hand, *ibid.*, pp. 183–185.

cluded from the curriculum at any given level? Is there, at present, undue emphasis on these activities?

5. How can we achieve an integrated curriculum, particularly on the secondary level, to avoid the waste of time resulting from overlapping courses and from barriers between subject departments?

6. "If a visitor entered your classroom he shouldn't be able to tell whether you're teaching religion, history, or government." (A supervisor of education). Discuss.

7. In the high school is the forty-minute or the fifty-five-minute period preferable?

8. Should less talented high school students take general mathematics or simple algebra? Should they be put into either of these courses on the basis of previous grades, tests, etc., or should they be allowed to try their hand at regular algebra and geometry courses?

9. Should science projects for school and community competition receive class credit?

10. Are school boards currently requiring more subjects than can be properly taught? Should a classroom curriculum aim primarily at breadth or at depth of instruction?

11. Should freshmen choose electives (*a*) in high school, (*b*) in college?

12. Should the student be tailored to the curriculum or the curriculum to the student?

13. Should the curriculum be modified when two grades are in one classroom?

14. Is there such a thing as a "model" curriculum?

15. Can education be integrated without a special course? If so, how? If not, what should the course be?

16. Should there be departmentalization on the elementary level?

17. Can history and sacred doctrine be woven together in the curriculum to produce students who have an awareness of their Christian heritage? If so, how?

18. "We try to hold a balance between a subject-centered and a child-centered curriculum." What meaning would you attach to this statement? Would you agree or disagree with it as the statement of an objective? If you agree, what suggestions would you make for implementing it?

19. "The purpose of graduate training is to make the student a scientist in his field, supposing that field to be a science." Discuss.

20. How does a teacher meet the needs of all children in a classroom in which the IQ may vary from 75 to 135?

21. Comment on the following teachers' statements concerning school or classroom curriculum on:

   a. The elementary level

   "I think geography and history should be eliminated from grades 1 to 6 and taken up later. The day isn't long enough for all the subjects, and we should concentrate on reading, writing, and arithmetic in the early grades."

   "Music is one of the arts and definitely has a place in the elementary classroom curriculum. But it must be taught properly. Intellectual training and development in music center around the ability to read a musical score. This involves note singing rather than rote singing. The choir taught in this way may not sound as finished in church, but the children will have learned more music."

   "We confine our extraclass activities to one afternoon a week, from 3:00 to 4:30; this is for Brownies, Cub Scouts, choir practice, and altar-boy instruction. An exception is the sport in season; teams practice five days

a week. The teachers remain in their classrooms for an hour and a half each day after school for guidance."
b. The secondary level

"Our vocational subjects are typing, shorthand, book-keeping, general business, homemaking, foods, and clothing. I think these last three should be dropped from the curriculum; they could and should be learned at home. The time could better be devoted to a regular academic subject or a fine-arts course. Some of the girls who go into these courses are very bright; they should be in classes which would challenge their intellectual capacities."

"I would make provision in the students' day for more study time, to be devoted to the 'core' subjects. A schedule set up on hour periods would eliminate some electives (we're overstocked with commercial subjects anyway) and allow part of the period to be devoted to study under the supervision of the class teacher and in the same classroom in which instruction in the subject had been going on. One of the things the students should get from this arrangement is some notion of how to study, and some of them might even do some studying at home."

"In order to satisfy college entrance requirements we teach so many subjects in our academic course that religion has to alternate with physical education, each averaging 2½ periods a week. I am afraid of the implications that the students may read into this arrangement. What do you think we should do?"
c. The undergraduate level

"I would rather give methods of orderly writing than a course in logic. Most students have strange notions about how one thing should follow from another.

They can learn this by reading and by practice in writing. Formal logic is too difficult for freshmen."

"We have given up the notion of an integrated course in social science. We have not succeeded in getting sociologists, political scientists, and economists to come up with anything truly integrated; each teaches only the field he knows."

"To what extent is the teaching of apologetics important for the student? My personal tendency would be to diminish the importance of this teaching because they are Catholic students; they have the Faith; they don't need to be converted. And the questions of apologetics are of such a nature as to raise doubts in the mind."

"Theology is an analysis of revealed truth, not of the personality of Christ or of His emotional appeal or of the warmth of His virtues and His love. I think one could hope to communicate this, but not to teach it directly."

"The student will fruitfully study dogma only when he sees some reason for doing so. This motivation is best supplied by a study of the life of Christ."

"Mathematics should not be regarded chiefly as a tool placed at the disposal of the useful arts, of external aims, even of other sciences."

"Interdepartmental courses tend to be superficial. The student needs the specialized course in order to come to grips with complexity, with an advanced level of thought, as part of a liberal education."

"A physics course in a liberal program should be a course *in* physics and not just a course *about* physics. It should use mathematics and contain laboratory work. The student should be a participant in the enterprise and not just a spectator."

"A competent physicist generally regards research as his most important work, the training of physicists as a secondary job, and the teaching of nonscientists as someone else's responsibility."

"It's all very well to talk about insisting that each student take no more than five courses. But unless such a reduction is to do anything more than give him even more time to waste, the courses must be beefed up, at the cost of a great deal of time and effort on the teacher's part. If the school either doesn't give him a light teaching load or rewards publication rather than teaching, it's talking out of both sides of its mouth at once."

"Some of these jokers who keep insisting that every student must have a course in this or a course in that (and it always turns out to be what they happen to teach) should sit down and try to make out a course of studies under real conditions. According to their requirements, not one school in the country can ever have turned out a properly educated person."

22. "All subjects are, ultimately, related to all others." Explain in what sense, if any, you consider this statement true. What implications would your explanation have for the curriculum at any level?

✳✳✳

chapter nine

Some Contemporary Philosophies of Education

In the Foreword it was stated that this book attempts to present a particular philosophy of education rather than a survey of other doctrines in this field. Yet there is a place in such a book for at least a single chapter devoted to an outline and evaluation of a few fairly recent works in philosophy of education. Its purpose is to introduce the student to the various authors and positions touched on, in the hope that he will be led to read and judge these works for himself. It is definitely not meant to serve as a surrogate for such reading, both because a synopsis is never an adequate substitute and because the critical evaluations which the chapter contains are only one man's view and should themselves be subjected to equally critical evaluation in the light of a reading of the original works. In efforts of this kind there is always some danger of superficiality; the surest way to remove that danger is to read the men themselves.

Within the scope of a single chapter it is impossible to take into account all or even most of the books and positions that might profitably have been given attention. The fundamentally important work of John Dewey, for example, is omitted for two principal reasons: First, several references to his thought have already been made where it seemed to have a direct bearing on some topic discussed in this volume; and, second, an adequate treatment of Dewey's educational philosophy would certainly require at least another book rather than merely part of a chapter. The selection that was made does not pretend to cover the whole of an area in which a great deal of thinking and writing is going on at the present time. The chapter simply considers a few men and works that seem to be attracting considerable notice and probably exercising real influence. Further, it treats those considered on an individual basis rather than as representatives of some particular philosophical outlook such as realism or pragmatism. The latter approach is frequently used and has real merit in that men who philosophize about education, as about anything else, do so from a general philosophical position. But this approach also has a weakness, in that it risks distorting the often highly personal details of a doctrine and blurring its sharpest outlines in the effort to force it into a mold which it does not exactly fit. In any event, this chapter does not attempt to touch on all major philosophical positions, but simply to survey a few prominent works regardless of the position represented. There will, accordingly, be some mention of philosophical points of view as these seem pertinent to the book being considered, but the emphasis is on the individual man and his work rather than on the philosophical label, however convenient the latter may sometimes be.

SMITH: THE IMPROVEMENT OF VALUE
JUDGMENTS

First we shall consider the simple and reasonable though not profoundly philosophical position represented by Philip G. Smith, of the University of Tennessee. The thesis of a little study,[1] prepared for one division of the Co-operative Program in Educational Administration, is that administrators who have some philosophic insight will administer better than those who lack such insight. To support this position, it is necessary to find out, first, what this philosophic insight or philosophic-mindedness amounts to. Then one can conclude why administrators need this outlook and can make suggestions as to how they may cultivate it.

In his introduction, the author begins from the position that there exist two erroneous but widely held views concerning the relation of philosophy to school administration. The first is that philosophy is so abstract as to have nothing whatever to say concerning practical school situations. The second is that philosophy is so definite that it determines inevitably and almost automatically every concrete decision to be made during a school day.[2] The truth, like virtue, lies in the mean. An intelligent administrator will make his own decisions, and not accept them ready-made from

[1] Philip G. Smith, *Philosophic-mindedness in Educational Administration* (Columbus, Ohio: College of Education, The Ohio State University, 1956).

[2] *Ibid.*, p. x. Cf. p. 93. Whether these two views are as widely held as the author maintains they are remains an open question. It is possible that Smith is here simply setting up the straw man of two equally untenable extremes so that his own analysis can correct them and establish the true position. However that may be, his position itself makes excellent sense, though its superficiality raises some doubts about the accuracy of calling it philosophical.

A philosophy of education

any rigidly conceived philosophy (to do so, of course, would be to misconceive entirely the nature of philosophy); on the other hand, an intelligent administrator will make his decisions in the light of some philosophic principles and with some philosophic insight.[3] The burden of the argument to this point seems to be that intelligent administrative practice requires a theory behind it, an unexceptionable but not particularly earth-shaking conclusion.

Perhaps, though, philosophy constitutes a special kind of theory. One of the basic things that can be said about philosophy is that it is concerned with what is fundamental in all areas of thought, and is not itself coterminous with any particular science.[4] On the same subject, passing mention is made of the early Wittgenstein and his conception of philosophy as an activity rather than a theory, as concerned with the clarification of thought rather than the acquisition of knowledge.[5] The author's own position is that the aim of philosophy is the improvement of value judgments; in other words, the developed habit of philosophical inquiry should enable us both to know what is really valuable in particular situations and to make decisions about what to do here and now in order to realize those values. Further, whereas science concerns what *is* (which is here called matters of fact), philosophy concerns what *should be*.[6] Apparently based on a mixture of John Dewey, C. I. Lewis, an earlier position of Herbert Feigl,[7] and a sentence from George Santayana, Smith's conception of philosophy seems to be

[3] *Ibid.*, p. xi.
[4] *Ibid.*, p. 8.
[5] *Ibid.*, p. 10.
[6] *Ibid.*, pp. 11–13.
[7] *Ibid.*, pp. 13–24. For Feigl's later position on the meaning criterion, see his "Philosophical Embarrassments of Psychology," *The American Psychologist,* 14, 3 (March, 1959), 115–128; and his "The Philosophy of Science of Logical Empiricism," *Minnesota Studies in the Philosophy of Science,* 1 (1956), 3–37.

reducible to that of an exclusively practical as opposed to speculative discipline, something like a combination of ethics and prudence. Whether this rather simple notion is really that which is implied in Lewis's value theory,[8] for example, is questionable; what seems beyond question, at least in this writer's mind, is that Smith's position amounts to nothing more profound.

The most useful part of this book for the author's announced purpose is the third chapter, in which he brings his conception of philosophic-mindedness down to the level of problems faced specifically by administrators. Organizing his comments around the headings of comprehensiveness, penetration, and flexibility, Smith presents a series of well-formulated and well-explained characteristics that the thought of an intelligent administrator should exhibit. With a wealth of pertinent illustration he supplies much sound advice on particular attitudes and traits that should mark the thinking of a successful administrator.[9] This advice, however, remains on the level of common sense, and could be expected of any intelligent, balanced, and experienced observer. The latter part of the book, based on various surveys and studies, may be of real value to those whom it is intended to serve. The earlier part, at least in its adventitious and somewhat pretentious references to philosophical theories, remains much ado about very little.

Some years after the appearance of this little work, Smith collaborated with H. Gordon Hullfish, his former teacher at The Ohio State University, on a similar book, but one more far-reaching in both breadth and depth.[10] What was earlier called philosophic-

[8] See Clarence Irving Lewis, *An Analysis of Knowledge and Valuation* (La Salle, Ill.: The Open Court Publishing Company, 1946).
[9] *Ibid.*, pp. 28–52.
[10] H. Gordon Hullfish and Philip G. Smith, *Reflective Thinking: The Method of Education* (New York: Dodd, Mead & Company, Inc., 1961).

mindedness is now called reflective thinking, and, as their title suggests, the authors take the position that the primary task of the classroom teacher is to help the student develop the habit of critical reflective thinking. As with Smith's earlier book, there is a good deal of dependence, in the theoretical sections, on the value theory of C. I. Lewis, as well as incursions into logic and psychology, especially learning theory. There is also what purports to be an application of this theoretical matter to classroom instruction, though there occurs the same difficulty of recognizing the relationship between the speculative and the practical parts of this book, between theory and application. However, the material contained in the latter (part IV) is made up of such excellent comments on and illustrations of the art of teaching that one would do well to concentrate appreciatively on it rather than on the failure to connect it with the preceding theoretical material. Further, the final chapter makes a genuine contribution to the perennial problem of education for democracy. Though frequently not on a philosophical level, this whole section represents a mine of helpful advice for the classroom teacher and for the administrator, and could have come only from the fruitful combination of years of teaching experience and the habit of reflective thinking upon that experience. The authors have well exemplified their own theme.

SCHEFFLER: LINGUISTIC ANALYSIS

Israel Scheffler, of Harvard University, may be taken as representative of the position known as linguistic analysis or analytical philosophy. His interest in this school was earlier demonstrated by his editing of an anthology [11] featuring such names as Steven-

[11] Israel Scheffler (ed.), *Philosophy and Education: Modern Readings* (Englewood Cliffs, N.J.: Allyn and Bacon, Inc., 1958).

son, Hare, and Ryle; and the title of a later work [12] indicates a continuing interest in linguistic analysis as an approach to educational problems.

Flourishing especially in the English universities, linguistic analysis derives in part from the logical positivism of the Vienna Circle through Wittgenstein and Ayer (though analysts usually repudiate positivism vigorously), and in part from the critical and analytical work of Moore and Austin. For logical positivists, statements in what have traditionally been called metaphysics and ethics must be discarded as meaningless, as having nothing to do with truth or falsity, because such statements fall outside experience and hence cannot be verified one way or the other. Taking less extreme attitudes, linguistic analysts do not rule traditional normative ethics out of existence, though they substantially qualify its meaning. Their own interest, however, is with another conception of ethics which the traditionalist might see as a metaethics [13] or a logic of ethics or an analysis of the problems of ethical discourse. Thus considered, ethics does not arise from observation of what men do nor issue in conclusions about what they should do. Rather, it arises from the critical consideration of the language that men use when they attempt to express some intellectual justification of those actions which they consider morally right.

The function of philosophy, accordingly, is that of analyzing and thus clarifying the language in which men express their thoughts so that they may realize as accurately as possible the meaning (or lack of meaning) of what they are saying, and thus be

[12] Israel Scheffler, *The Language of Education* (Springfield, Ill.: Charles C Thomas, Publisher, 1960). Courtesy of the publisher and of the author.

[13] See Vernon J. Bourke, "Metaethics and Thomism," in Charles J. O'Neil (ed.), *An Etienne Gilson Tribute* (Milwaukee: The Marquette University Press, 1959), pp. 20–32.

enabled to carry on more intelligible and hence more fruitful discussion. In Aristotelian language, philosophy is reduced to a combination of epistemology and logic, with the emphasis on the latter taken in the sense of an organon. What the linguistic analyst calls philosophy the Aristotelian would see as an introduction to philosophy.

Scheffler calls his own book an essay in the philosophy of education, which he clearly differentiates from a history of philosophies of education. The aim is to apply what the author characterizes as philosophical methods to basic educational concepts. These methods turn out to be those of the linguistic analyst, and aim at the clarification of certain ideas and forms of discourse that recur in educational literature, so that, through these examples of the critical evaluation of such discourse, the reader may be the better able to analyze similar statements when he meets them himself. There is particular emphasis on relating statements to their context and on disentangling practical considerations and issues from their often confusing associations.[14] In a word, one might sum up, the point of philosophy of education is to instruct the reader in how to clarify statements occurring in educational literature and to avoid the mental confusions often present in it.

In his eagerness to justify this new conception of philosophy, the author is unfortunately led to do something less than justice to more traditional conceptions of philosophic activity. As he sees it, in the face of this notion of philosophy as the analysis of basic concepts for their clarity and arguments for their validity, "philosophers could no longer interpret their task as the deductive proof of factual theorems on the basis of self-evident axioms disclosed in intuition," nor could they any longer indulge themselves "in painting suggestive but vague portraits of the universe."[15] If Scheffler

[14] Scheffler, *The Language of Education*, *op. cit.*, pp. vii, 3, 4.
[15] *Ibid.*, p. 7.

honestly regards this as an accurate characterization of philosophical activity since Socrates (who is here, by the way, accorded the distinction—dubious in two senses—of being a forerunner of linguistic analysis), then one can but recommend further study. If he is deliberately setting up a straw man for rhetorical purposes, then he should revert to his own principles and subject these statements and ideas to the critical review which they badly require. Even the analysts, it seems, need analysis.

One may quarrel with the author's conviction that this work of the analysis of concepts and statements in the field of education constitutes a philosophy of education. But one can have very little quarrel with the manner in which the task is carried out, even if he sees it as constituting a kind of introductory logic rather than a philosophy properly speaking. For the author does, and does with admirable clarity and acuteness of thought and expression, what he says he is going to do. He critically examines definitions, dividing them into various types, and argues, for example, that what purports to be a descriptive definition of "curriculum" actually contains a hidden practical element and announces a program.[16] In the following chapter he applies the same careful analysis to such educational slogans as, "We teach children, not subjects," to the end that we may avoid interpreting such slogans literally and making them operational doctrines.[17]

Next there comes a similar critical examination of the educational metaphors of growth, molding, and sculpture as applied to the teaching-learning process, and an application of the conclusions reached to similar figures of speech that present themselves in educational literature.[18] The last two chapters are given over to an analysis of the notion of teaching, though the discussion is somewhat restricted by the author's eliminating, for the sake of sim-

[16] *Ibid.*, pp. 11–27, espec. 23–27.
[17] *Ibid.*, pp. 36–46.
[18] *Ibid.*, pp. 48–58.

plicity, any relation to success in that endeavor and confining the idea of teaching to that of making the effort to do so.[19]   Scheffler sees teaching as an art on the model of medicine or engineering or cooking, and insists that clarity about the meanings of teaching is necessary for anyone arranging a curriculum.   The book concludes with a summary and an indication of some further educational problems to which the method of analysis pursued and exemplified in this book could and should be applied.

If one looks at this work and the position that it represents as a sort of logic of education rather than a philosophy of education, as a clearing of the ground by the clarification of language and thought, then one can but applaud both the conception and its execution.   The astute observations in which the book abounds accomplish two things: First, they point out some confusions of thought and language in the field of education, and explain why they are confusions; second, through careful, step-by-step analysis and criticism of current examples of such confusions, they provide the reader with models of procedure for his own critical examination of professional literature.   Even though every careful reader has always done this in his own way, this is the only book that I know which tackles the task systematically.

On at least one further point, however, it is necessary to take issue with the author: that is, in his denial that a definition of man provides the basis for educational practice.   "The conclusion often drawn in educational theory," he states, "is that we must first decide what the correct definition of 'man' is, and that then practical educational consequences will only need to be inferred by us through the application of pure logic." [20]

<hr>

[19] *Ibid.,* pp. 60–61.   This amounts to what the author earlier (pp. 13–15) characterized as a stipulative definition. For a related analysis of teaching, see B. Othanel Smith, "A Concept of Teaching," *Teachers College Record,* 61, 5 (February, 1960), 229–241.
[20] *Ibid.,* p. 33.   Reprinted by permission.

The Question of Human Nature

The first criticism that Scheffler offers of this position is that of "postulating a simple deductive implication between definitions of human nature and practical educational consequences." [21] But this is simply another straw man; no competent philosopher of education has made any such claim, and even the incompetent ones that I can think of do not make this crass error. The book that you are now reading, for example, is built upon the theory that educational policy and practice must, in the nature of the case, take into account some notion, whether explicit or implicit, of the nature of man; but the remainder of the book is far from a simple logical deduction from that notion. What Scheffler seems to have in mind is something like the method of Spinoza's *Ethics;* but this is not a method used, to the best of my knowledge, by any philosopher of education.

The second criticism that Scheffler offers of this position is that there are many equally accurate definitions of man, and that to choose any one of them and then "to proceed to read off curricular counterparts to each dimension, as is often done, is to beg the whole question." [22] Apart from the inaccuracy of "as is often done," one may question the statement that various alternative definitions of man are "all equally accurate." If by various definitions the author means, for example, a historical definition, an anatomical definition, an economic definition, then, of course, each may be equally accurate because it is looking at the object defined from a different point of view and for a different purpose, and is expressing a partial truth about man by describing some aspect of his being. But each of these is not equally accurate in the sense of being equally pertinent to the purpose of the definition, a purpose which, in this instance, is that of deciding how this man who is being defined

[21] *Ibid.* Reprinted by permission.
[22] *Ibid.,* pp. 33–34. Reprinted by permission.

should be educated, in the broadest meaning of that term. In this context the appropriate definition is the one that says most completely what man is, since the problem is how to educate the man and not just one aspect of his being. The appropriate definition, then, is a philosophical and, ultimately, a theological one (though one may, in a work in philosophy of education, restrict himself to the former). In this sense, the definitions are not equally accurate.

Further, it is possible that the statement under discussion might be taken to mean that all philosophical definitions of man are equally true (or equally false). But unless he sees words as the ultimate reality, one does not start with a definition, not even one based on prior usage of the term being defined. One starts by observing men, by analyzing carefully what they do, and by making inferences from these observations to the nature of the being that is doing these things. This is, in oversimplified terms, what the philosophical psychologist attempts to do, and it is what a full chapter in this book was devoted to doing. One does not, then, wind up with a definition of man based on prior linguistic usage; rather, he winds up with a descriptive statement, inductively arrived at, on which a reasonable educational program may be built, though not by pure deduction. And it is going to make a great deal of difference to the educational program concerned whether the conclusion is that man is a rational and responsible animal, different in kind from other animals, or whether the conclusion is that man is simply another biological entity determined by his environment. Other possibilities exist, but these two will serve as examples. Scheffler sees the choice of a definition of man (as though it were something to be picked out of the air almost at random rather than arrived at through painstaking examination of evidence) as, in part, depending on "the very consequences for educational practice to be expected of such a definition."[23] This

[23] *Ibid.,* p. 34. Reprinted by permission.

evaluation of consequences, however, will itself be possible only in the light of a previous notion of the nature of the man affected, whether that notion is explicit or only implicit.

The author has indeed made a powerful case for the importance of critically analyzing ideas and arguments. Those contained in his own book, as he himself insists, are no exception.

PHENIX AND OTHER PHILOSOPHICAL SURVEYS

Frederick C. Gruber, of The University of Pennsylvania, presents a comparative and historical survey of various philosophical positions as these relate to the educational enterprise; his purpose is to provide the student with a foundation on which to build his own philosophy of education.[24] Apart from perhaps inevitable oversimplifications and a few inaccuracies in reporting the doctrines of others,[25] the author provides useful material for his announced purpose. His own preference for relativism appears in the last twenty pages of the book, and for pragmatism in Appendix B, entitled "Modern Philosophies and Education"; in this appendix, the book's customary objectivity noticeably breaks down.

Writing from a position that seems to be much the same as that revealed by Gruber, V. T. Thayer [26] takes a largely historical —and well-documented—approach to the many educational problems that he discusses. Though he does not formally and explicitly spell out a position that could be called philosophical, he consistently approaches problems from a naturalistic point of view.

[24] Frederick C. Gruber, *Foundations for a Philosophy of Education* (New York: Thomas Y. Crowell Company, 1961), p. vii.

[25] For example, that of St. Thomas on teaching (p. 66) and on freedom (p. 259).

[26] *The Role of the School in American Society* (New York: Dodd, Mead & Company, Inc., 1960).

A Number of Possible Positions

Philip H. Phenix, of Teachers College, Columbia University, is another who sees the function of the philosopher of education as that of raising questions rather than answering them, of explaining a number of possible positions instead of only one, in order that the student may be led to examine the grounds on which each position rests rather than accept any one of them uncritically.[27] In general, the author succeeds in presenting various possible positions clearly and, for a work in one volume, adequately. On most issues he does not pretend to be neutral, but does make a real and largely successful effort to present other views as possibilities, though with disconcerting frequency his own position turns out to be the reasonable mean between what are presented as extremes.

One of the features of this book for which many readers will be grateful is that it recognizes the immense diversity of philosophical thinking and spares them the rigid and largely artificial organization of positions under such labels as idealism, essentialism, and the other familiar ones. One of the features for which many readers will not be grateful is the author's avoidance of documentation on the theory that the weight of someone's authority might get in the way of an objective appraisal of the arguments them-

[27] Philip H. Phenix, *Philosophy of Education* (New York: Henry Holt and Company, Inc., 1958), pp. v, 178. Here again is the fallacy of the false dichotomy, for these are not the only real choices. It is also possible to outline a philosophy of education in a doctrinal rather than a historical or comparative way, while yet presenting reasons for the conclusions reached. In such a presentation one does not at all ask the student to accept unthinkingly the position outlined, but rather to examine critically the reasons given as part of the doctrine expounded. The comparative approach to philosophy of education has its advantages, but it is not the only alternative to indoctrination.

selves.[28]   But there is more than one passage in this book in which
one may legitimately wonder just what doctrine the author is sum-
marizing; whether it was ever, in fact, found in just the form that
it is here given; and whether, in consequence, the reader is being
asked to evaluate a genuine position or one that has been inadver-
tently misrepresented.   Footnotes are more than window dressing;
in a book of this sort, which expressly presents alternative views
for consideration, they would constitute the reader's guarantee that
he was being asked to judge among real positions.   No author,
however honest and however competent, should deny his readers
a chance to check the sources and to study the doctrines involved
at first hand; and for this purpose, a bibliography is not an adequate substitute.

Perhaps the most prominent example of a weakness induced
by this lack of documentation occurs in the author's consideration
of positions on what he calls the uniqueness of man and the resulting difficulties in accounting for the apparent interaction of mind
and body.[29]   Any reader with some experience of philosophical
literature will recognize the problem, but he will not necessarily
recognize the various interpretations and solutions of the problem
that are here given.   In ostensibly describing the doctrine which
holds that man is different in kind and not only in degree from
the rest of the natural order, Phenix is led to exaggerate the degree
of discontinuity between them that is proper to this doctrine in its
classical Aristotelian form.   His presentation and criticism of a
dualistic position would come closer to accuracy if applied to those
in the Platonic tradition; but it either ignores or mistakes the doctrine of those in the Aristotelian tradition, who see man as specifically distinct from the brute yet in many respects continuous with
the natural order.   Further, this position does not rest, as it is here
suggested that it does, on the "ethical and religious insights of

[28] *Ibid.*, p. vii.
[29] *Ibid.*, pp. 462–470.

mankind," but on careful analysis of evidence and on inference from that evidence. Nor may the position reasonably "lead to the acceptance of unanalyzed concepts about it." [30] What is really unanalyzed is the position itself that is being criticized on such a distorted basis, and it is left unanalyzed by the author. Documentation would at least have allowed the reader to find out what sources were being used and thus to do his own analyzing; it might also have enabled him to add to those sources so as to gain a more adequate picture of the possible positions on this basic problem.

The author's ignorance or misunderstanding of some of the solutions that have, historically, been advanced in connection with this problem lead him to regard it as, in its historical form, insoluble. He then advances his own solution, which turns out to be a form of monism that explains the problem by explaining it away. But to adopt a metaphysical position on a question concerning one phase of the ultimate nature of reality in order to avoid facing a difficulty which one gives up as insoluble on the basis of an ignorance or misunderstanding of historically existing positions, is to do less than justice to readers to whom one supplies no adequate alternative source of information.

The same weakness is evident in the explanation of a theory of human development which the author calls that of divine creation.[31] This position, as here described, corresponds to nothing within the range of literature known to this writer. Proper documentation would allow one to examine the sources and thus to discover for himself where interpretation ends and interpolation begins. The same may be said for the assessment of religion as believers conceive it, an assessment which presents religion as a form of totalitarianism which should logically issue, in the political order, in a form of theocracy.[32] "Thus," we are told, "there can be

[30] *Ibid.*, p. 463. Reprinted by permission.
[31] *Ibid.*, pp. 504–505.
[32] *Ibid.*, pp. 79–84.

no matters of public policy which are outside of and irrelevant to the system of actual religious faith," including "the procedures by which the society is to be governed." [33] Unless its apparent meaning can be explained away, this is a serious and a dangerous misconception of any religious doctrine with which this writer is familiar, and, in view especially of the current debate concerning the position of religiously oriented schools in this country, an irresponsible one. To a believer, this statement is not an explanation but an accusation; he might reasonably ask that it be substantiated.

It would, however, be unjust as well as ungenerous to overlook the general balance, the fairness, and the depth of learning that characterize the book as a whole. On the functions proper to the school (p. 38), on the curriculum (chap. 4), on the secular school (p. 86), on education as a profession (chap. 9), and in his respect for speculative as well as for practical knowledge (pp. 9, 18–19, 405), the author displays what to this writer appears a sane, sound, and balanced outlook. And his chapters on education and the fields of knowledge (part III) constitute a series of essays on the classical subject matters of the classroom curriculum that, though inevitably open to dispute on some points, constitute as a whole a learned and illuminating discussion that will prove genuinely helpful to any student of education.

A Moral Philosophy of the Curriculum

In a later work [34] Phenix deals with the notions of education and curriculum in the broadest meaning of these terms, as well as their application to that particular form of education which is schooling. In effect, he essays the ambitious project of saying what those agencies of education which are the home and the

[33] *Ibid.*, p. 84. Reprinted by permission.
[34] Philip H. Phenix, *Education and the Common Good: A Moral Philosophy of the Curriculum* (New York: Harper & Row, Publishers, 1961).

school should teach and why they should teach it; and he does an impressive job. His position, in brief, is that children should be so taught that they may successfully meet the challenge posed by the problems of contemporary society. And since problems exist as problems only because people hold certain values, education must concern itself with values, and must lead to correct choice and action. It is in this sense that education is a moral enterprise aiming ultimately at the improvement of conduct.[35]

The next question concerns the standard by which values may be distinguished and judged. In general it is that values arising from the selfish interests or desires of the individual are bad and those arising from something having objective worth are good. Apparently thinking of the eighteenth-century misconception of natural law and mistaking it for an Aristotelian conception of moral science, Phenix denies the existence of any abstract moral laws and maintains that all value judgments are made in particular circumstances. In Aristotelian language, one could say that he admits only prudence, with no possibility of a moral philosophy behind it. The fact remains that the whole book is an effort to reach value judgments which have some degree of universality, to say what the home and the school considered abstractly and generally should teach children, precisely so that those who must carry out the work of teaching may make better choices of procedure in the particular circumstances in which they find themselves. *Education and the Common Good* is a book in moral philosophy and particularly in social ethics in the Aristotelian and Thomistic understanding of those expressions. It is unfortunate that a misunderstanding should lead to insistence that all value judgments are particular, though the author also insists that this does not mean that value judgments are thereby entirely relative. For some degree of generalization is possible, he thinks, and the very existence of the moral enterprise, the concern of men to learn

[35] *Ibid.,* pp. 3–5.

what it is right to do and then to do it, testifies to the existence of at least a potential universality of judgments about values.[36]

Education, then, aims at changing persons so that they will effectively choose and do what is good rather than selfishly pursue their individual desires.[37] Here is a clear echo from the *Nicomachean Ethics:* the ideal of the virtuous man who lives the good life because he is a good man, a man devoted to the pursuit of objective goodness rather than the fulfillment of his own desires, a realist rather than a sophist. Such a man belongs to and helps to build what the author calls a democracy of worth as opposed to a democracy of desire.

The remainder of the book makes explicit this purpose by concentrating on the four basic values which the author designates as intelligence, creativity, conscience, and reverence. It is under the heading of these values that he considers the various contemporary problems to which the values are to be applied: Under intelligence come intellectual excellence and the mass media of communication; under creativity are considered aesthetic excellence, manners, work, and recreation; under conscience are included the uses of nature, health, sex and family life, social class, race, economic life, political organization, and world responsibility; finally, the value of reverence is applied to religion.

In general, it can be said that each chapter presents a thoughtful and relatively thorough analysis of its topic. Even though there are fundamental points on which he is open to strong dissent, the same sanity and balance that characterized Phenix's earlier book are here evident again. Here, too, is the same combination of penetrating insight and incisive expression. And here, above all, is an eloquent plea for moral education that reveals its author's lofty motives and sincere devotion to that common good of which he effectively writes.

[36] *Ibid.*, pp. 5–6. Cf. pp. 27–28.
[37] *Ibid.*, pp. 6–7, 10.

BROUDY: A FORM OF CLASSICAL REALISM

Harry S. Broudy, of The University of Illinois, considers that his function is more than that of presenting the student with a variety of philosophical positions, both because the beginning student is not yet in a position to judge intelligently among these positions and because the positions themselves are not equally defensible. Accordingly, Broudy offers, for the student's consideration, his own philosophy of education, which he calls a form of classical realism. It is a realism, he explains, because it acknowledges the existence of an objective truth independent of the knowing subject and the existence of a structured universe within which it is man's function, partially through education, to strive for the good life; it is classical, he adds, because its fundamental notions concerning the nature and goals of men are derived from the doctrines of Plato and Aristotle.[38]

Broudy sees philosophy of education as the ultimate level on which educational problems may be considered, one not reached by dialogue of a nonphilosophical kind. The lowest plane on which educational discussion occurs he calls the emotional or uncritical, and offers as an example people voting against a proposed school innovation out of a sense of insecurity, even though they may rationalize their emotional attitude as the outcome of logical thought. A second stage is called the factual or informational, for example, the relative economic costs of each of two proposed programs; disagreements of this kind can be settled by getting the facts. A third is the explanatory or theoretical or scientific level, on which, for example, one school program may be preferred over another on the basis of a psychological theory of learning. The

[38] Harry S. Broudy, *Building a Philosophy of Education,* 2d. ed. (Englewood Cliffs, N.J.: Prentice-Hall, Inc., 1961), pp. vii–viii.

final point is reached when the discussion turns on such questions as the nature of reality, of truth, of value. Is there, for example, any changeless being underlying the observable flux, or is there only process and becoming? Are there, then, any eternal verities, any objective good and beauty, or do all these depend on and change with the individual and his circumstances? In educational terms, should the church, for example, or the state or the family have final responsibility for the educational program? The level on which this problem can be discussed goes beyond factual information or even scientific theory to an ultimate conception of reality, to the nature and the relations of various societies, and to the goods or values or goals which are proper to each of those societies. This is not the same kind of question as one concerning the best age at which to introduce instruction in reading. Philosophical problems are of a special kind, and problems of this nature arising in the field of education constitute the material of a philosophy of education.[39]

Among other questions, that of the aims of education may be considered on each of the levels outlined above. On the philosophical level, the aim of education could be said to be the living of the good life. The good life, the happy life, the virtuous life —as Aristotle has explained it—will consist in the cultivation of human capacities to their fullest reach by processes which Broudy calls self-determination, self-realization, and self-integration. This aim for education makes sense, he continues, only if we see human nature as being everywhere the same, and the good life as being accordingly something objective, to some extent independent of the vagaries of individuals and their personal and cultural circumstances.[40]

An analysis of the human personality yields evidence that there is such an objective reality as human nature, characterized

[39] *Ibid.*, pp. 15–19.
[40] *Ibid.*, pp. 37–39.

especially by the ability to rise above conditioning to the choice, within limits, of the pattern of one's own life. The roots of this freedom lie in the power of symbolization (what we have been calling the power of abstract thought), which raises man above the level of the purely biological and the determined into the area of self-determination, self-realization, and self-integration.[41]

To find out how the school can contribute to the student's capacity for the good life, one must first distinguish the school clearly from other educational agencies. Thus the school is not the government, nor the family, nor the church. Each of these has its proper educational functions and a legitimate interest in the educational enterprise. Yet the school retains an autonomy because its primary task, that of the development in its students of intellectual habits, is a task peculiar (not exclusive) to itself. Anything that the school can contribute toward the good life beyond helping its students develop their intellectual capacities, their power of symbolization, is in the nature of a fringe benefit; but no matter how many fringe benefits it supplies, failure to perform its primary task will leave it, as a school, without any justification for existence.[42]

In part II Broudy outlines the values—for example, the economic, the aesthetic, the moral, and the religious—that may be expected to flow from an educational enterprise fashioned and operated according to the philosophy of education which the author has outlined.

How shall the school bring about these results? By arranging its curriculum (Broudy seems here to be confining himself to what we have called above the classroom rather than the wider school curriculum) so that the student may best develop the desired intellectual habits and skills. The author rejects the traditional subject-centered curriculum on the grounds that it does not supply

[41] *Ibid.*, pp. 42–72.
[42] *Ibid.*, pp. 100–103.

sufficient motivation to learn, does not even lead to the retaining of information, does not develop the ability to think, is not well integrated, and omits current social problems. He also rejects the problem-centered curriculum on the grounds that the problems which are real for immature students usually do not require formal knowledge and any particularly scientific method in order to be solved by the students themselves on a level that will be satisfying to them.

In place of these, Broudy suggests a form of general education which aims at developing in the student the habits and skills of acquiring knowledge, of solving problems, and of using knowledge imaginatively. This goal will require four general kinds of educational activity: the systematic study of organized subject matter, especially the symbolic (abstract) disciplines of reading and mathematics; problems courses aiming at enabling the student to understand, to deliberate about, and to judge problems more effectively; and opportunities for aesthetic creativity, which, along with the natural joy of knowing and being able to think, will contribute to the enjoyment of knowledge.[43] The curriculum that is intended to help bring about these results is presented as a rather drastic revision of the elementary and secondary course of studies organized according to six major categories. Since the aim is general rather than specialized education, work in any area of study should not attempt to cover anything like all the material available, but should concentrate on the basic concepts, facts, principles, and methods of investigation proper to each.[44]

Broudy then devotes a chapter to showing how teaching methods are rooted in educational psychology, and another to the consideration of some of the advantages and disadvantages of various ways of organizing an educational system.

Very little in the way of comment seems called for here. The

[43] *Ibid.*, pp. 283–310.
[44] *Ibid.*, pp. 311–332.

author's conception of the nature of philosophy of education and of the steps required in developing one parallel closely what is found in the early part of this book. His analysis of the nature of man and, consequently, of the kind of education proper to him, are in general and often in particular agreement with positions taken in this book. One possible point of criticism concerns his rejecting the traditional subject-centered curriculum on the ground that it does not develop the student's ability to think. In view of his own later insistence on organized subject matter, it would appear that his objection to what he conceives as the traditional curriculum springs from its failure to include the problems courses that he recommends as helping the student learn to use his knowledge. But surely even subject-matter courses can be taught, where the subject itself calls for it, in such a way as to include consideration of the problems involved. Indeed, how else could they possibly be taught intelligently? It would appear that the author's basic objection is not really to a theory of curriculum but to bad teaching. Apart from this tentative criticism, however, Broudy's position is sound, at least if the arguments given in the earlier part of this book are themselves sound. And the point is not just that the name of Aristotle is mentioned early in both books; it is that a basically Aristotelian interpretation of reality stands up under careful scrutiny better than any other.

Though there is a certain amount of literature on the relations between existentialism and education, the varieties of doctrine usually included under the existentialist caption would render difficult the reaching of any generally applicable conclusions. Since those philosophers who are accounted existentialists have little or nothing to say about education in the sense of schooling, one must turn to some of their interpreters for suggestions along these lines. These tentative interpretations are often intelligently made and intrinsically valuable; yet, as their authors usually point out, they can amount to no more than inference and implication. For this reason, we shall simply refer to two of those interpreters [45] and turn to another man and another doctrine.

ULICH: COSMIC REVERENCE

Making wide use of his earlier work, Robert Ulich, lately retired from Harvard University, has presented the definitive expression of his philosophy of education in a single volume.[46] It is not easy to place his position in any definite category, especially since that position is marked by highly personal insights and convictions. One notices a definite reluctance to adopt what the author would regard as extreme positions, a reluctance based on more than mere compromise. It might be reasonably accurate to characterize Ulich's philosophical outlook as a form of humanism [47] —certainly not a Christian humanism, but not a crudely anti-Christian one either. Throughout the book there is an air of humaneness, of civility, of urbanity, that should guarantee its author's position a sympathetic hearing.

The Hegelian strain in Ulich's outlook shows itself in a general tendency to synthesize apparently antithetical positions or approaches. Thus religion and humanism, he thinks, could ideally be united, since both have the same goal of leading men beyond a

[45] See, for example, George F. Kneller, *Existentialism and Education* (New York: Philosophical Library, Inc., 1958), espec. pp. viii, 41, 122; Ralph Harper, "Significance of Existence and Recognition for Education," in Nelson B. Henry (ed.), *Modern Philosophies and Education,* part I, 54th Yearbook of the N.S.S.E. (Chicago: The University of Chicago Press, 1955), pp. 215–258.

[46] Robert Ulich, *Philosophy of Education* (New York: American Book Company, 1961).

[47] In another volume, Ulich wrote from the point of view of an existentialist. See his "Comments on Ralph Harper's Essay," *Modern Philosophies and Education,* pp. 215 ff.

merely biological existence to ever higher and transcendent notions of themselves and the lives proper to them. Indeed, they lend themselves to union, for the religious concern with infinity necessarily involves consideration of finite humanity, and humanistic concern with humanity must take into account men's relation with the infinite. The value of such a higher synthesis for education would be that it could do justice to different philosophical and religious positions without identifying itself with any one of them.[48]

The weakness of this last statement lies in the fact that the adherents of the various positions in question could hardly be expected to see this higher world view, this cosmic synthesis, as really doing justice to a position that it is synthesizing out of existence. A pagan humanist, for example, might have difficulty in seeing the need for any reference to an order of transcendence and infinity; and a believer might also have difficulty in discovering any constructive approach to religion in a position that looks upon religion as a species of myth. And these difficulties need not be a result of prejudice, as one of Ulich's oversimplifying phrases suggests.[49] They could be a result of conviction, reached honestly and carefully, and reached after, not before, an examination of evidence. Not all judgment which happens to be contrary to one's own is prejudgment.

Ulich presents this vaguely pantheistic form of monism under the title "cosmic reverence," and claims Albert Schweitzer as its modern apostle. Its relevance to the educational process is that it would supply the public school with the universal and unifying notion on the basis of which its students could be united without any disturbance of their various religious beliefs.[50] It is not a

[48] *Ibid.,* p. 114.
[49] *Ibid.*
[50] *Ibid.,* pp. 121, 125–127.

question, he claims, of the exclusive alternatives of religion or secularism, but rather of the personal and social integration that come from the development of the natural virtues of justice and devotion and love and reverence for life.[51]

Once more, one may question Ulich's claim that continued adherence to a religious or to a secularistic position is necessarily the result of intolerance and dogmatism. Yet one can have nothing but sympathy and admiration for his vision of human beings, becoming through a better education ever more conscious of the heights as well as the depths implied in that humanity, cooperating on the natural level for the achieving of common goals which they share precisely because of their common humanity. Maritain has seen that such cooperation on the practical level is possible among men of good will in spite of irreconcilable differences, largely theological and philosophical in nature, on the theoretical level.[52] Ulich's failure to see this point, the practical importance of which simply cannot be exaggerated, leads to his insistence on transcendence, on cosmic reverence, as the higher synthesis in which both religion and secularism, as partial views of the whole of reality, will realize themselves by losing themselves. In spite of its author's evident devotion to the democratic ideal, it is monism of this sort that is the most dangerous enemy of democracy, for it insists that men must overcome all differences before they can successfully cooperate in the pursuit of common political and other goals. Though Ulich would no doubt repudiate any such imputation, his plan for the direction that schooling should ideally

[51] *Ibid.*, pp. 171–173.
[52] See Joseph W. Evans and Leo R. Ward (eds.), *The Social and Political Philosophy of Jacques Maritain* (New York: Charles Scribner's Sons, 1955), pp. 116–144, espec. pp. 123–136: "The Possibilities for Cooperation in a Divided World."

take is in many ways similar to the reconstructionism of Brameld, and contains many of the same implicit dangers to the kind of society that he himself prizes so highly.

Weak as Ulich may be on the theoretical side, his suggestions for the practical implementation of his philosophy of education are well worth study and reflection. The difficulty is to see these suggestions as flowing from *his* philosophy of education, though they do everywhere evince his distaste for extreme positions and his sense of balance and harmony. Like the similar remarks of Smith and Hullfish, they are the mature and thoughtful reflections that one might reasonably expect from any teacher of intelligence and experience, but which one seldom finds expressed so clearly and forcefully. There are, for example, pointed and practical observations on popularizing (p. 160), on the dropping of the classics from the program of studies (p. 179), on the importance of the practical in a human education (p. 186), on the place of art in that same education (pp. 188–196), on methods of teaching (pp. 198–224), on the curriculum or program of studies (pp. 225–228), and on the education of teachers (pp. 230–240).

One may have doubts about the value of Ulich's theoretical statement of his philosophy of education; one can have nothing but respect for his intentions and for his sane and sound suggestions for improvement in the day-to-day work of the schools.[53]

MORRIS: EXPERIMENTALISM AND PROGRESSIVISM

Another contributor to contemporary literature in philosophy of education is Van Cleve Morris, of Rutgers University, who

[53] A similar statement might be made concerning the admirably balanced comments contained in a work which claims Whitehead as the inspiration of its theoretical position. See Frank C. Wegener, *The Organic Philosophy of Education* (Dubuque, Iowa: Wm. C. Brown Co., 1957).

maintains a position which he calls experimentalism in philosophy and progressivism in educational policy. Experimentalism he takes as closely allied to pragmatism or instrumentalism. Insisting that practice depends on a previous theory, that policy depends on a previous philosophy, he first outlines his experimentalist philosophy and then his consequent progressivist educational policy. Philosophy, as Morris sees it, is primarily concerned with three questions: What is real, studied in ontology; what is true, studied in epistemology; and what is good or of value, studied in axiology through its divisions of ethics and aesthetics.[54]

Man Is the Measure

In his attitude to reality the experimentalist is a naïve realist, straightforwardly describing what he sees and eschewing any "superstructure of metaphysical presumption." It is at our peril that we go beyond the primary data of our experience, beyond the level at which our description of reality can be repeatedly put to trial in a public manner. Morris insists that this conception of experience includes "quiet reflection" as well as sense knowledge; yet it can never bring us beyond "human experience in its raw form," so that "reality is simply what we experience it to be." Indeed, reality in itself is unknowable, and the real world is actually constituted by our experience of it. We control our experience by a systematized inquiry through which we act on whatever lies beyond us, experience the reactions or consequences, and thus grow in intelligence. And what we experience is never a thing but rather a process, so that objective truth (here called "pre-established truths") is impossible. Morris quotes approvingly the dictum of Protagoras, the Sophist, that "Man is the measure of all things." [55]

[54] Van Cleve Morris, *Philosophy and the American School: An Introduction to the Philosophy of Education* (Boston: Houghton Mifflin Company, 1961), pp. 5–8, 20–21.
[55] *Ibid.*, pp. 68–73.

It is interesting to notice that in the doctrine of Protagoras this statement had meaning only on the basis of the materialism that he inherited from Democritus, and in the doctrine of Morris or of anyone else it can have meaning only on the same basis. Reality, for Protagoras, is exclusively material; hence, all knowledge is sense perception and nothing more. Qualities, moreover, reside not in matter but in us, who perceive matter; hence, what is hot to one man will be cold to another, and truth, if it has any meaning, will be entirely subjective and relative. We can never know what things are in themselves, but only the manner in which they affect us.

Is this the position of the experimentalist? As Morris describes that position, the only difference lies in the intellectual consistency with which the Sophist maintained it. It is impossible to say with certainty whether Protagoras was first a convinced materialist and then drew the logical consequences in the realms of knowledge and of action, or whether, on the other hand, he simply adopted materialism as the theoretical justification for the pragmatism and relativism that he wanted to teach Greek youth as tools for their worldly success. What can be said is that he clearly saw the connection involved, a relation of strict cause and effect between materialism and subjectivism. Morris tries to avoid the charge of materialism and sensism by stating that his concept of experience includes more than sense knowledge. Yet the statement remains unsupported by evidence; for all the further propositions about reality that he enunciates are intelligible in his doctrine, as they were in that of Protagoras, only on the supposition that knowledge is nothing more than sensation. To characterize this doctrine as subjectivistic, relativistic, and skeptical, is not to call names; it is to apply accurate descriptive adjectives to the doctrine as enunciated. It is no wonder that "one man's metaphysics is as good as another's," [56] for there is, quite literally, no meta-physics,

[56] *Ibid.,* p. 71.

no reality beyond the physical, and hence no knowledge of any such reality. It will also follow, of course, that one man's truth is as good as another's and that one man's values are as good as another's, for there is no objective truth or goodness, and man is indeed the measure of all things.

Possibly the experimentalist can escape the charge of relativism (though perhaps he would not regard it as an accusation) by pointing to the possibility of checking one's private experience against that of other people, by reminding us that "the nobility of this ontology is its *public* character." [57] This might make some sense if it meant that a man could be more sure that he was approaching objective truth in his investigations if his findings coincided with those of others who were undergoing the same experience; there would still be the possibility of attaining some measure of objective truth, through group rather than individual effort.

At one point it looks as though this is the experimentalist criterion of truth. "The great advantage of Experimentalism," we are told, "is that it is a *public* epistemology; it is a method of knowing which is out in the open, available to all. . . . The sort of experience which is common to all men, testable, and warranted is the only kind of experience that is capable of yielding what we call knowledge." [58] The catch is that this knowledge, of whatever kind it is, should not be identified with objective truth. Indeed, "the word *truth* is an equivocal term," which should be qualified by the adjective *tentative*.[59] It is the scientific method which makes this adjective always necessary, a method that begins in the consciousness of a tension or difficulty and follows along with a diagnosis of the situation, a listing of possible solutions, a projection of the consequences of each possible solution, a testing of each solution to see if the projected consequences really occur, and

[57] *Ibid.*, p. 68.
[58] *Ibid.*, p. 165.
[59] *Ibid.*, pp. 158–159.

a final judgment on the basis of this method.[60]   In view of the fact that the phenomena to be investigated constitute a process or flux, it is inevitable that any judgment, any solution, any knowledge can be only tentative in character, for the reality to be investigated is not only constantly changing but actually is change or process itself.

A Simplification of the Scientific Method

What the author is really doing here is misusing a highly simplified version of a method of investigation used in the physical sciences in order to bolster his own philosophical interpretation of reality, an interpretation which has no direct connection with any scientific method.   A methodology of science is not itself a philosophy; it does not of itself give rise to any particular account of reality and our knowledge of it; and it does not depend for its existence on any particular philosophical convictions about the ultimate nature of reality.   One need not, for example, be a materialist to be a scientist, any more than one need be an idealist or anything else to be a scientist.   The scientific method, in and of itself, is independent of any philosophy, and the effort to use it in support of a particular philosophical interpretation of reality reveals intellectual confusion about what is involved.

Indeed, the whole effort of science, whether physical or other, is to overcome as far as possible the tentative nature of knowledge, to abstract from the flux of phenomena some intelligible generalizations that will, as far as they then go, reduce many phenomena to one law, that will find the outline of a cosmos within what would otherwise remain a chaos.   Granted that the effort to penetrate and understand reality is never finished, for the fundamental reason that the human mind is finite and hence limited in its capabilities.   Yet the scientist ordinarily considers himself to be contributing to an effort at understanding that is making some

[60] *Ibid.*, pp. 160–162.

progress, that has nailed down some positions and will nail down more, even though it will never succeed in nailing them all down. To see the always unfinished nature of the scientific enterprise is simply to see that man is not God; it need not at all involve the denial of the possibility of reaching any objective truth, a denial which makes nonsense of the whole work of science.

A further and related weakness in the experimentalist position is that it seems always to restrict science to the physical sciences, and then to see these as what we have been calling practical rather than speculative. In regard to the first point, one wonders whether the experimentalist would regard the conclusions reached in various mathematical sciences as merely tentative truths; if so, he would be taking a position that most mathematicians themselves would not subscribe to. Modern mathematics may be to a large extent postulational, but its conclusions are certainly not looked on as merely tentative. In regard to the second point, the examples of science and of the scientific method that are used seem invariably to deal with what is to be done rather than with what is, and thus to rule out of existence the whole area that we have designated as speculative knowledge. Such a view, far from being arbitrary, follows logically from the basic Sophistic position regarding the world and the impossibility of our knowing anything as it is. "Since we can never really know 'it,' let us turn to the study of how to *manage* 'it.'" [61]

The Good and the Public

One of the difficulties with trying to manage what you do not understand is that you can get no hint about procedure from what you are trying to deal with. Actually, anyone who literally took this position could do nothing except grope in the dark; for example, anyone who thought that he literally knew nothing about what human beings are could not even begin the process of edu-

[61] *Ibid.*, p. 72.

cating them, for he would have no basis for any plan of action and no criterion for judging any results. The subjectivism of Protagoras leads logically to the nihilism of Gorgias. In reality, as the dogmatic tone of progressivist books in education indicates, even the experimentalist holds many conclusions as far more than tentatively true, and guides his practical activities accordingly. Yet his criterion of success is still subjective, and the good, like the true, is a matter of what appears rather than of what is. Consistently, he can never say *est* but only *videtur,* and man is still the measure of all things.

Just as men construct their own truth, so do they construct their own values or conceptions of the good. That is true which works, and that is good which one wants; the morally right course of action is the one that yields desirable consequences. (One thinks of Phenix on "the democracy of desire.") The evident objection is that one is once more landed into a thoroughgoing relativism, and this time into a moral relativism that, since it concerns action rather than knowledge, has more immediately evident effects than epistemological subjectivism. To counter this charge, the experimentalist says that we should regard as good "not just what works for me but what works for all." "The scope and intensity of public consequences are what help us to measure the morality or immorality of the act." [62] Since, however, circumstances change, there can never be any moral absolutes, and such acts as stealing, lying, and murder cannot be absolutely forbidden, for sometimes these would lead to the public good. [63]

Again, this position is consistent with the author's basic skepticism. For if you cannot know what reality is, neither can you know how to manage it; if you do not know what something is, neither can you know what you should do with it. What you should do with it can only be what you want to do with it, and the

[62] *Ibid.,* p. 271.
[63] *Ibid.,* pp. 267–272.

word *should* really ceases to have meaning. Men create their own values, and create them according to their own choice, that is, arbitrarily. And one does not rescue such a doctrine from its objectionable consequences in the practical order by setting up the public as arbiter. What public are you talking about? Do you take into account people of one city, or one school district, or one nation, or the whole world? Do you take into account only those who are presently living, or past and future generations as well? If the public of one nation regard themselves as a master race whose historical mission is to subjugate and thus civilize the public of other and inferior nations, which public is right? If public knowledge and consequent ability to judge have been carefully corrupted through years of propaganda, are the controlled judgments that result still right? If a public demand arises that progressivist schools eliminate the more extreme practices that the experimentalist philosophy has led them to and return to more traditional methods of education, is the public right? On this last issue, it seems, the public consensus somehow fails, and we return to the previously scorned "saints and prophets," [64] except that this time they are the saints and prophets of experimentalism, a fact which seems to make all the difference. If man is the measure of all things, you finally have to decide which man.

In general, it can be said that this book, which we may fairly consider a superior representative of experimentalism and progressivism, presents its case well. Almost alone among the progressive educationists that I have read, Morris has a sure command of the language and a lively and readable style which lift his work far above the deadly dull pedestrian prose that one comes to associate with his position. Unfortunately, when his exposition deals with positions other than his own, his work is marred by repeated examples of either incompetence or dishonesty. In better circles it is customary to make some effort to understand and to present

[64] *Ibid.*, p. 68.

297

fairly a position which one is going to criticize; yet time after time Morris substitutes distortion for description and invective for comment.

In the whole of part VI, for example, in which applications of previous theory are made to teaching and administration, the progressivist is constantly presented as the hero and all others as reactionaries who want what every reader would agree is bad teaching. Throughout the book, other positions are described as absolutistic in outlook and as stupidly offering a final prescription for solving all educational problems forever. This travesty eliminates any need for the author's critical assessment; it also confuses the issue by its inaccuracy. In one of the sections devoted to Neo-Thomism, for example, the old ghost of the faculty theory (also misunderstood) is again dragged out, to the accompaniment of the following: " 'canned,' unscientific answers," " 'Impositionist' approach," " 'answer-chopping,' " " 'logic-chopping.' " [65] Even the abundance of quotation marks leaves this an exhibition of mere name-calling rather than of reasoned criticism. In other passages, technical doctrines which are important for the theme of the book are cavalierly criticized on the basis of a complete misunderstanding of the doctrine concerned: the Aristotelian teaching on virtue (p. 63, note 19), the relation of reason and revelation (pp. 344–345), the relation of church and state (pp. 345–346), the meaning of the expression, "a government of law instead of men" (p. 361, note 2). In addition, there is the gratuitous insult of the author's slighting references to the sacrament of confession (pp. 263–264, 277–278), a subject concerning which he also displays a pronounced ignorance. The editor's introduction to Morris's book uses the words "solid scholarship" (p. v). Among experimentalists this sort of exhibition, professionally incompetent and personally offensive, might well pass as scholarship; among scholars it would not pass at all.

[65] *Ibid.*, pp. 196–197.

chapter ten

A Few Perennial Problems

It would appear that there should be room, somewhere near the end of this book, for the consideration of a few assorted problems of the kind that we have always with us. The number of educational questions worth considering is indefinite, as the pages of educational journals attest. Only those problems with a philosophical dimension would properly have a place in this volume; accordingly, such important topics as school admissions policies or the education of the gifted will not be included. Further than this, the choice of those few problems that are included is rather arbitrary, and represents, as will become clear, my personal interests rather than areas of professional competence.

There is a further reason for the somewhat tentative nature of the positions that will be taken in this chapter. Near the beginning of this book it was argued that philosophy of education is part of social ethics. It was also maintained that the more immersed in particular circumstances an ethical conclusion becomes, that is, the nearer it approaches the realm of prudence and of the singular event, the more difficult it becomes for us to see, to grasp intellectually, the necessity of the relation between the conclusion and the principles in which it is resolved. A conclusion in ethics, even one that is near the prudential order, may be just as necessary as a mathematical conclusion, and, in itself, as little open to doubt or to debate. In relation, however, to the one who is trying to understand it, the necessity of the conclusion will be much less clear, and, in that sense, more open to doubt and to debate. In the present circumstance, that lack of clarity and of subjective certainty extend also to the one who is trying to explain and to justify the conclusions. In brief, I am much less certain of the validity of the positions taken in this chapter than of those taken in earlier chapters, both because of the host of particular circumstances involved and because of a relative lack of technical competence. It is true that there is some philosophical dimension to the problems considered, but their treatment here will amount to a few personal observations rather than to any full philosophical consideration. The idea is to get a train of thought and discussion started, not to lay down anything like the final word.

EVALUATION AND REPORTS

The first of the problems on which a few remarks will be made is that of measuring and evaluating and reporting students' progress or lack of it.[1] No attempt will be made to offer gratuitous advice

[1] Useful suggestions are to be found in J. Stanley Ahmann and Marvin D. Glock, *Evaluating Pupil Growth* (Englewood Cliffs, N.J.: Allyn and Bacon, Inc., 1958), and John W. Rothney, "Evaluation of Learning," in Charles E. Skinner

on the highly technical matter of constructing adequate tests or other means of measurement. There are, however, some questions with a philosophical bearing; for example, the questions of what one is trying to measure and evaluate and report, and for what purpose, involve a consideration of the aim of education at any given level. Thus, one who sees the school as primarily a socializing agency will give more emphasis to measuring and reporting such moral virtues as cooperativeness and respect for authority than such intellectual virtues as history and arithmetic. School authorities will try to measure what they think the school should be doing, not what they do *not* think the school should be doing; and they will evaluate and report student progress in these areas rather than in others. Once again we are back to the various possible meanings of education, and to the goals proper to each of the agencies of education.

Effort, Relative Standing, and Knowledge

It has been pointed out by Hand,[2] among others, that the notions of measurement and of appraisal are not identical, and that the same measurement may give rise to different appraisals of accomplishment depending on the purpose for which the measurement is being made. Thus, he goes on, the appraisal of a student's work in, say, English or mathematics will vary according as the purpose is, first, to show which student excels which other student or, second, to show how much each student learned in relation to his intellectual capabilities. The appraisal, then, will depend on whether one is considering the student as competing with other students or as competing with himself. It would appear, however,

---

(ed.), *Educational Psychology*, 4th ed. (Englewood Cliffs, N.J.: Prentice-Hall, Inc., 1959), pp. 676–693.

[2] Harold C. Hand, *Principles of Public Secondary Education* (New York: Harcourt, Brace & World, Inc., 1958), pp. 220–224.

that there is a third possibility which is not mentioned here (though it is later in Hand's chapter), and that is that one could appraise the degree of mastery of a given subject matter that the student exhibits on the test or whatever is being used as a means of measurement. Indeed, only after the degree of competence has been measured and expressed in some symbol such as a number or a letter will it be possible to arrive at the standing of any student in a given group. The relative excellence of each student can be established only in terms of an objective criterion against which each is first measured.

It is true that to some degree a teacher may raise or lower his standards of achievement—perhaps unconsciously—to take account of the general mental level of his students; to the extent that this happens the test is primarily telling who excels whom in the group. But this adjustment need not be and is not always made; the teacher may have a quite definite notion of what degree of competence in a given area of knowledge a group of students at a certain level might reasonably be expected to exhibit, and can measure and evaluate their performances accordingly. Even where the teacher does adjust his demands up or down according to the abilities of the group, he is still measuring their relative ability and is still finding out who excels whom in terms of mastery of subject matter. The only difference will be that his results will more logically be expressed in percentiles than in percentages. The point I am making, though, is that the percentile depends finally on the percentage, even if the latter is not explicitly calculated; the rank in class depends upon one's mastery of subject matter. Students can be related to each other only if they have first been related to something else.

The point of this argument has been to defend the practice of measuring, evaluating, and reporting a student's knowledge of a given subject matter at a given educational level. This practice is frequently and erroneously equated with that of assigning relative class standings to students and thus fostering an unhealthy spirit of competition. It will be maintained later in this section that such competition is not necessarily and always unhealthy. Here, however, it is merely being argued that the choice is not exclusively between competing with others and competing with oneself. In presenting only these alternatives, Hand offers another example of what we have been calling the fallacy of the false dichotomy. Whatever one may think of competition with others and the practice of assigning relative class standings, the point being made here is that in the guise of eliminating this practice one is also and first eliminating the evaluation of and report on the student's comprehension of a given subject matter. And if schools are primarily intellectual institutions, this is an evaluation that simply must be made. Effort is good, but it is not a substitute for competence.

If education is growth, then what any educational agency should try to measure and evaluate is the kind of growth it sees itself as helping the student to achieve. And what it should report is the kind of growth, from among those which it has evaluated, which the people to whom it is reporting are interested in. Further, account will have to be taken of the effect of the system of evaluation and reporting on the very growth with which it is concerned, that is, on the development of the children themselves. Finally, the educational agency should really measure and report what it claims it is measuring and reporting, and not anything else. Let us consider each of these points in turn, though to some extent they interweave.

What the School Should Measure and Report

With the first point we are back again to that educational agency which is the school, and the aims which are proper to it. If the school is primarily an intellectual institution, centered in the classroom and its work, then the school will primarily measure, evaluate, and report the growth of its students in knowledges and skills. Since the school is a broader agency than the classroom, it will also measure, evaluate, and report the growth of its students in moral and social qualities, particularly, though not exclusively, as these affect the student's intellectual development. These moral and social qualities will probably need greater emphasis with younger than with more mature students. In any event, however, both the evaluation and the report should clearly distinguish between the moral and the intellectual.

In regard to the second point, the school will have to vary the nature of its report according to the interests of those to whom the report is being made. A university that will admit students only from the upper third or quarter of their high school graduating class will have to have a report that includes class standing. The dean of a particular professional school—engineering, for example—will be interested in and should receive a report that includes a percentage rating in mathematics courses, and perhaps an estimate from his teachers in these subjects of the applicant's probable aptitude for engineering studies. A prospective employer may be interested in, among other things, the student's extraclass activities and social qualities, and should receive a report geared to these interests. Parents, to whom most of the reports go, are probably interested in all the aspects of their children's development that the school helps to achieve, and should so be kept informed.

When we come to consider the form of these reports to parents we find ourselves concerned with the last two of the points mentioned above. It was there suggested that the school should try to evaluate and report the student's mastery of a given subject matter. Is it possible to make such an evaluation objectively and accurately? If the school attempts to do this, should it also translate the results of these measurements into relative class standings? Would such rating probably produce bad psychological results for many of the students? Should the report rather try to indicate a student's achievement in terms of his own potentialities, so that he competes only with himself? Does this last system really measure anything more than the moral virtues of industry and perseverance, and is it possibly a poor preparation for the hard realities of advanced study and of a fiercely competitive world? It is probably impossible to answer these questions with any degree of certainty, even though one's convictions may be rather definite; one can but try to judge in the light of his own and of others' observation over the years.

Largely on the basis of such experience, it is my own present conviction that the teacher of any given subject matter can make a reasonably accurate and objective evaluation of a student's mastery of the work of a course, and that the school can and should report that evaluation to the student, to his parents, and to any other legitimately interested parties. Whether the evaluation and report should be made in terms of letters, of honor points, of percentages, or of anything else does not seem to matter too much as long as those to whom the report is made understand the system that is being used. Standardization would obviously be desirable here, especially for the sake of those students who are seeking admission to high school and, even more, for those seeking admission to college or graduate school, and also for the sake of those school officials who are in charge of admissions. Since, however, many of the people concerned are passionately convinced that it does matter in what terms the report is made, but are not agreed on what those terms should be, the prospect of standardization remains pretty remote.

These are merely observations based on personal experience; other people's experience has led to different conclusions. Whatever system of measurement and evaluation and reporting is under discussion, it will usually be found easier to attack than to defend it, for human fallibility enters into each one of them; it shows up in relation to some subject matters more evidently than in relation to others, but it inevitably haunts them all to some degree. And until that distant day when cybernetics pushes us all out of the classroom and into an honest living, some uncertainty will remain with us. One of our jobs is to reduce that uncertainty as much as we can and to keep an open mind about ways of doing so.

Eliminate Competition Among Students?

Another question about which no universally valid conclusion seems possible is that of the psychological effects of percentage and percentile ratings on the students themselves. Examples can be adduced in which a neurotic or psychotic condition can be traced, with a high degree of probability, to the traumatic experience of failing a course or achieving a low class standing or both. Less extreme examples can be given of those who were so discouraged by poor grades that they gave up trying and failed to develop further their limited but real potentialities for intellectual growth. From the other end of the scale, examples could be given of highly gifted students who also gave up trying, but this time for the reason that they didn't need to work in order to pass a particular course or stand well in class. The result here was also the failure to develop potentialities, as well as the development of the moral vices of laziness and pride.

Further instances could be given of the harmful effects on students of the effort to reach an assigned level of accomplishment that is perhaps beyond their powers, and also of the harmful effects of academic competition, especially when the latter is heightened by ambitious parents whose real motive is to use their children as instruments for their own competition with other parents. Perhaps the strongest argument against this system of evaluation and reporting is the dreadful memory of the pain that it has inflicted on some of our students. It is a hard thing to be the instrumentality through which another human being is hurt, especially a defenseless child. The alternative looks appealing: to measure each student's achievement in relation to the standard of his native capability rather than in relation to the standard set by the teacher for all members of the class, and to eliminate class standings so that the student competes with himself rather than with other members of the class. There would probably be fewer frustrations and broken hearts, and the only ones hurt would be those who deserved to be hurt because they weren't doing their best.

It has been claimed that this system is "based on sound Catholic educational theory and practice," and that "a child may fail in comparison with other children, but as long as he does the best he can with what God and his environment have bestowed upon him, he does not fail." This latter statement is no doubt true if we take one sense, and the most important sense, of the word "fail." But it is possible to succeed in one respect and to fail in another. The weakness implicit in this position is that it confuses the various meanings of the term education and equates the education proper to the school as a specific institution with the education proper to life as a whole. The second notion of education is infinitely more important because its end is the ultimate, supernatural end of human life. Yet the first is also important, even though its end is the merely proximate and natural end of the development of human powers.

One could also question the psychological effects of this system of evaluation on the student. For some purposes it may be true that "the most desirable competition for a child is competition with himself alone," but for other purposes it is not. Children cannot forever be shielded from the hard facts of a highly competitive world. In most high schools, in any college or university that I have heard of, and definitely in the competitive jungle of the workaday world, each person must place his abilities on the line and learn to face up to and live with the often disappointing results. So far as the traumatic results of the experience of failure are concerned, it is quite possible that these would be more severe when met unexpectedly after early years spent in the insulated world of competition only with oneself. Life in this world takes courage and perseverance and the ability to face reality as it is. One does not develop these virtues suddenly, but gradually; one does not develop them by avoiding the facts of life, but by taking his lumps, licking his wounds, and coming back for more. It is a terrible thing to see a child hurt, and any of us would be happy to take the blow instead and protect the child. In the long run, however, this is not a kindness to the child; it is protecting him from present hurt (and yourself from the pain of watching him) at the expense of leaving him unprepared for the bigger disappointments that will inevitably come his way in the future. There are psychological dangers to grading on relative mastery of a subject matter and to reporting class standings; most of them, however, should be able to be alleviated by intelligent and sympathetic counseling. There are also psychological dangers to grading on achievement as measured only against personal capacity, and these are not likely to be alleviated by any counseling.

Further, there is the question of justice, not only to the student himself, but to his parents. When parents receive a school report they are legitimately interested in finding out not only how hard their children are trying but how much they are learning. They are understandably concerned with their children's preparation for more advanced study or for a career in the world, and they want to know how they are shaping up and what improvements they could and should be making in that preparation. A number of teachers who have had to evaluate and report on their students' work on the introvert system have stated that parents do not like the system because they do not understand it. My own reaction is that the parents may dislike the system precisely because they do understand it and do not want any part of it.

It is, of course, important that parents should also know how hard their children are working, whether their conduct at school is acceptable, and, in general, whether they are making progress in the development of moral virtues and social graces as well as in knowledges and skills. But there is no need to confuse these areas and to suppress evaluation of one in order to achieve evaluation of another. A common, simple, and workable practice is to have one page or one section of a report card devoted to a report on the student's achievement to date in a given subject matter, with that achievement evaluated in terms of the mastery of that subject matter which the teacher considers reasonable for that period. The other page or section is devoted to moral and social virtues, and lets the parents know how their children are progressing in these areas. Parents want to know whether their children are developing reasonably well in both intellectual and moral virtues, so far as the school can assist in their development and measure the result. Further, they have a right to know these things, and when school authorities deny them this information and confuse the issue in the name of a questionable psychological theory, they are doing the parents as well as the students less than justice. If they consider moral virtue important in the work of the school, this seems a peculiar way of inculcating it.

AUTHORITY AND DISCIPLINE

At first sight the philosophical roots of the notions of authority and discipline[3] may seem to be buried a long way beneath their daily application and its immediately practical demands. Yet those philosophical roots do exist, and perhaps a brief examination

[3] In this section the term discipline is being used in meanings that *Webster's New World Dictionary* gives as follows: "training that develops self-control, character," "acceptance of or submission to authority and control," and "treatment that corrects or punishes." In other parts of this book the word has generally been used in its primary sense of "a branch of knowledge or learning." See note 1 in Chapter one.

of them may enable those of us who must exercise authority to do so a little more intelligently and a little more equitably.[4]

The place to begin is with the notion of society.[5] Throughout our lives we all belong simultaneously to many societies: family, church, civil society, school, basketball team, business firm, bridge club, PTA, and many others. The common mark of all these societies, what constitutes each as a society, is the fact that here many persons are united in the pursuit of a common end. In fact, it is this common end, this unity of direction, that makes the many persons in some sense one, that makes them a society. In philosophical terms, the final cause of a society is also its formal cause; the common end or goal is what constitutes the many members as one society.

The unity of order that is a society may range from the unity of husband and wife in one family to the unity of the countless numbers of people in all times and places in one human race. Whatever the size or the type of society, however, some form of authority will have to exist if the many are to direct themselves consistently to one end. Authority may be exercised in any one of a wide variety of forms, but it will have to be there in some form if the society is to remain in existence.

One reason, though a subordinate one, why there will have to be a principle of order in any society is that a certain number of the members may be lacking, relatively speaking, in the moral virtues,

[4] A classic exposition of the origin and nature of authority is Yves R. Simon, *Philosophy of Democratic Government* (Chicago: The University of Chicago Press, 1951), espec. pp. 19–33. Cf. Joseph W. Evans and Leo R. Ward (eds.), *The Social and Political Philosophy of Jacques Maritain* (New York: Charles Scribner's Sons, 1955), pp. 89–100.

[5] This and the following three paragraphs are adapted from Herbert Johnston, *Business Ethics,* 2d ed. rev. (New York: Pitman Publishing Corporation, 1961), pp. 250–252. Reprinted by permission.

may be interested in their own good rather than in the common good, and may even be willing to sacrifice the common good to their private advantage. These people have to be restrained and, if necessary, punished for the protection of the society. Another, and a similar reason, is that a number of the members may be relatively lacking in the intellectual virtues, may be incapable of the maturity of judgment necessary to run their own show, and will therefore have to be guided by others who are wiser and more experienced than they are.

The principal reason, however, why authority is necessary in any society has nothing to do with the shortcomings of the members. For even if the members of a society are truly devoted to the common good and are unusually intelligent in their pursuit of that good, yet, unless consistent unanimity can be guaranteed, a principle of authority will be necessary to decide what means are to be followed in securing the common good. In this contingent order in which we live, however, unanimity in the face of several means of attaining the common good cannot be guaranteed, because no demonstration is possible.[6] It is impossible to show why this means as opposed to that must necessarily be the one selected. It follows that authority has an essential function, not because of any shortcomings on the part of the members of the society, but because of the very nature of the situation itself. In short, authority is essential to any society, including the academic one.

The very nature of authority demands that it be exercised for the common good of those who are subject to it; it is a responsibility rather than a privilege. Government is always for the sake of the governed; when turned to the advantage of the governors it loses its moral authority and becomes mere tyranny. The laws of a civil society are made for the good of those who are to obey them, not for the advantage of those who enforce them. The

[6] See in Chapter one the section on Philosophy of Education, Prudence, and Conscience.

rules of a school or of a classroom are made for the good of those who are to keep them, not for the convenience of those who administer them. In an academic society it is important that rules exist and be obeyed; but they exist and must be obeyed so far as they help the students in their work, not so far as they save administrators and teachers from getting ulcers. This basic distinction, sometimes forgotten, should underlie each individual disciplinary action.

A further distinction, though, might also be made. The rules laid down for the guidance of the members of any society should be restricted to those that will guide them to the end proper to the society in question. Thus, the laws of a civil society look to the good of that society and not of any other; they aim at the temporal common good of the citizens, not at their supratemporal common good. The state is not the church, and it is interested directly in the natural rather than the supernatural virtues of its members, and immediately in the civic virtues which lead to the attainment and preservation of the common weal. Neither is the school the church, and it, too, is interested directly in the natural rather than the supernatural virtues of its members, and immediately in the virtues which lead to the development of a successful academic life in common. It is true that the school, as a more inclusive educational agency than the classroom, is directly concerned with the development of moral as well as of intellectual virtues in its students. Further, the church-related school is properly engaged in furthering the supernatural virtues in its students, at least indirectly, through the provision of opportunities for religious practice. Yet the school remains a school, and exists for the sake of knowledge before it exists for the sake of goodness. It is possible, then, that school officials might sometimes go too far in zealous and well-intended efforts to see to it that their charges flourish in all aspects of moral goodness. Since the church, the home, the state, and probably other educational agencies are also directly concerned with helping their members, among whom are the school's students, to develop morally, the school might perhaps leave some of this work to these agencies. It would be difficult to provide a definite example to illustrate this point. In any particular instance involving school discipline, however, it might be useful to bear in mind the fact that this discipline exists and is to be administered not primarily for the moral reform of the person involved but rather for the common good of the whole academic society and for the personal good of the student as a member of that society. The school deals directly with the person as student, and some of the phases of his personal conduct are none of the school's business.

Reflections on Justice

Up to this point, the material of this section has rested upon an analysis that could be called philosophical in character, concerned with the nature of authority and with the school as exercising authority. The rest of the section will be nothing more than personal reflections. For whatever value they may have, however, those reflections lead to the conclusion that the hallmarks of good school and classroom discipline are fairness and firmness, that is, justice, administered without fear or favor.

Fairness in the administration of discipline grows out of the realization that authority exists for the sake of those over whom it is exercised. The administrator or the teacher who keeps this fact in mind will avoid becoming personally involved in any situation to the extent that his anger or his pride come largely to dictate his disciplinary action. He will not award the English prize to A rather than to B because A's father has a million dollars or will not hesitate to bring pressure to bear on higher authorities. He will not let C get away with murder in the classroom because C happens to be related to the principal. He will not let racial or religious prejudice or social snobbery influence his treatment of any student in any way. He will not take advantage of his supe-

313

rior knowledge to humiliate any student either publicly or privately under the guise of administering discipline. He will not allow himself to be flattered into a convenient coma by student operators who will polish even crabapples for higher grades. In brief, he will deal honestly and fairly with his students. Most young people, as yet uncorrupted by the cynicism of their elders, have a passionate sense of justice. They do not ask that it be easy, but they do ask that it be fair. And they have a right so to ask. School discipline is very largely school morale; and school morale is very largely student reaction to what they see those do who are telling them what to do.

Firmness in the administration of discipline grows from the same realization of its purpose. If authority is for the sake of those over whom it is exercised, then it must be exercised when the situation calls for it. When a school administrator or a teacher is convinced in any given situation that he is right and that he should carry out this or that disciplinary action, then he must carry it out, however unpleasant the task is personally. Anyone who exercises authority had better forget about personal popularity. The better members of his society will respect him, and respect is something far more solid. In exceptional circumstances they may even love him. If this happens, however, it should be strictly a by-product. The point of exercising authority is to get the job done, and to get it done for the sake of the governed, even in the teeth of their opposition and at the sacrifice of one's own popularity. This need not involve harshness or cruelty or even personal coldness; kindness and firmness are compatible. Ultimately, however, the teacher exists for his students, the parent for his children, the officer for his men. It has been said that a man who holds a commission really becomes an officer when he is no longer afraid of the soldiers under his command. The same is true of teachers or parents or any others in authority. If more parents were concerned with demanding that their children do what is right rather than with whether the children love them—that is, if they were concerned with their children rather than with themselves—family life would be better. Parents who are afraid of their children cannot run a family successfully. Administrators or teachers who are afraid of their students or of anyone else cannot run a school successfully. What matters is not whether you are popular; what matters is whether you get the job done. And that means firmness when firmness is necessary.[7]

PUBLIC MONEY FOR PRIVATE SCHOOLS?

This book is taking the position that students in both public and private schools, at all levels of education, who wish to include instruction in sacred doctrine in that education, have a right to assistance for that purpose from the public treasury, whether Federal, state, or other. If such assistance would be interpreted as a violation of any present constitution, whether Federal or state, then either the interpretation or the constitution should be amended.

In Chapter four [8] the reasons why the government should help parents who wish to provide a religious education for their children [9] were summarized thus:

Parents have the primary obligation to educate their children and hence the primary right to choose the means of doing so. The state, like the Church, is in the field of school education primarily to help the family. Parents who wish instruction in sacred doctrine for their children should have the help of

[7] For a tragicomic account of seventh and eighth grade students' attitudes to school authority exercised over their social activities, see Katharine M. Byrne, "Our Dear, Dear Children," *America*, 104, 11 (Dec. 10, 1960), 369–371.

[8] See above, p. 99.

[9] "The structure of the argument is not complex. Its principle is that the canons of distributive justice ought to control the action of government in allocating funds that it

the state in this as in other forms of education. To provide this help is not to confuse Church and state, since the state acts for the family, not for the Church, and does not itself espouse any religious doctrine. To refuse this help is to deny to the parents who wish it the public assistance in education to which they have a right as citizens.

---

coercively collects from all people in pursuance of its legitimate interest in universal compulsory schooling. The fact is that these canons are presently not being observed. The 'solution' to the School Question reached in the nineteenth century reveals injustice, and the legal statutes that establish the injustice are an abuse of power. So, in drastic brevity, runs the argument.... For my part, I have never heard a satisfactory answer to it." From *We Hold These Truths: Catholic Reflections on the American Proposition* by John Courtney Murray, S.J. (New York: copyright Sheed & Ward, Inc., 1960), pp. 17–18. Reprinted by permission. Cf. *ibid.,* pp. 143–154.

"Sharp distinction between church and state does not mean that the church and the state must live in ignorance of and isolation from each other. On the contrary, they have to co-operate. But this distinction means that the proper domain of the state is lay or secular and that no privileged treatment, contrary to the principle of the equality of all before the law, can be given by the state to the citizens of any given creed, their activities, or their institutions.

"Accordingly, the solution, in the educational sphere, is to be sought in a sound application of the pluralist principle. Religious training should be made available to the student population—not in a compulsory way, but on a voluntary basis—in accordance with the wishes of the students and their parents, and given by representatives of the various faiths." Jacques Maritain, "Thomist Views on Education," in Nelson B. Henry (ed.), *Modern Philosophies and Education,* part I, 54th Yearbook of the N.S.S.E. p. 84. Copyright 1955 by the University of Chicago. Reprinted by permission.

"It is radically unjust, and in violation of the abiding spirit of constitutional government, to allow a reasonable

In Chapter five [10] some workable methods of including instruction in sacred doctrine in the college curriculum were described. A forcefully argued book [11] has presented practical means whereby the state could, without violating existing constitutional law, assist students at all levels to obtain an education that would include instruction in sacred doctrine. Very briefly: [12]

The certificate plan provides that government make direct money grants in the form of vouchers or certificates to parents or guardians of all children attending approved independent schools. . . . The tax credit plan, on the other hand, provides that government give a tax offset to parents of all children attending approved independent tuition-charging schools. . . . From this analysis, it is clear that the certificate or tax credit plan involves no government aid or support of church-related schools. The government subsidy is given directly to parents to enable them to pay in part their children's tuition at the

exercise of parental and religious liberty to entail a burdensome inequality before the laws determining government's relation to education." William Gorman, "A Case of Distributive Justice," *Religion and the Schools* (New York: The Fund for the Republic, Inc., 1959), p. 34. For differing views, see the other three essays in this pamphlet. See also William F. Lynch, S.J., "Divisiveness in American Civilization," and John Courtney Murray, S.J., "The Problem of Pluralism in America," *Catholicism in American Culture,* Semicentenary Lectures (1953–54), College of New Rochelle, New York; Bernard J. Kohlbrenner, "The Controversy over Public Support to Parochial Schools," *School and Society,* 89, 2193 (May 20, 1961), 238–242; The American Assembly (Columbia University), *The Federal Government and Higher Education* (Englewood Cliffs, N.J.: Prentice-Hall, Inc., 1960), pp. 196–198.

[10] See the section on Catholic Education.

[11] Virgil C. Blum, S.J., *Freedom of Choice in Education* (New York: The Macmillan Company, 1958).

[12] *Ibid.,* pp. 26–28. Reprinted by permission.

school of their choice. Parents and their children alone are the beneficiaries of the subsidy.

Conflicting Opinion

This last position is by no means universally accepted. In January, 1961, a proposal was introduced before the legislature of the state of New York to make a grant of from $100 to $200 a year to help college students in the state pay their tuition fees at private, church-related schools as well as at public ones. Press reaction to the proposal varied. One columnist wrote: [13]

> The action New York State is considering is in principle the same as that adopted by Congress in providing the funds for education to veterans of World War II and the Korean War under the "GI Bill of Rights."
> The grants are allotted to the individuals, and they pay the money directly to the school of their choice, which can be a public, a private or a church-related institution as long as it meets prescribed academic requirements.

On the other hand, a lead editorial strongly condemned the proposal as a mere evasion of the law: [14]

> It is a shocking thing that high officers of the state government would offer a proposal that is nothing less than an attempt to evade the constitutional bar to aiding denominational colleges with public funds. . . . So far as the substance of the present proposal goes . . . we are against it because we are against any intermingling of state and church, even for so beneficial a result as education.

In another connection a *Time* writer said: [15]

[13] David Lawrence, *The South Bend Tribune,* January 20, 1961, p. 8. Reprinted by permission.
[14] "State Aid to Church Colleges?" *The New York Times,* January 26, 1961, p. 28. Reprinted by permission.
[15] *Time,* 77, 5 (Jan. 27, 1961), 62.

One possible compromise is direct grants to Catholic students, patterned after the G.I. Bill of Rights, which paid many a veteran's tuition at church-related colleges after World War II. There may be other constitutionally permissible compromises.

On March 14, 1961, the legislature approved grants to New York students in New York colleges, both nonsectarian and church-affiliated, of from $100 to $800 a year, depending on the financial status of their parents.[16] Some doubts have been expressed that the bill, as actually worded, applies to students in church-related schools; only time will tell how the bill works out.

The public assistance referred to is, of course, available to students of any religious persuasion. In practice, however, it seems to be almost exclusively Catholic spokesmen who lay claim to such aid. For example, in the same month in which the foregoing proposal was presented to the Albany legislature, a group described as an educational task force recommended to the incoming Kennedy administration a four-year program of Federal aid to education to the extent of $9.3 billion, with all of the money going to public schools. Cardinal Spellman objected to this qualification as an indirect but real pressure on citizens to transfer their children to public schools and as discrimination against the constitutional rights of parents: [17]

> "For many millions of American parents, this means that they will be taxed more than ever before for the education of their children but that they cannot expect any return from their taxes, unless they are willing to transfer their children to a public grade or high school. . . . Such legislation would discriminate against a multitude of America's children because their parents choose to exercise their constitutional right to educate them in accordance with their religious beliefs. . . . It is unthinkable that any American child be denied the federal

[16] *U.S. News and World Report* (Mar. 27, 1961), 14.
[17] Cardinal Spellman as quoted in *The South Bend Tribune,* January 18, 1961, p. 18. Reprinted by permission.

319

funds allotted to other children which are necessary for his mental development because his parents choose for him a God-centered education."

Among others, however, Lutheran and Jewish spokesmen lost no time in expressing dissent from Cardinal Spellman's position and in disclaiming any wish for public assistance for their schools. Reverend Dr. Oswald C. J. Hoffmann, public relations director of the Lutheran Church–Missouri Synod, "which operates the largest system of Protestant elementary schools in the country," is quoted as follows: [18]

> "As Americans who accept the traditional American policy of church-state separation, we Lutherans would not feel discriminated against if federal funds were appropriated for public schools only. In fact, we think that federal assistance, if there has to be such assistance, should be restricted to public schools."

A representative of "five national Jewish organizations" is quoted to the same effect: [19]

> "We feel the maintenance and furtherance of the Jewish religion to be the responsibility of the Jewish community, a responsibility which we have no desire to impose either in whole or in part upon the American taxpayer."

The Methodist Council of Bishops also opposed the "use of federal funds for support of private or parochial schools." [20]

And so it goes, with many Catholics feeling themselves to be the victims of persecution and religious bigotry and many non-Catholics feeling themselves called on to forestall a sectarian grab for political power. It is extremely doubtful that the differences will ever be resolved to the satisfaction of everyone concerned.

[18] *The South Bend Tribune,* January 19, 1961, p. 2. Reprinted by permission.
[19] *The South Bend Tribune,* January 20, 1961, p. 20. Reprinted by permission.
[20] *The South Bend Tribune,* April 7, 1961, p. 7.

Meanwhile, the situation seems to call for an honest effort to understand the position with which one differs coupled with firm adherence to the right as one sees it and, further, the resolution not to tear apart the civil society itself in the course of the debate.[21] And, as Rabbi Robert Gordis has put it, "If the discussion is conducted on a rational level, we may hope that the solution finally achieved will be both moderate and just."[22]

The Rights of the Family

Perhaps one of the points of difference that has not always been sufficiently clarified concerns divergent notions of what a church-related school is. The Jewish spokesman quoted above seems to see it as essentially a religious institution, an extension of the church, for he speaks of "the maintenance and furtherance of the Jewish *religion.*" Cardinal Spellman, on the other hand, seems to see it as essentially an academic institution, for he speaks of the use of funds "which are necessary for his [the American child's] *mental* development."

In Chapters four and five above, it was maintained that the fostering of religious practice, however important in itself, is only a secondary reason for the existence of a church-affiliated *school.* Precisely because it is and remains a school, its primary reason for existence is an intellectual one, concerned with knowledge. If God exists, then the most important knowledge that anyone can gain is the knowledge of God through sacred doctrine. The primary reason, then, for the existence of the church-related school

[21] For a sharp warning on this point, see Theodore Powell, *The School Bus Law: A Case Study in Education, Religion, and Politics* (Middletown, Conn.: Wesleyan University Press, 1960).

[22] "Education for a Nation of Nations," *Religion and the Schools* (New York: The Fund for the Republic, Inc., 1959), p. 33.

remains an intellectual one concerned with knowledge and with "mental development." If one sees the school as primarily the auxiliary of the family,[23] aiding the family chiefly in the development of its children's intellectual virtues, then there is no reason why tax support should be withheld directly from students and parents who are interested in theological instruction and withheld indirectly from the schools which furnish such instruction.[24]

Civil or political society, and its organ which is government, exists to secure the temporal common good of its members. The members have the obligation to contribute to that common good in the way in which the government asks them to do so—by

[23] "By natural law, the primary obligation to educate children rests with parents. The Church, the State and the school possess rights, each in its proper sphere, to aid the family in the discharge of this duty. These rights do not conflict but should be in perfect harmony in ordering the education of the child." Very Rev. J. William Lester, Diocesan Superintendent of Schools, Diocese of Fort Wayne–South Bend, *Our Sunday Visitor,* The Fort Wayne–South Bend Diocesan Edition, 50, 18 (Sept. 3, 1961), 3A. Reprinted by permission.

[24] For a detailed consideration of the constitutional issue involved, see the synopsis of a study made by the legal department of the National Catholic Welfare Conference, reprinted in *U.S. News and World Report* (Dec. 25, 1961), 67–69. The possibility of extending Federal aid to church-related schools below the college level, Cardinal Spellman's comments on proposed Federal aid to public schools only, and the Bailey Bill, which would dump the problem in the laps of state rather than Federal legislators, are all discussed briefly in *U.S. News and World Report* (Feb. 19, 1962), 47. Cf. "Federal Aid and Freedom," *The Commonweal,* 75, 23 (Mar. 2, 1962), 594–596. Cf. also Charles E. Sheedy, "How Meaningful Is the Religious Tradition?" *Liberal Education,* 46, 1 (March, 1960), 50–53.

obeying the laws, by paying taxes, by risking their lives in war. The members have the corresponding right to share in the common good to which they have contributed, and to ask the civil society and its government—at whatever level—to do just what they were constituted to do. In general, this means doing what needs to be and can be done for the achievement of the common good and what the individual citizen or such a smaller group as the family cannot do itself. Included under this heading is education, and particularly, though not exclusively, intellectual education. This is a function which falls by nature to the family, but one which the family alone is unable to carry on to the required degree. As part of that common good in which it has a right to share, the family may call upon government at the appropriate level to help it in this important task.

To help the family, however, does not mean to absorb it and usurp its rights. Except on the totalitarian premise that the citizen is totally the creature of the state and has duties but no rights in regard to it, the obligation of government is to help parents obtain for their children the education that the parents want, not the education that the government wants. The government has, of course, rights in the education of its future citizens. But the primary rights are the parents', and parents who wish, for moral or for intellectual reasons or for both, an education for their children in a church-related school have a right to the same assistance in providing that education as those parents who do not wish such an education for their children. Parents are as unlikely to be professional theologians as they are to be professional mathematicians; they need and have a right to assistance in the provision of both kinds of instruction. The fact that they may form a minority within the political society does not remove their rights. A majority vote determines who will administer the machinery of government; it does not determine whose rights that government will recognize. The tyranny of a majority is no less heavy and no less unjust than the tyranny of one man or of a few, and a government is no less totalitarian for going through the outward forms of democratic procedure in the attainment of an undemocratic end.

The government that systematically denies public assistance for what are called private schools is, in effect if not in intention, gradually if not immediately, closing down church-related schools and forcing citizens to send their children to schools that are not of their choosing, thereby denying their basic natural rights. For, with education costs rising as dramatically as they are, you do not have to padlock religiously affiliated schools to force their closing tomorrow; you have merely to provide needed funds to public schools and deny them to any others to achieve the same result the day after tomorrow. Massive Federal aid to public education exclusively is a case in point.

"Separation of church and state" is not a doctrine or an explanation or an appeal to reason; it is a slogan that dispenses with reason, an appeal to the emotions of fear and suspicion and hatred. The first amendment to the Constitution originally meant that no government should establish and support any one religion as official, but that there should, instead, be liberty of conscience and of worship. As now misinterpreted, the first amendment means that government shall be actively hostile to every religion, not so far as religious practice is concerned, but so far as theological teaching is concerned. It means that, indirectly but effectively, the official government doctrine as promulgated by the practice of the schools that it maintains is that theology is intellectually unimportant and that the ultimate intellectual interpretation of reality is a form of naturalism. This is not religious neutralism; this is active irreligion, with the worship of a misunderstood democracy as a substitute for religion. It can happen here, and, if you want *1984*, this is the way to get it.

QUESTIONS

1. Is end-of-semester testing necessary to maintain high achievement standards? In all grades? In some grades?
2. Has the school administration the right to control student activities which are not part of the school curriculum?
3. Should there be an entrance examination as a prerequisite for admission to secondary (public, private) schools?
4. How many years should be devoted to elementary schooling? To secondary schooling?
5. Should a student who has not maintained the required scholastic standards be retained in a grade when his record indicates that he will derive little or no benefit in the way of increased knowledge from this course of action?
6. Should there be uniform state tests as a requirement for graduation from (public, private) high schools?

chapter eleven

꧁

The Teacher's Vocation

The preceding chapter, made up of odds and ends left over from the earlier portions of this book, was already a sort of epilogue and should perhaps have rung down the final curtain. However, there remain a few final remarks about teachers and teaching.

SOME RESPONSIBILITIES AND
SOME RIGHTS OF TEACHERS

As was briefly suggested above,[1] it is the claim to the necessary and effective means to a given end that constitutes a right. Rights, considered personally and subjectively, are based upon the objective existence of a given end and upon a man's or a society's obliga-

[1] See in Chapter four the section on The State.

327

tion to work toward that end. A right is founded upon and explained by a need, the need of available means to reach an end that exists as a fact. You cannot reasonably lay claim to (that is, you do not have a right to) what will lead to an end that you do not happen to have. A teacher, for example, cannot reasonably ask for a permit to carry firearms on the plea that it will enable him to guard the money in the ABC Bank, for the good reason that he has no responsibility for guarding that money. The safety of the money is not, for him, an end; therefore he has no need of the means of achieving that end, and hence he has no right to that means because he has no need of it. Likewise, one cannot reasonably lay claim to what will *not* lead to an end that he does have, something that is not an effective means to that end. As another example, a teacher cannot reasonably ask his students to bring him a polished apple every day, since this does not assist him in the performance of his teaching functions. A right may be said to be a moral claim on what you need to get where you have to go. If either of these elements is lacking—if you don't have to get there, or if you do have to get there but don't need these means to do so— then you have no right to these means. If, and only if, it is objectively right that you should take the means to reach a given end, then you have, subjectively, a right to access to those means. You *have a right* to do what *it is right* for you to do.

Once again we are back to end and means. Like anyone else, the teacher is responsible for doing his job, and has a right to the means which will allow him to do it. Before we can say what his rights are we must know what his responsibilities are, what his job is, what ends are proper to him as one of the agents of education. This book has been maintaining that the primary function of the teacher is to teach; it is to help his students acquire knowledge, the ability to gain further knowledge, and, so far as possible, the desire to do so. Secondarily, and perhaps mostly by example, the function of the teacher includes increasing in his students the moral vir-

tues and the social graces, and doing what he can to help them
maintain a sound emotional balance.

A Duty to Know and a Right to Study

How accomplish these things? If the first job of the teacher
is to teach, his first need is knowledge. This means that it is his
primary moral responsibility, precisely as a teacher, to master to the
best of his ability the subject matter in which he is instructing his
students. Staying a chapter ahead isn't good enough. Neither
is a knowledge of the subject which is confined to the content of the
textbook being used./ On anything except the most elementary
levels, the teacher who cheerfully proclaims, "Give me the book
and two weeks and I'll teach anything," indicates either a hope-
lessly shallow intellectual depth or an irresponsible attitude toward
his job. Neither alternative promises much for the student. There
is a point in constantly broadening and deepening one's knowledge
of what he is teaching, even though this knowledge may go far
beyond what is likely to be directly required in the classroom.
Any area of knowledge worth studying and teaching has a context,
has perspectives, has relationships with other areas of knowledge,
has depths that the students cannot plumb at their present level
but of whose existence they can and should become conscious.
Without any specific effort on his part, a teacher who knows something of these depths and of these perspectives will suggest them
to his students, thus revealing to them ever-widening horizons and
ever-deepening possibilities. It is glimpses such as these that save
at least the better students from the danger of intellectual parochial-
ism, of imagining that they have effectively mastered some subject
after exposure to a single textbook. It is glimpses such as these,
again, that recreate for some students the excitement with which
most of them originally came to school, the curiosity, the desire to
know more, the refusal ever to be content with present knowledge,
perhaps the determination to devote their lives to being pioneers

and explorers in the realms of the mind. One cannot expect every teacher to strike the sparks that enkindle this enthusiasm; one can, however, be certain that a teacher who is not thoroughly knowledgeable and competent will rather douse the fires than light them.

If the teacher's first responsibility is to know, so that he may better teach, then his first right is the opportunity to study as the means that lead to knowledge. If the preceding paragraph has any validity, a teacher who is not constantly expanding and deepening his knowledge cannot do an adequate job. This statement will apply more strongly the higher one goes in the academic hierarchy; but it will apply to some degree at all levels. One cannot, though, expand and deepen his knowledge without time to acquire it and to reflect upon it and gradually to make it part of himself.

To what extent does this opportunity now exist in fact? It depends upon the particular situation, but one man's personal observation says that the extent is pitifully small. Teachers in large universities with genuine graduate schools are expected to do research as a necessary preliminary to their teaching and publication; their academic duties are ordinarily tailored to this end. Smaller liberal colleges often simply cannot afford to support scholars while they do research or provide them with adequate library or laboratory facilities. Some of them cannot even afford to support them while they study the results of other men's research, but can allow them only enough time for a desperately hurried preparation for the too many classes in too many subjects that they must be asked to teach. This is teaching on a quantitative rather than on a qualitative basis, and the students inevitably suffer. On the high school level the problem has changed only in degree. There is a genuine intellectual content to any subject worth teaching in high school, and a chemistry teacher, for example, who knows only high school chemistry cannot teach even high school chemistry effectively. Fields such as these are developing rapidly, and the teacher who is so swamped with classes or with extraclass activities that he cannot find time to read more than the current textbook in his field is being denied the chance to teach well, to do the job that is required of him. He has a right to something better, to access to the means of reaching the end for which he is being held responsible. On the grade school level there is a further change in the degree of urgency of the problem, but, again, in degree only. The grade school teacher, like any other, is primarily engaged in the process of instruction, and needs time to keep up with developments in his areas of teaching and especially with developments in methods of presentation. He needs, as do other teachers, time and energy that are not exhausted by too many duties, especially those not directly connected with the classroom. Doubling as nursemaid and policeman and bookkeeper, with the cheering prospect of summer school at the end of the year, is not conducive to encouraging deep or extensive study.

The problem is that there just aren't enough teachers for the number of students, and that to provide them, and then further provide the conditions in which they can teach properly, would be staggeringly expensive. Meanwhile, teachers try to bear an impossible load, and students suffer because the load is impossible. For both private and public schools (though the burden is heavier and becoming even more so for private schools) those who pay the financial bills will have to make up their minds how much they can afford for the schooling of their children, and should expect to get what they pay for. They have so far enjoyed and no doubt will continue to enjoy something that simply cannot be paid for— the selfless devotion of teachers at all levels and in all kinds of schools who are teaching because they really love God's children and who want, in their generosity, to give them that precious insight into reality that they themselves prize so highly. Yet even devoted people have to recruit their strength and increase their knowledge, and for both purposes they need some leisure. Good teaching takes devotion to the job and a real love for it; but it also takes physical endurance and intellectual knowledge. Neither of these requisites lasts long accompanied by overwork. Our usual reaction to being required to perform impossible feats is to pitch in and do our best. There is a question, however, whether this is good for the students in the long run. As long as we continue to spread ourselves thin in the hopeless effort to reach on everything, we simply cover up the problem and thus enable it to be ignored a little longer. If more of us did what we were able to do well and refused to try to do the rest of it at all, perhaps the situation of too many students and too few teachers and dollars would be dramatized to the point at which something effective would be done. If this be treason, make the most of it.[2]

The Art of Teaching

If the teacher's first responsibility is to know what he is teaching, his second one is to know how to teach it. Whereas the first requirement would be more evident at the higher levels of instruction, the second would be more evident at the lower levels. Yet both are necessary at all levels, and the difference is one of degree only. Ability as a research scholar is a *sine qua non* for anyone teaching a graduate course, for unless he can give his students something resulting from his personal discovery or interpretation, and unless he can also show his students something of how to go about research in the field, he is not really teaching on the graduate level. But ability as a scholar is no excuse for lack of ability as a teacher, and a genuine responsibility even of a graduate teacher is to present what he teaches as effectively as possible, and to put real effort into that presentation. Parenthetically, a justified criticism of most graduate schools is that they neglect this part of the formation of future college teachers.[3] If teaching methods can

[2] Cf. David D. Henry, *What Priority for Education?* (Urbana, Ill.: The University of Illinois Press, 1961).

[3] See Earl J. McGrath, *The Graduate School and the*

themselves be taught—and they can—then they should be taught to apprentice college teachers as well as to apprentice elementary teachers. It is true that the importance of pedagogical method increases as one gets into the lower grades and that its importance seems, roughly, to vary inversely with that of knowledge of subject matter. Yet at all levels a close attention to teaching method is of vast importance and can make a tremendous difference to the effectiveness of the teaching involved. One can legitimately criticize most graduate schools for largely ignoring this factor in the training of college teachers, just as teachers' colleges have recently been criticized for overemphasizing this factor at the expense of further training of their students in subject matter. It is all very well to hold that "All there is to teaching can be learned through a good education and being a teacher," [4] but experience indicates that the art of pedagogy is a difficult one, and that it both can and should be taught.

Whatever a particular teacher's knowledge of this art, however, there is one thing in this line that remains strictly within his control, and that is preparation. His first job, again, is to know what he is to teach. His second is to organize what he is to teach in what he considers, on the basis of whatever training he has had in this art, to be the most effective form of presentation. Preparation of classes and careful reading of assigned exercises take time and effort, but they are an essential part of the teacher's work, and he has a strict moral obligation to do his work as effectively as he can.

Decline of Liberal Education (New York: Bureau of Publications, Teachers College, Columbia University, 1959), p. 27. See also Bernard Berelson, *Graduate Education in the United States* (New York: McGraw-Hill Book Company, Inc., 1960).

[4] Robert Maynard Hutchins, *The Higher Learning in America* (New Haven, Conn.: Yale University Press, 1936), p. 56. Reprinted by permission.

Yet preparation, too, takes time and energy, and if one holds a teacher responsible for a competent job in this respect he must also give him the means of doing the job. Just as teachers need and have a right to time to learn, they also need and have a right to time to prepare the presentation of what they learn. It is unreasonable and unjust to demand that someone achieve a given end when he does not have access to the means of doing so. Is it better, in both public and private schools, to continue to do a job that is not as good as it should be and not as good as it could be for lack of material and human resources, or to bring the situation more into the open by doing part of the job properly and the rest of it not at all? My guess is that students would gain in the long run by the second alternative, and the students are the only reason why the schools exist. It is true that passive resistance brought jail to Gandhi, but it is also true that it brought independence to India.

Developing the Means and the Love of Learning

So far we have been looking at the obligations and the corresponding rights of teachers to learn and to teach as well as possible the subject matter—the arts or sciences or skills—which they are given to teach so that their students may increase in knowledge. Another function of the teacher mentioned above [5] is to help his students learn how to gain further knowledge for themselves. And in almost any example that one can think of, this second function stands out as more important than the first. So far as teaching the skills and the arts is concerned, there probably is not too great a practical problem. Anyone teaching reading, surely, will have in mind and will point his activities toward the student's becoming able to develop his reading skill, to pass beyond the material then being used and to read with comprehension more difficult material

[5] See pp. 211–213, 238.

in the future. Anyone teaching, say, literature, will surely have in mind the student's appreciating and later comprehending more deeply much more than the particular poem or essay then being read.

The practical difficulty seems to arise in the teaching of the sciences, especially those whose conclusions involve some degree of personal commitment on our part. When we teach national history, are we more concerned that the students will come to understand something of how their own country came to be what it is and something of what the historical enterprise involves, or that they will adopt the same set of heroes and villains as our own and the same interpretation of the same event? It will, of course, make a difference on what level we are teaching; yet, if history is more than chronology, this distinction will have some application at any level, and will largely determine whether the student will be equipped, on the basis of our instruction, to pursue further study of history on his own. When we teach philosophy, including the philosophy of education, are we more concerned that the student accept without question and dutifully repeat for us the conclusions that we have reached on controversial problems, or that the student come to understand on what premises these conclusions rest and be invited to examine the premises anew and perhaps to find further ones?

Examples could be multiplied indefinitely. Many of us are tacitly convinced that our own conclusions represent the ultimate point in the understanding of a subject matter, and are concerned that when our students leave us they should be equipped with a set of eternal verities with which to face the world. Accordingly, we rather artificially try to supply them with something that we wishfully imagine to be effectual weapons of defense against the assaults of a world whose ideas and values are not ours. This is a kindly and well-meant endeavor, but one wonders what its final

335

results will be for the student. As Cardinal Newman put it concerning education on the university level (though it applies to a lesser extent on lower levels): [6]

> We cannot possibly keep them from plunging into the world, with all its ways and principles and maxims, when their time comes; but we can prepare them against what is inevitable; and it is not the way to learn to swim in troubled waters, never to have gone into them.

For one thing, the subject matter which we are teaching may have much more room for contingency and much less for necessity than we have believed, and perhaps the verities of which we are presently convinced are less eternal than we think. Just possibly we do not have the final word that absolves our students from the hard necessity of further thought. The world into which they are going is an open world, a world so indefinite in its diversities and its potentialities that we cannot possibly say anything like the final word about very much of it. Our job is rather to equip our students to carry on from the point to which we can bring them, to teach them how to think rather than what to think. The negative attitude of teachers who are unwilling to aim primarily at this end reflects a lack of confidence in the students themselves, an unspoken suspicion that, really, only the teacher can be trusted to think for himself and must therefore think for others as well. Since almost all teachers have in almost all classes students whose basic intellectual equipment is superior to their own, this lack of confidence seems a bit misplaced. True, the student is immature, but the teacher's job is not to try to keep him immature by doing his growing up for him. The student should indeed come from a school at any educational level equipped with certain basic knowl-

[6] John Henry Cardinal Newman, *The Scope and Nature of University Education* (New York: Dutton Everyman Paperback, E. P. Dutton & Co., Inc., 1958), p. 202. Reprinted by permission.

edge, both factual and other; much more, however, he should come equipped with the ability to increase that knowledge and his facility in acquiring it.

Even this, however, is not enough. The most difficult part of a teacher's job, and perhaps the most important, is that of instilling in the student the desire to learn more. His success or lack of it in this area will be achieved by much the same means as his effort to help his students develop moral virtue. The thing can be done, but not by talking. The only effective way in which a teacher can help his students develop a love of learning is by having a love of learning himself. If ideas are important and exciting to the teacher, that enthusiasm will be communicated to the students through the teacher's obvious concern that they learn and learn well. And no substitute will do, especially no façade. Perhaps the most important thing that any teacher can inspire in his students is a genuine love of learning; for without it schooling is a mechanical thing, a process exclusively of preparing for an occupation, of getting the right union card. The whole notion of speculative knowledge will then be lost, to the great impoverishment of the student and, ultimately, of society. The Latin root of the English word "student" implies zeal, eagerness to know. But you can't give what you don't have, and you can inspire zeal for learning in students only if you yourself have the pure love of learning. Do you?

Professional Obligations

It would take too long to try to cover all aspects of a teacher's function. Something has already been said of his responsibility to respect the human personality of the student, with a reminder that this does not necessarily involve a close personal relationship. One further obligation, out of many more that could be mentioned, concerns the careful use of speech and the avoidance of gossip. A teacher holds a position of trust in more than one way, and has

337

corresponding obligations. One of these ways is that a teacher, because of his position, has access to information concerning students that is definitely confidential, classified information. We all expect that what we tell our physician in the course of our professional relationship with him will be held in strict confidence, since he has this information as a physician rather than as a private individual and has it for our advantage rather than for his. He simply does not have this knowledge in a private capacity, and is not at liberty to divulge it to anyone. We take this sort of professional conduct for granted. If teaching is also a profession, as we all maintain it is, then it also imposes certain professional obligations. The information that a teacher has concerning a student's academic progress, for example, either is or shortly will be public property and need not be guarded as private. But such things as the student's results on tests that are supposed to be kept confidential, the student's perhaps unfortunate behavior on a particular occasion in the classroom or outside it, a delightful morsel of inside information about his family conditions that the student has trustingly confided to the teacher—all these are items that the teacher does not know as a private person and has absolutely no right to reveal. We all love to gossip and to build ourselves up by confiding inside information to an admiring audience. To do so at a student's expense, however, is a serious betrayal of a serious obligation. The tragedy is that so few of us see it as a serious obligation. If in doubt about whether we have a right privately to reveal any particular matter, we have merely to ask ourselves whether we have this information in a private or in a professional capacity. If in further doubt, the safe thing is to say nothing.

The final point to be made in this section may sound like a complaint, and perhaps it is, though it also involves both rights and responsibilities of teachers. The point is this: If teachers are asked to perform such professional though extraclass services as tutoring or public speaking, they have a right to demand payment for services rendered and an obligation to the other members of their profession not to sell those services short. There still seems to be, in what is sometimes called the public image of the teacher, more than a remaining trace of the stereotype of the wandering scholar turned village schoolmaster, impecunious and therefore exploitable, a latter-day Ichabod Crane. The teacher has not really attained professional standing in the eyes of the public or in the eyes of his fellow professionals, though strictly professional conduct is demanded of him. A lingering credence is still accorded the jibe attributed to Shaw, that those who can, do, and those who can't, teach. Credence will continue to be accorded it as long as teachers allow themselves to be imposed upon.

Teaching is one of the oldest and noblest of the professions. Its practitioners are, by and large, devoted first to their jobs and only incidentally to any reward they draw from it. Yet the hard fact is that in our contemporary society a profession and its members are judged largely on the basis of their own estimate of themselves and their work. When physicians drove their buggies through the night on errands of mercy, they were taken for granted. Now that they have moved up to the country club and you can't get a house call out of one of them unless you're on the hospital board of directors, they have become respected. When teachers begin placing some importance on their services they may also become respected members of the community. Tutoring and public speaking are, for teachers, professional services, and they owe it both to themselves and to their fellow teachers to charge for them accordingly.

TEACHING AS A VOCATION

Years of offering teachers what little I can myself teach them have convinced me that I am not the one to tell them what their vocation means,[7] but rather that they are the ones whose dedicated

[7] See Etienne Gilson, "The Eminence of Teaching," in Anton C. Pegis (ed.), *A Gilson Reader* (Garden City, N.Y.:

lives disclose to me the boundless possibilities of the vocation which we share. Years of association with teachers, and especially with high school and grade school teachers, have left me with a profound sense of admiration in the Latin as well as the English meaning of the word. How they do it, I shall never know.

Every real teacher knows what his calling involves; it involves making persons. The making of man is the culminating point in the creative act of God; cooperation in that creative act is the high privilege and the source of the dignity of the parent's vocation; a different cooperation in that same creative act is the source of the dignity of the teacher's vocation. Through aiding parents in the great work of education which is theirs by nature, the teacher plays his indispensable role in carrying forward the continuing work of creation, the work of making men through the development of that power by which they can be said to be made to the image of God. In a properly analogical sense, the students whom we teach are our boys and our girls; it is here that Mr. Chips has the advantage of Elia.

To those teachers who frequently find the going tough—and who doesn't?—a word of encouragement. You have to be a born optimist to be a teacher; or, failing that, you have to talk yourself into it. The teacher is a sower of seed, some of it falling on good ground and some on barren. Most often he will never know which, for this is a seed that is long in the growing; and when the harvest is finally gathered in, for good or for ill, the sowing belongs to the long ago and the far away. The teacher must live on hope and on trust. On rare occasions he sees the fruit of his sowing in the intellectual flowering of his former charges; more rarely, he sees one of them return to express gratitude and appreciation. Mostly, though, he lives on the hope that he has had a hand in the making

Image Books, Doubleday & Company, Inc., 1957), pp. 298–311. In the same volume, see also "The Intelligence in the Service of Christ the King," pp. 31–48.

of a man, and on some days, especially as his years of service lengthen, he finds that hope can be pretty thin nourishment. On those days I would recommend to him the words of one of Bruce Marshall's characters, "It's only the men who are still apostles at forty who ever do anything." [8]

To those teachers who see their true vocation as being missionaries in a more basic sense—and many do who teach under religious obedience—a different word of encouragement. The confessor as well as the martyr has stormed the gates of heaven. The world is wide and its works are varied, and any one of those works can be turned to the service of God through the service of His creatures. There are many apostolates, and not the least of these is the twin apostolate of study and teaching. *Contemplata aliis tradere*—that is no small thing. It is not given to all to bring the saving waters of baptism to pagan souls. To teachers it is given to bring the light of learning to those entrusted to them, to help them begin in this life the contemplation that will find its final fulfillment in the eternal knowledge of the essence of God. They also serve.

SUPPLEMENTARY QUESTIONS

1. What students should be admitted to school (at various levels)? Should those be admitted for whom nothing can be done intellectually? Can motivation change this situation?
2. Should all students be passed? Should a definite percentage be passed?
3. Should students be placed in homogeneous or heterogeneous groups? How can one handle different intelligence levels so that each student gets as much as possible?
4. How can school discipline be improved?

[8] *The Fair Bride* (London: Constable & Co., Ltd., 1953), p. 198.

341

5. Can high academic standards be maintained in the face of the large numbers of students? If not, which should be sacrificed?

6. Should everyone be admitted to secondary schools?

7. If crowded classrooms and shortened recreation periods make personal contact with individual students and their needs very difficult, should fewer students be admitted to school?

8. What place does guidance have in the curriculum?

9. Should a school principal also teach?

10. Should grade levels be abolished?

11. Should students who try hard but cannot get the material be graduated? Should they be encouraged to leave school?

12. Should Communists teach in American schools?

13. Is there such a thing as a right to go to college? If so, who has it?

14. Does a school overstep its authority in dictating policy governing such things as dating, smoking, hair style, and dress?

15. Are parent-teacher conferences beneficial in schools?

16. Should the high school base its acceptance of students on their ability to fit into the existing program offerings, or should provision be made for all regardless of learning potential?

17. Is a coinstitutional or a coeducational high school to be preferred? Can either be reconciled with Pope Pius XI's position in *The Christian Education of Youth?*

18. What should the high school do for its very few extremely gifted students, e.g., in music or in mathematics?

19. Is it true that modern education is drifting without direction? If so, what should be done?

20. Should modern educators guide more and more students toward scientific courses?

Index

Abstract knowledge (*see* Knowledge)

Academic freedom, in church-related schools, 109–110
as related to problem of art and prudence, 171

Activity or experience curriculum, 249–252

Adler, Mortimer J., vii

Administration, as academic function, 105–107
as art, 15
of authority in school, 311–315
and extraclass activities, 255
and moral example, 111–112
relation to philosophy of education, 3, 15
Smith on, 265–268

Aesthetic creativity, Broudy on, 285
(*See also* Fine arts)

Analytical philosophy, 268–275

Appetites, and nature of animals, 53
perfectible by habits, 50–51, 53–54, 61

Appraisal and measurement, 301–302

Aquinas, St. Thomas, on disposition as distinguished from habit, 164–165
on *habitus,* 49
on intellect, 30
on learning and teaching, 192–215
on moral philosophy, 280
on speculative knowledge of operable object, 6
on speculative and practical intellect, 3–4
on the state as developing moral virtue, 41–42

Architecture both useful and fine art, 74, 156

Aristotle, in doctrine of Broudy, 282–283, 286
on intellect, 30
and linguistic analysis on philosophy, 270
on metaphysics, 150, 152
on moral science, 280
Morris on, 298
and notion of liberal knowledge, 149–152, 168–170
on reality, 193

343

Facts, function in learning and
teaching, 161, 218–219
Faculty (*see* Powers of soul)
Faculty theory, 298
Faith, and fideism, 183
function in learning and
teaching, 2, 218–219
relation, to knowledge, 2, 218,
229–230
to science and opinion, 163,
198, 206, 229–230
to theology, 127
Fallacy of false dichotomy, 239,
303
Family, as agency of all forms of
education, 84, 99–100
and education for domestic relationships, 248–249
and emotional development,
101–102
and intellectual education, 103
and moral education, 43, 100,
248–249, 312–313
as natural society, 86
and physical education, 99
primary educational agency,
and basis of right to educate, 94–96, 99, 315–316
relation, to Church, 95–96,
104
to state and school, 90,
94–96, 104, 315–316,
322–324
and social education, 102–103
Federal aid to education, 319–
321
Feigl, Herbert, 266
Fine arts, composition as one,
155–156

Fine arts, nature of, 74
and nature of man, 33
as part of liberal education,
156
related, to liberal arts, 75, 154–
157, 171
to useful arts, 75, 171
teaching of, 222–224
teaching of appreciation of,
156–157, 223–224
First Amendment to Constitution, 324
Formal discipline, 48–49
Fortitude, 60–61
(*See also* Moral virtue)
Freedom, academic, 109–110,
171
Fusion in curriculum, 245–246

General education, Broudy on,
285
relation to liberal education,
157–158
Geography, teaching of, 246–
247
function of faith in, 218
Geometry as liberal art, 73–74,
154
(*See also* Liberal arts)
Gordis, Rabbi Robert, 321
Gorgias, 296
Gossip and teachers, 337–338
Graduate school teaching, history, 161
liberal arts, 154, 222
literature, 157
and research, 330, 332
sciences, 158, 162–163, 165

359